# REINVESTING in AMERICA

# Reinvesting in America

## The Grassroots Movements That Are Feeding the Hungry, Housing the Homeless, and Putting Americans Back to Work

*Robin Garr*

**Foreword by David Osborne**

ADDISON-WESLEY PUBLISHING COMPANY

Reading, Massachusetts • Menlo Park, California • New York • Don Mills, Ontario
Wokingham, England • Amsterdam • Bonn • Paris • Milan • Madrid
Sydney • Singapore • Tokyo • Seoul • Taipei • Mexico City • San Juan

*Library of Congress Cataloging-in-Publication Data*

Garr, Robin.
Reinvesting in America : the grassroots movements that are feeding the hungry, housing the homeless, and putting Americans back to work / Robin Garr.
p. cm.
Includes index.
ISBN 0-201-40756-6
1. Charities—United States. 2. Voluntarism—United States. 3. Nonprofit organizations—United States. I. Title.
HV91.G339 1995
361.7′0973—dc20 94-47421
CIP



Jacket design by Jean Seal
Jacket illustration by Lyle Leduc/Gamma Liaison
Text design by Wilson Graphics & Design (Kenneth J. Wilson)
Set in 10-point New Century Schoolbook by Weimer Graphics, Inc.

1 2 3 4 5 6 7 8 9-MA-9998979695
First printing, May 1995

# Contents

Foreword by David Osborne vii

Preface REINVESTING IN AMERICA xi

Introduction GIVE A MAN A FISH 1

**1** PEOPLE NEED FOOD 11

**2** PEOPLE NEED SHELTER 43

**3** PEOPLE NEED DECENT HOUSING 75

**4** PEOPLE NEED EDUCATION 99

**5** PEOPLE NEED HEALTHY CHILDREN AND FAMILIES 119

**6** PEOPLE NEED POLITICAL POWER 151

**7** PEOPLE NEED JOB SKILLS 185

**8** PEOPLE NEED WORK 205

Conclusion LESSONS FOR ALL AMERICANS 229

Appendix GETTING INVOLVED 239

Acknowledgments 255

Index 257

# Foreword

WASHINGTON IS ABLAZE WITH DEBATE ABOUT antipoverty policy. Welfare reform is on the front burner. The Department of Housing and Urban Development wants to reinvent public housing. The Clinton administration and Congress both want to shift categorical programs in housing, training, and other areas into block grants for the states.

But much of this debate misses the point. Most of the noise, particularly in the media, focuses on welfare. What work requirements will we impose on those on welfare? Who will we throw off the rolls? Will we hand the whole system over to the states to run?

The welfare system *is* dysfunctional, and it *is* refreshing to think that fundamental welfare reform is possible. But welfare is only part of the poverty picture. If we are to combat poverty in America, we must do far, far more than reform the welfare system. We must shift our efforts from *maintaining* people in poverty—which is, after all, what welfare is all about—to creating *development* in poor communities, so people can climb out of poverty.

*Reinvesting in America* gives us a glimpse of how we might do that. Robin Garr did what so few policy experts in America ever do: He got out of the office and went into the communities where solutions are being crafted. He spent several years traveling across America, visiting successful community organizations that ran everything from homeless shelters to job training programs. And he learned a fundamental truth. He puts it this way: "Based on the programs I've seen and the hundreds of creative poverty-fighters I've met across the nation, I'm convinced that we can look to these small-scale, local efforts to find responses to hunger and poverty that are not only more effective but more humane than our current social-services and welfare programs. These new responses are not based on the inventions of office-bound bureaucrats or policy gurus but the common-sense ideas of everyday Americans who've seen a problem and done what needed to be done to fix it."

The answer, Garr argues, has two basic components. First, we must shift from maintenance to development. "We must build on the strengths of poor people rather than assume that their weaknesses will forever defeat them," he writes. "We must foster individual self-reliance. . . ."

Second, we must shift from the old government model of bureaucratic programs to a new model of public funding for private, community-based organizations. "We must take fullest advantage of every opportunity to build *partnerships* between government and the nonprofit groups that have demonstrated creativity, competence, and skill at what they do."

Over the past two decades, Garr points out, a quiet revolution has taken place in America's low-income communities—a revolution the media has largely ignored. In 1970 there were only a few dozen viable community development organizations in America. Today there are many thousands, from community development corporations to food banks, homeless shelters to self-help credit unions, job training organizations to banks. Many of them operate four, five, or six different initiatives to spur development in their communities—constantly reaching to fill new needs and solve new problems.

*Reinvesting in America* is their story. This book makes it obvious why there are better weapons in the war on poverty than public bureaucracies. Like Cafe 458 in Atlanta, they take the time to deal with people on a personal, one-to-one basis—something government programs seldom do. They care more about individuals than programs. Like Esperanza Unida in Milwaukee, which runs businesses through which young people get jobs *and* training, they tailor their services to the needs of their customers. Like Ohio's Open Shelter, they force people to deal with the consequences of their behavior—something government is often afraid to do. Like Habitat for Humanity, Jimmy Carter's favorite charity, they involve people in building the solutions to their own problems, rather than simply giving them hand-outs.

Above all else, the hundreds of community groups profiled in this book exceed government bureaucracies in that indispensable quality called creativity. Their stories burst with the seat-of-the-pants ingenuity that emerges whenever motivated, pragmatic people sit down together to solve problems. This creativity is the real secret that Robin Garr has uncovered, and it is impossible to read his book without appreciating its power.

Unfortunately, *Reinvesting in America* makes it equally clear that these organizations cannot succeed on their own. They may be "points of light," as President Bush liked to say, but on their own they will never burn as brightly as they must if they are to succeed.

Our challenge today is to wire them to government resources without strangling them in red tape.

In his conclusion, Garr provides a set of principles to guide such efforts. He argues, with great insight, that government should support organizations that:

- are guided by clear objectives
- foster self-reliance by building on people's strengths
- use a 'holistic' approach, bringing a full array of tools to bear on each individual's problems
- deal with individuals, one-on-one
- focus on prevention
- demonstrate strong leadership

Garr adds that these organizations are most successful when they network with other local organizations fighting similar battles. These insights suggest an approach to the battle against poverty far different from that being debated in Congress.

Imagine a strategy in which each economic region within a state had its own Economic Opportunity Council. That council would engage in strategic planning, define its mission (or missions), and agree on a set of desired outcomes and benchmarks with which to measure progress. It would not carry out operations itself, but would act as a catalyst, broker, and convener for the entire community.

It would engage many different organizations and individuals to carry out elements of its strategy, using a variety of mechanisms: contracts, grants, vouchers, tax breaks. It would fund organizations that had clear objectives, fostered self-reliance, used a holistic approach, crafted solutions tailored to the needs of individuals, emphasized prevention, and exhibited strong leadership. And it would force these organizations to compete for their funds based in part on their results—while turning them free from regulations and red tape.

This is the kind of strategy that emerges from Garr's work. Unfortunately, it is light years away from the welfare reform debate. And yet, only two years ago, the Clinton administration passed a major initiative built along these lines: Community Empowerment Zones. It slipped quietly through Congress, while welfare reform has created a predictable storm. *Reinvesting in America* suggests that we would be wise—once the sturm and drang of welfare reform has abated—to see how we could expand Empowerment Zone funding from a handful of communities to hundreds.

For those who care about the poor—as opposed to those who simply want political credit for reforming welfare—*Reinvesting in America* is an important book. If we can figure out how government can empower the grassroots, bottom-up initiatives captured in this book, we *can* make a dent in poverty.

*David Osborne*
*Essex, Massachusetts*

# Preface

IT'S BEEN MORE THAN TEN YEARS NOW, BUT I STILL remember vividly a tough old fellow in Louisville's battered West End who survived most of the harsh winter of 1982 with no income other than the twenty-seven crumpled dollar bills that his daughter gave him for Christmas. He burned boards ripped from an abandoned house next door for heat, and his only complaint was that he wouldn't be able to do much reading until he had enough money to replace his broken glasses.

I wrote a story about him in the *Louisville Times,* and donations of cash, canned goods, used eyeglasses, offers of prayers and wishes of hope came pouring in. That made me feel good—though the fact that a man had to live like that in Louisville, Kentucky, U.S.A., in the 1980s made me feel bad. Interviewing food stamp recipients and unemployed people as a newspaper reporter in my own home town, I'd seen up close how bad things were getting for poor people. I wouldn't have minded mounting a journalistic crusade to change all that, but I could never impress my editors that things like this were really happening to real people in Louisville—or that they were important.

Move forward a few years, add one Pulitzer Prize to the newspaper's collection for the news staff's coverage of a fiery bus crash that killed twenty-seven youngsters on a spring night in rural Kentucky. The *Times* was dead, merged into the morning *Courier-Journal,* and Gannett Corporation had bought the local media empire from Louisville's Bingham family. Things were changing fast, and not even a piece of a Pulitzer could keep me from feeling restless. When I learned in 1989 about an unusual project being sketched at a nonprofit group in New York City, I knew I had to get in on it.

The leaders of World Hunger Year (WHY), a nonprofit organization that had long focused its efforts on international hunger, were deeply concerned about how badly hunger and poverty had gotten out of control here in the United States. Bill Ayres, a former Catholic priest and longtime radio talk show host, had founded the organization in 1975 with his friend and partner, the late folksinger and songwriter Harry Chapin. Ayres and Dr. James Chapin, Harry's older brother, a college professor and expert on poverty issues, noticed a surprising development as they reviewed applications for the organization's small grants program, the Harry Chapin Food Self-Reliance Award. Over just a year or two, a remarkable number of grassroots groups had suddenly outgrown their original single-purpose operations as soup kitchens or rescue missions. They weren't just providing emergency food and or shelter anymore. Suddenly they were dealing with housing, job training, economic development. They were teaching poor people how to become self-reliant again. What's more, many of the organizations weren't just relying on private contributions and volunteers. They had formed partnerships with government, getting at least part of their support from local, state, or federal agencies.

No national organization, public or private, was tracking this development or even, apparently, aware that it was going on. Certainly no one was making any effort to identify the most innovative and successful grassroots organizations with an eye toward replicating their efforts.

I enlisted, and within weeks, we had designed the program we would call Reinvesting in America. It would be a hybrid of advocacy and journalism: I would travel all over the nation, using a reporter's tools to find as many grassroots programs fighting hunger and poverty as I could. I would single out the most innovative, visit them, interview the people in charge and the people they served. I would write down whatever I found, and we'd assemble my findings into a computer database that we hoped would show us new and exciting patterns. We refined the concept as we went along. We would introduce grassroots activists to each other so they could share their ideas. We would tell reporters about these individuals and their groups, and teach activists how to get media attention. We would urge foundations and corporate grant-makers to support the best initiatives with cash. We would hold the best grassroots programs up to government policymakers to consider as models for new and better ways of delivering social services. We would make the database comprehensive and user-friendly, and we would offer the information it contained free to anyone interested in fighting hunger and poverty in America. And, when we got it all figured out, I would write this book.

Too impatient to wait for funding, I hit the road, relying on the float time before credit card bills came back and on a little help from our friends, like the Harry Chapin Foundation, which pledged to pay my salary, and singer Bruce Springsteen, an old friend of

Harry Chapin's, who told Ayres that he liked this idea—and proved he meant it by writing a generous check.

On my first trip, a swing through Tidewater country, Washington, D.C., and the Appalachian regions of Virginia and Kentucky, I filled a fat notebook with my first batch of stories. There were outstanding efforts going on out there, and it wasn't hard to find out about them. Interviewing the people involved was no different from what I'd done as a reporter. Neither was the task of turning interviews into articles and assembling the information I found in usable form.

After a short stint back in New York and another flurry of telephone calls, I was off again, this time to northwestern Ohio's pickle-growing country, where I met the dedicated folks at the Farm Labor Organizing Council and learned that fighting hunger can take the form of organizing migrant farmworkers to fight for fair salaries and decent working and living conditions. This, I thought, was definitely better than passing out leftover restaurant food at soup kitchens. I met Kent Beittel, one of the most colorful individuals in the national fight against homelessness—a guy who threw away the rule book in order to help people recover their lives at the Open Shelter, within sight of the Ohio state capitol in Columbus. Next, a foray to the Rust Belt regions turned up the Milwaukee job-training program Esperanza Unida, a nonprofit auto repair shop that produces skilled technicians capable of earning high pay on the local economy. I continued traveling monthly, spending about a quarter of my time on the road and the rest digging up information about outstanding programs and writing down what I learned. Now, four years later, I've been to more than two hundred cities, towns, and villages in all fifty states, visited more than five hundred programs, and become increasingly aware that we are only scratching the surface. But the shape of things is coming clear, and there's hope in it.

In the pages that follow I tell the stories of the nation's best grassroots programs and policies, and show how we can use the lessons they teach us to fight the problem of poverty efficiently and well. This isn't just one story but scores of stories about people who thought they could make a difference, and did. And it's my story, too: the story of a reporter who suspected that a lot of Americans weren't happy about stepping over homeless people or closing their eyes to Depression-style poverty on the nation's streets. It's the story of a reporter who found those people, asked them what they were doing and why, and wrote down what they said.

# Introduction

# Give a Man a Fish

"GIVE A MAN A FISH, AND YOU'VE GIVEN HIM A *meal. Teach him to fish, and he'll have food for a lifetime."*

I was munching a corn muffin and sipping black coffee at Third & Eats, a nonprofit delicatessen run by a church, where homeless people learn to cook and serve and work their way off the streets, when I saw the T-shirt tacked to the ceiling. The shirt (it looked like an extra-large, Beefy T) uttered its message in green and white, restating the old wisdom in politically correct first person: GIVE ME A FISH AND I'LL EAT FOR A DAY . . . TEACH ME TO FISH AND I'LL EAT FOR A LIFETIME.

Later I heard it quoted at a food bank in Ohio, in the original form: "Give a man a fish." I saw it in fund-raising material for a program in Boston that trained Spanish-speaking workers in computers, and I heard it again from Red Gates, a Lakota Sioux activist in North Dakota, who presides over a galvanized-iron warehouse filled with surplus government commodities, canned fat pork and butter and beans, where he worries about feeding the people and ending the grinding poverty that keeps them down.

"Teach a man to fish." It seemed as good a way as any to sum up in a few words the story I wanted to tell.

But it wasn't as simple as I thought. I figured this out one sunny afternoon in Alaska, when the short Arctic summer was hurtling toward autumn and I found myself standing on duckboards on a vacant lot in Anchorage, talking to a guy who looks like a young Abraham Lincoln and who *gives people fish*.

Right there while I was watching, he reached his bare arms into a big white plastic bin full of ice and fish, hauled out an eighteen-inch-long silver-scaled beauty, and *whap!*—threw it into the back of a hungry college student's station wagon, where it joined a growing pile leaking blood and fish guts all over her spare tire. She smiled and thanked him, then put the car into gear and drove off, happy to be fed for far more than a day. That was when I figured out the truth behind the old saying. Clichés are sometimes right, but you can never trust 'em. Just when you think you've got the conventional wisdom figured out, it'll turn around and bite you.

I had found my way to something like forty-five states by then, still hoping that sooner or later I'd run into someone who'd found the secret everyone else had overlooked. I'd ask questions, joking that I was using the tools of journalism for a benign purpose. I worked sources and culled clippings and followed word-of-mouth reports to trace the bright, creative, committed people who were working out of church basements and storefront food pantries and burned-out industrial buildings and, here and there, actually making a difference in the lives of poor, hungry, and homeless people. If I could find enough of them, and study their ideas until they fell into some kind of pattern, I reasoned, perhaps the lessons they'd have to teach would come so clear and pure and demonstrably sensible that *everyone* would want to try them.

## *Giving Away Fish*

That's the way Michael O'Callaghan sees it. He's the Lincoln lookalike in Anchorage, a lean, mutton-chopped man with a mission who calls himself "a rowdy" and says every salmon he hands out to a hungry Alaskan carries a message. "Here in Alaska, we have a tremendous abundance of fish, but the people don't have access," he said. "These people here can't go out and get fish. Licenses, regulations—it's bullshit! The people should be able to get their fish. So the deal is, this is a common property resource, it belongs to the people. Rich, poor, they belong to everybody."

This is no sweet, turn-the-other-cheek philosophy but a hell-raising, do-what's-right approach that has led O'Callaghan to salvage and give away hundreds of thousands of pounds of fish that would otherwise have been left to rot—and prompted the Alaska state legislature to cough up $30,000 to help him do it.

And so, when the word goes out that Mike's got fish to give away, hungry people come from all over Anchorage and out in the bush country, converging in station wagons, vans, rusty sedans, and pickup trucks on the muddy lot at Fifth Avenue and Barrow Street, just down the block from the city's pride, the sparkling new

Alaska Center for the Arts, a $60 million edifice where Alaskans who can afford it spend $50 and more to see concerts and plays. Promptly at noon a rumbling semitrailer truck pulls in, bearing waist-high white plastic bins filled with fat, glistening pink salmon carcasses in salt water on ice. They're free for the taking for anyone who wants them—just bring your own bag—and they're good food—food that was being thrown away by the ton until Michael O'Callaghan got into the act.

O'Callaghan confesses that he started doing this kind of thing for a simple reason that had little to do with charity or sending the government a message. He was unemployed, and he and his family were hungry. This condition led him first to dumpster diving and then into EARTH, a nonprofit, zero-budget organization of volunteers that he heads. He doesn't spend much time keeping count, but EARTH has surely fed thousands of Alaskans. The whole thing started when the Carr's grocery store near his home fenced off a dumpster that previously had been a reliable source of stale baked goods, discarded food in dented cans, and other edible but unsalable items. O'Callaghan suggested that the store manager remove the fence so the people could eat, and received an unsurprising refusal. So, he said, "I put on a suit and came back as 'the Reverend O'Callaghan,' and I went to a bigger guy." The grocery executive agreed to let O'Callaghan's group, with permission, take usable produce and canned goods from one department of one store to distribute to poor people.

This limited effort worked so well that Carr's—with O'Callaghan's nudging—soon extended its permission to the full store, and then to its entire Anchorage-area chain. EARTH now coordinates more than a hundred volunteers who report regularly to Carr's outlets, pick up discarded canned goods and other food, and dispense it to hungry people through churches and civic groups. No muss, no fuss, no red tape, no paperwork. In 1993 alone, O'Callaghan estimates, the group passed along close to a million pounds of food that previously would have gone to the dumpster.

The fish giveaway started in much the same way. Three years ago an Alaska hatchery spawned controversy when it was revealed that, because the market was oversupplied, it intended to dump an entire year's migration of pink salmon, an edible but commercially undesirable species known as humpies. Appalled by this waste, O'Callaghan scouted up a fish boat and a crew to run it, headed for the salmon grounds, got out in front of the hatchery's boats, and captured 20,000 pounds of fresh salmon, which they brought back to Anchorage and gave away within twenty-four hours.

Learning that hatcheries routinely discard tons of humpies after stripping the females of their eggs and the males of milt for breeding, the following year O'Callaghan's group won the permission of several hatcheries to take the carcasses for free. They persuaded the state legislature to allocate $30,000 to cover truck rental, and EARTH started trucking salmon to downtown Anchorage. During the August and September season, they gave away 585,000 pounds of salmon. The following year, armed with a $75,000 grant, the group gave away more than 800,000 pounds, at a rate of more than 40,000 pounds a day during the peak of the season.

"You know anybody with a pickup?" O'Callaghan asked the woman from the University of Alaska, who said her carload of salmon, stored in the freezer, would feed her all winter. "If they've got a pickup, they can take a truckload back to the university and give it away."

O'Callaghan sees beyond the joy of helping people to the policy implications of what he's doing. He would like to see the Alaska fishery project replicated in every region where commercial fishing is practiced, and he's lobbying to have the Department of Commerce's National Atmospheric and Oceanic Administration add a tax on commercial fisheries to finance it. It's a mighty big dream; but as he says, fist pounding the air to punctuate the point, throwing away millions of pounds of fish every year is a mighty big waste. A big enough waste, indeed, to justify giving fish to quite a few people. Time enough to teach them to fish later.

## *Change Versus Charity*

EARTH is unusual, but it's hardly unique. It's part of a quiet revolution that's been going on all over America, effectively but without much notice, during the past dozen years.

There's nothing new about charity. People have always dispensed it more or less freely to those less fortunate than they. But what's going on here is a little different from charity, and a little more than charity. Concern for the poor has traditionally been a function of churches and, sometimes, the government. But EARTH is neither. It is an unusual partnership bringing together individuals, a nonprofit organization, state government, and private enterprise in a common effort.

Such partnerships between government and the nonprofit sector—a slight twist on the notion of privatization that is inspiring government during the 1990s to seek entrepreneurial solutions to problems by contracting with the private sector—recur again and again throughout this book. They are central to the most effective grassroots initiatives in the fight against poverty.

Here's another of the secrets of the quiet revolution that started suddenly and with little notice, all over the nation during the 1980s: It was an instinctive, pragmatic reaction by everyday people to a sudden visible increase in hunger and poverty. Pragmatism and a commonsense, roll-up-your-sleeves approach to local problems has been a part of American culture—and one of which we're justly proud—for centuries. It still is. The revolution has little to do with government and nothing to do with social policy, but it has quickly spread from the nation's largest cities to smaller cities, suburbs, and farm towns.

Many elements spurred this change. The increase in poverty can't be pinned entirely on either political party. Tax-weary citizens shouted through referendums like California's Proposition 13 in 1978 to limit taxation—and many of the government programs that taxes pay for. Well-meaning reformers opened the doors of state mental institutions, which they accurately described as warehouses; but local governments declined to finance halfway houses and support programs to move newly released mental patients back into community life. Inflation in the wake of the OPEC oil embargo hit the economy hard, and the Reagan administration brought a minimalist view of government to bear during the 1980s, cutting deeply into federal spending for social services, particularly low-cost housing. The result? *More* homelessness.

While the richest 5 percent of Americans saw large increases in their incomes during the Reagan era, most working people saw no real increase in inflation-adjusted income after 1979. Before long, the growing class of working poor—people who earn at or near the minimum wage—could no longer maintain their families at the poverty level even by working full-time. As Harvard public policy professor David Ellwood, who later took a post overseeing welfare reform in the Clinton administration, was fond of saying, "People who work shouldn't have to be poor." This simple truism strikes a chord in the American spirit, and yet most of us have learned to quell this awareness, much as we learned to look the other way as beggars and homeless people proliferated on the streets of our cities. In fact, nearly 27 million Americans were receiving food stamps in 1994, and fully 40 percent of the adults below the poverty line had jobs.

Meanwhile, manufacturing jobs fled overseas. Toward the end of his term, even President George Bush acknowledged that the economy was in "free fall." The problem transcends party politics, of course. Things didn't look up for poor people in America when Bill Clinton moved into the White House. A full year into the Clinton administration, a poll by the Marist Institute for Public Opinion, a policy study organization based in New York, found that an estimated 2.5 million New Yorkers said they had to sacrifice clothing, medical care, living arrangements, or food to make ends meet. "The hardship extended above the poverty line and beyond the working poor to include middle-income families," poll director Barbara Carvalho said. The survey found that more than one-third of New Yorkers with family incomes under $25,000 couldn't afford to buy needed clothing. More than one-fourth reported passing on necessary visits to the doctor, and one in seven said they sometimes had to do without food. Even one in six New Yorkers with family incomes between $25,000 and $60,999 said they had to sacrifice clothing and medical care, according to the poll. (The median family income in the city is $34,000.)

So familiar has the sight of homeless street people and soup kitchens become in our cities that we forget these everyday realities were uncommon after the Great Depression and through most of the postwar years. Until the 1980s, Americans assumed that it was common for people to live and sleep on the streets in places like Calcutta, but certainly not New York City or Wichita, Kansas. Our grandparents had stood in soup lines during the Depression, but it couldn't happen now . . . or so we thought.

When poor people started turning up at rectory doors begging for food and cash during the 1981 recession, the initial response came from the traditional sources: religious and charitable organizations, which began passing out meals and finding room to set up cots in church basements, offering charity to help people get through the hard times. But something different happened, something that had never happened during any previous postwar recession: the hard times didn't end, and the same people kept coming back for more. It wasn't long before the ad hoc lunches grew into soup kitchens and the rooms of cots evolved into congregate shelters. Emulating a model that spread by word of mouth, most larger cities opened food banks, nonprofit organizations that coordinated donations of food and cash and distributed foodstuffs to soup kitchens and food pantries.

And then, mirroring a development that had mixed success in the Great Society programs of the 1960s—when nonprofit organizations formed partnerships with government to provide better services together than either could do independently—these grassroots initiatives started to change. Instead of merely providing emergency services, many of them evolved into multiple-purpose organizations that didn't just feed hungry and homeless people, but sought to identify their problems and do whatever was needed to move them back into the mainstream.

These initiatives did not trickle down from the federal government, or from foundations, or from think tanks or academe. They rose *up* from the grass roots. They developed out of the commonsense ideas of foot soldiers in the war on poverty, drawing on good old-fashioned know-how, creativity, and American can-do spirit.

George Bush praised these efforts as "points of light." But in doing so, he also perpetuated a myth: that private groups and individual charity could replace government in ensuring that no American would go unhoused, unclothed, and unfed. Bipartisan recognition of government's duty to provide basic support for every American, a tenet of the New Deal that was refined in the Great Society, had made significant progress toward erasing domestic hunger and poverty by the 1970s. But it unraveled during the next decade, which saw Wall Streeters build fortunes while literally stepping over an increasing throng of homeless people sleeping under cardboard on the side streets of the Financial District.

Now, creative partnerships between government and nonprofit organizations—with government providing financing and appropriate oversight to the grassroots organizations providing competent, caring services at the local level—may offer a road map back to a healthy American society. It is time for government to pay attention to the outstanding ideas coming from the grassroots geniuses who know best how to fight the war on poverty in their own cities and towns. It is time for government to reevaluate its social service programs and to separate effective initiatives from those that are obsolete or that never worked well, looking away from tradition and toward the new ideas that have been tested and proved in the nation's neighborhoods. It is time for government to call a truce in the turf wars that are inevitable when poverty programs are dispersed among such disparate cabinets as Agriculture, Health and Human Services, Housing and Urban Development, Labor, and even Defense and the Interior. It's time for the grass roots and government to come together to create new, more effective forms of social services, and to eliminate the worst poverty in the United States once and for all.

There are hundreds of effective models all over America. If any community elected to replicate them all, that community could put hunger and poverty on the run. As necessary as shelters and soup kitchens are while thousands of Americans remain without adequate housing or sufficient food, they do little to attack the deeper problems that cause hunger and poverty. The best of these new models go beyond merely providing handouts. They don't simply extend charity but foster social change. They build self-reliance.

At Esperanza Unida, on Milwaukee's predominantly Hispanic South Side, young men like Gilbert Sanchez learn how to repair cars. With trainees working alongside experienced mentors, the nonprofit venture operates a commercial auto shop as a thriving business. Sanchez had stitched together a résumé featuring long gaps of unemployment between short-term jobs at minimum wage—for example, as an errand boy in a print shop for just over $4 an hour. Now he has a skilled job at a Milwaukee Oldsmobile dealership where he earns $17 an hour, and has his eyes on the management track. Esperanza Unida found its approach so successful that it has added hands-on training in many marketable skills, from auto body repair to welding, building trades, and family day care. Esperanza Unida doesn't give people food. It gives them the tools to earn a good living. That's self-reliance.

In rural Alabama, where isolated Sand Mountain's slopes rise to form the southern end of Appalachia in the pine woods northeast of Birmingham, a group of tiny church congregations, too small to do much for their poorer members independently, banded together as Sand Mountain Parishes. It established a cooperative cannery to help stretch the region's seasonal bounty of produce through the winter. The group also started a building program that puts up small but sturdy solar-powered houses for the mountain's most ill-housed families. Now it is helping a group of single mothers form a home-building cooperative. That's self-reliance, too.

A quiet revolution is going on, all right, so quietly that hardly anybody outside the grassroots organizations themselves knows it is happening—and they aren't talking much about it. The media, the government, even most funding organizations don't get it at all. This is a shame, because some of this stuff is working, and way too many of the traditional welfare programs aren't. Are there lessons here? The more I traveled and the more I saw, the more I thought so.

# 1

# People Need Food

I MET BEN IN ATLANTA. HE WAS A THOUGHTFUL fellow whose life had pretty much gone to hell after he killed his mother one morning when he was a teenager. It was an accident, but that didn't make him feel any better. It sent him into a spiral of drug and alcohol abuse and depression that lasted quite a few years and didn't ease up until the loving people at a little place called Cafe 458 helped him crawl out of the gutter.

Ben's story serves about as well as any to show how this whole thing isn't about handing out free lunch or even about welfare programs and social policy. What it's really about is individuals.

"So here I am," says Ben. "I love it here. I love the people here, you know? I'm going on two years clean and sober. Who would have thought it?"

He shakes his head. He can't help smiling. His buddies Ray and Phil and Andrew cluster around the table, their words spilling out and tumbling over one another's in their eagerness to tell their own stories, how they hit bottom and bounced back up again, clean, employed, and looking to the future.

What makes Cafe 458 so special? On the surface it appears to be a fairly routine, if admirable, effort: a soup kitchen for street people. But it is one that attaches dignity to charity by dressing it up in fancy clothing in the belief that people—even homeless street people—respond favorably to being treated well.

Atlanta's Sweet Auburn neighborhood, where Martin Luther King, Jr., grew up and the nation's civil rights leaders laid plans in the historic Ebenezer Baptist Church, has gone a bit gritty, as have too many inner-city neighborhoods around the nation. Set incongruously amid the liquor shops and frame houses in need of paint, Cafe 458 pops up as a surprise. A one-story building decked out in broad bands of pastel pink and green, it looks like a chic bistro, and it reinforces the image with a discreet sign in a side window: SEATING BY RESERVATION ONLY. Smiling waiters bustle around the airy dining room in crisp white aprons, straightening the fresh flowers on the tables. A blackboard lists the entrées of the day: a pasta dish, of course, or roast beef *au jus*.

But Cafe 458 is a bistro with a difference. A nonprofit operation, designed and built by volunteers in what used to be a cheap liquor store, it serves a select group of diners, who get reservations through referrals from social service agencies. They earn the right to eat at the café by agreeing to participate in programs aimed at getting them back into the community. Run by a ten-member commune of volunteers who aren't satisfied merely to feed people in decent surroundings, Cafe 458 does more: It uses the attractions of good food and a pleasant atmosphere to get luncheon guests talking about their problems and starting to think about goals. "We say the food's not the focus; it's just the hook to get people together for conversation," explained Betty Voight, who with her husband, Dave, is a member of Community of Hospitality that directs the organization. "It's a way to develop relationships, from which emerge the other issues that have to be addressed."

A participant's initial goals may seem achingly simple to anyone who's never been on the street—replacing eyeglasses, for instance. Or lining up at social service agencies to retrieve the two forms of ID that a person needs to fill out the necessary forms for benefits. "You tell us where you want to be in three months, six months, a year, and we'll work with you," said A. B. Short, the executive director of Cafe 458. "Tell us your goals, and we'll help you reach those goals."

Toward that end, the café's menu includes more than just good things to eat. Participants can take advantage of free services, all provided by volunteers. Meetings of Alcoholics Anonymous, Narcotics Anonymous, and other twelve-step groups are held regularly. Volunteer barbers offer free haircuts. A medical van visits weekly, as do volunteer lawyers offering no-cost legal services. "We're talking about very basic, fundamental, short-term, achievable goals," Short said. "Self-esteem is a major problem when you're poor and homeless. If you get small victories to build on, you'll start getting back that sense of self-worth, and then you can control your life."

That's the idea behind Recovery, the residential program for treating long-term drug and alcohol abuse that Cafe 458 provides for men like Andrew, Ben, Ray, and Phil. Ten men at a time, recruited from the café's guests, live in a safe, clean home provided by a church, where they receive intense, ongoing group and individual therapy and work in small in-house businesses—a bulk mail operation and a housing renovation program. The program lets recovering addicts ease back into the routine of taking responsibility for daily work. Its success has been stunning: while as many as 90 percent of the graduates of drug and alcohol programs nationally relapse after six months, Short said, nine out of ten Recovery graduates stay clean.

Open only for lunch on weekdays, Cafe 458 was serving sixty-five meals a day within weeks of its opening in 1988. During the last six months of 1992, its workers dished out more than five thousand meals and brought happiness and a little hope to hundreds of Atlanta's street people. And, with its unpaid, communal staff, it did it on a budget of about $135,000 a year.

Betty Voight also serves as one of the Recovery counselors. A sturdy woman with apple cheeks and a round face, whose dark hair is rapidly giving way to gray, and who always wears a smile and a carved wooden ankh on a silver chain, Betty ponders a question: Why has Cafe 458 worked so well to change people's lives?

"Relationships," she concludes, after a long silence. "What we're really about is building relationships with people. Food is the bait; it brings people together. Eating around the table becomes the medium for what we really do, which is work with people, network, make something good come out of it. It's not just putting food into homeless people's bellies, but making them feel welcome. We play music. We put flowers on the tables. We listen. People tell us their stories and we tell ours. It opens people to the process of transformation.

"I think another secret is that the more we become involved in drug and alcohol abuse, the more we learn how entrenched homelessness and chemical abuse and poverty and loss of self-esteem all mesh together," she said, interlocking her fingers, pulling them apart, meshing them together, underlining the point and underlining it again. "So we're a little more tough on those doing drugs and alcohol. It's crazy, a part of our success, and our failure—well, not failure; we could have more guests if we weren't tough. When people admit substance abuse, we say, 'Look, we won't feed you if you don't do something about this.' We give them a schedule, make it easy. If there's any success here, that's an important piece of it.

When folks are ready to change their lives, we're here to form some structure for them. So many folks, out there homeless, save all their money to buy booze and crack. They go to soup kitchens and shelters to eat and sleep so they can save whatever they've got for drugs. We try not to enable that."

Dave Voight joins us. A quiet man, his nature balances Betty's openness. He's snug against a chilly January day in Atlanta in a red-and-blue plaid shirt, tail out over brand-new jeans with the cuffs rolled up. His graying beard is two shades lighter than the longish, sandy hair that flops down over his high forehead. Tall and short, slim and sturdy, talkative and quiet, they're a complementary pair, but what they share is a deep sense of optimism; they are full of smiles and hope.

Asked to think about some of the café's greatest success stories, they nod and agree that Phil is one. But Betty adds, "I have to be honest. It wasn't necessarily our program as much as that he finally let go of the feeling that he had to do it all by himself. One night, at his wits' end, he woke up crying, asked God to help, almost desperate. That's usually the way; it's God's spirit—we're just here to help."

Phil, however, believes the café deserves a big share of the credit. "I had no idea I'd come this far," he said. "I'll be clean three years in March. I came to the café program with an open mind. I said, 'I want to know what's making me do this to myself.' I asked myself these questions, prayed a lot, and it seems a lot of answers started to come. Therapy, one-on-one sessions that went on for a year, facing some things I'd never faced. Some things I'd never want to mention to other people.

"The café was different from every other program. Others wanted you to go out and work. I know daily, long-term, that is what's needed. You can't do it in a short period of time. After twenty-three years, you're not going to get self-esteem and self-confidence in a couple of weeks. It takes building a foundation, and the café is effective at that. Six months, all I had to do was stay clean. All they wanted me to do was work on myself, and that was a lot to offer. 'Stay clean for six months and work on yourself'—and I was able to do that.

"I never forget where I came from. I'm thankful every day because I know what I've got. It's not so much feeling proud; it's made my life a lot better. To have come this far in a few years—I've got a wife, a family. I've reconnected with my son, all these things. It's given me a lot of hope, you know, and a lot of faith that I can make it through without using drugs to mask it or escape it.

"Put this in your book: Statistics-wise, the café is the most successful place of any in this city. Why? The dedication of the people who work here. And it's long-term. They don't let up until the job's done, and when the job is over, they're still there, and the door's always open. It's a special place, it really is."

## *Food Banking*

Cafe 458's approach is only one of many. It's repeated in similar forms in a handful of other cities. In Chicago, former police officer Laura Nigro hosts breakfast, lunch, and dinner at the Inspiration Cafe on the city's multiethnic North Side. The St. Joseph Center in Venice, California, offers dignity to its homeless clientele with flowers, tablecloths, and table service. But it's the extra step from free lunch to building self-reliance that makes Cafe 458 unique.

The same kind of distinction divides the nation's food banks into two categories: those that simply distribute food efficiently, and those that are committed to change.

Food banking, which first arose during the late 1970s, has become institutionalized in America. A national organization, Second Harvest, oversees the activities of food banks in most major cities. Generally operating out of warehouses, food banks hustle donations of excess food from major food corporations, groceries, farms, private donors, and the government. They store it briefly, and, for a nominal handling fee, they then distribute it to neighborhood soup kitchens, food pantries, and other groups that provide emergency food directly to the public.

Constrained by the whims of charity and the season, food banks frequently find themselves, and their clients, in a literal feast or famine. Flooded with fresh produce during the harvest, some find it impossible to process tons of fruits and vegetables before they spoil. Weeks later, fresh produce is impossible to find. In 1990, when the bottom abruptly fell out of the commercial market for oat bran products, major food processors dumped hundreds of tons of bran on the nation's food banks, claiming significant tax deductions and, it is to be hoped, aiding the cardiovascular health of thousands of poor and hungry Americans. Shortly after the quick end of the Desert Storm conflict in Kuwait, the government, staggering under a vast oversupply of dehydrated military meals, donated them to the Second Harvest network.

The idea of taking to the barricades to encourage social change, however, comes only reluctantly to many food bankers. Many of them are older men who came to the work after retiring from the world of commerce, and their inclination is to run the banks like a business. "We can't really get involved in issues and advocacy. Our board says getting food out is the priority," said Howard Cawein, formerly executive director of Miami's Daily Bread Food Bank, a network that apportions more than a million pounds of food each month to some 350 agencies in south Florida. Similar principles apply at the Greater Chicago Food Depository, which, founded in 1979, is among the nation's oldest and largest food banks. According to former director Stephen Whitehead, the group now distributes nearly twenty million pounds of food a year through neighborhood organizations in the region.

It's easy to trace the conservative, don't-rock-the-boat approach of many urban food banks to the background and experience of the typical director. But there's been some shift of philosophy at the national level since the arrival in 1991 of Sister Christine Vladimiroff, a longtime activist in the peace and justice movement for Central America, as Second Harvest's executive director. With a new attitude at the top, many of the nation's food banks—some more readily than others—are starting to get involved in advocacy and public education.

The most creative food bankers, like Rachel Bristol Little in Portland, Oregon, Bill Bolling in Atlanta, and Carolyn Lanier in Lubbock, Texas, needed no prompting. "They always called us 'the rebel food bank,'" laughs Lanier. She recalls that when a group of Lubbock citizens proposed a food bank a decade ago, Second Harvest was unwilling to allow it to affiliate, arguing that there was little hunger and not much need for food banking in this dusty west Texas town where the oil patch meets bean-growing country. A decade later, the South Plains Food Bank consistently wins Second Harvest's top awards, and it serves as a model to help pull less aggressive food banks along.

But now and then, it still makes the folks at headquarters nervous. "They nearly flipped when we started our voucher system," Lanier admitted.

In that program, a startling departure from customary food bank procedures, half of the food bank's warehouse on the city's industrial west side distributes food directly to hungry people, defying the conventional wisdom that food banks shouldn't deal with the public directly but only through intermediate nonprofit agencies.

"Why not?" shrugs Lanier, noting that direct distribution offers a simple solution to a consistent problem: many of the city's neighborhood food pantries don't have any good way of picking up produce in quantity from the food bank, and often can't distribute any more food than can be carried in the trunks and back seats of volunteers' cars. The standard argument against allowing citizens to come to the food bank in person is that local groups like pantries and soup kitchens are in a position to deter fraud by screening participants for eligibility. No problem, says Lanier: The neighborhood groups now issue paper vouchers instead of food, which the bank accepts as payment for boxes each containing a week's groceries for a family of four. Through this and other standard programs, the South Plains Food Bank distributed eight million pounds of food in 1992, serving 180 organizations in Lubbock and another 50 or so in the surrounding area.

But, says Lanier, "Food is only a small portion of what we do." An array of needed services has spun off from the food bank, ranging from weekend congregate meal centers in the inner city to a recycling program. The food bank also owns its own farm—a five-acre spread on the outskirts of town run by Roy Riddle, a burly army retiree, who oversees a crew of volunteers to get more than a hundred tons of fresh produce in off the property in three separate harvests a year. It is developing an orchard that will not only raise fruit but train unemployed people in new skills. Yet another of Lanier's projects strings together apparently unrelated elements in a remarkable pattern: Prisoners at the Lubbock Correctional Facility earn minimum wage by collecting pruned grapevines from the nearby Cap-Rock Winery and fashioning them into decorative wreaths. The wreaths—several thousand of them in 1994—are sold through a national catalog by a commercial floral broker in Denver, raising enough money to pay the workers and help support the program. The workers in turn get a little work experience and something more attractive to list on their résumés than Lubbock City Jail.

Rather than seeing the region's poor and homeless people as mere recipients of charity, the South Plains Food Bank gets involved in their lives, aggressively recruiting them as volunteers who learn job skills through work. More than one hundred formerly homeless people have been able to move from volunteer posts at the food bank into full-time jobs.

Realizing that homeless people were going to be around the food bank, Lanier also quietly arranged to fill a few simple but essential needs, making showers and a washing machine and dryer available to the volunteers. A literacy training course, also taught by volunteers, is surprisingly full. Finally, in its most ambitious project, the Lubbock food bank raised nearly $5 million to resurrect a vacant industrial building as a high-tech food dehydration plant. Because dehydrated food is easily transported and stored—one hundred pounds of fresh green beans can be processed and packed in a bag not much larger or heavier than a pillow, and will remain nutritious without cold storage—it is particularly well suited for food banks and soup kitchens. And from the food bank's standpoint, it converts the harvest-time glut of perishable produce into a stable product that can be stored for months.

The South Plains Food Bank offers a particularly good example of two more of the principles that run through many of the most effective grassroots programs: first, it draws a balance between mere charity and programs that assist people in changing their own lives; and second, it demonstrates the critical importance of bold, creative leadership that's willing to try unusual initiatives to make a difference.

## *From Food to Jobs*

The cavernous Mitch Snyder Shelter for homeless men in Washington, D.C., among the nation's largest and perhaps one of its best known, houses a much less familiar program that deserves wider recognition. At first glance, DC Central Kitchen might appear to be just another of the more than 120 local groups nationwide that collect usable leftover food from restaurants and institutions and redistribute it to soup kitchens and other nonprofit groups to feed poor and hungry people. But it goes beyond the routine, thanks to the creativity of its director. Robert Egger, who grew up as an army brat, always dreamed of getting into the nightclub business and still can't quite believe that he's running an organization that feeds poor and homeless people and teaches them to work.

The group doesn't simply collect and pass on whatever food the community makes available in its random kindness each day. To overcome the unpredictability of such largess, which can result in recipients dining on croissants and pumpkin pie on Tuesday, pork and beans on Wednesday, and perhaps nothing at all on Thursday, Egger's staff follows the simple expedient of using the Snyder Shelter's twenty-thousand-square-foot kitchen as a staging and storage area. Donations of food are inventoried, checked for cleanliness and purity, frozen if necessary, and eventually combined with previously collected food and some purchased goods to put together complete, balanced meals for distribution.

Another innovation is even more noteworthy. Rather than enlisting part-time volunteers, DC Kitchen hires homeless people—mostly men from the Snyder Shelter, but also homeless women from other shelters—as staff. In exchange for minimum-wage work, participants get thorough training in food service. Although some view burger-flipping as unfulfilling low-skill and low-wage employment, Egger insists that the program goes beyond that: Graduates gain entry to a career path that may start hard and low but that offers quick advancement to people who are willing to work.

Hilton Hunter, a chef with ten years' experience in Washington restaurants, including at the posh Watergate Hotel, oversees the training program, which takes ten students at a time through a ten-week course, using a curriculum devised in partnership with the Cornell School of Hotel Management. The course includes practical experience preparing meals in the organization's kitchen as well as classroom work covering basic cooking techniques—making stocks, baking, and all the other skills a trained chef needs—and ranging to kitchen sanitation and the safe use of knives. The still-young program already boasts considerable success, with all but a few alumni having moved into restaurant jobs and kept them.

"It's hard work," said Greg Miller, a formerly homeless man from North Carolina who completed the program last winter and is now a line chef at J. Paul's restaurant in Washington. "It's hot. You get the hair burned off your arms. You get grease burns. And I love it. I go in, I work hard, and I'm trying to improve myself." Indeed. He's earning $8.50 an hour and hoping to move up soon. His employers have no doubt he'll do that.

Besides distributing more than a thousand full meals daily to three dozen emergency-feeding programs in and around Washington, DC Central Kitchen pays its rent for the Snyder Shelter's facilities by cooking fourteen hundred meals a day for the shelter's own residents. And it does all this with a lean, permanent staff of seven and a $250,000 annual budget.

For Robert Egger, the difference between DC Central Kitchen's approach and that of similar but more traditional operations is the difference between pity and empowerment. Redistributing food is only the short-term concern; in the long run, lives are being saved. But empowerment is not an easy sell. Most nonprofits willingly provide charity, but talk about social change makes a lot of people uneasy. Still, Egger is beginning to make inroads, perhaps because his program is too successful to ignore. The Donner Fund of New York gave him a $65,000 grant to send him around the country in an effort to convince five other nonprofits to adopt his job-training model. When I spoke with him in the early spring of 1994, plans for potential copycat programs in Boston, Kansas City, Los Angeles, and western Connecticut were under way, and initiatives were already gearing up in Sacramento and on the Purdue University campus in West Lafayette, Indiana. Around the same time, Egger finally succeeded, after years of nagging, in persuading Foodchain, the Atlanta-based national association of programs involved in recovering perishable food, to adopt job training as a top priority for its organizations. "Waste is wrong," Egger says. "Everybody knows that. Be it food, money, or men and women, we can't afford to waste any of them."

DC Central Kitchen embodies another critical premise of successful grassroots efforts: the most successful way to help people grow is to build on their strengths, not cater to their weaknesses. Knowing that homeless men who've whipped their problems with drugs and alcohol *want* to work, Egger gives them a chance to prove it, and to learn a useful skill.

## *Getting Food to People: Soup Kitchens and More*

When Lynn Bellew and her daughter migrated to Anchorage from the Lower Forty-eight in the late 1970s, rattling northward along the AlCan Highway, they ate a lot of canned beans out of the back of their station wagon. "Bean's Cafe is open," the girl would chirp from the back as she handed her mother a lukewarm helping. When they arrived in boomtown Anchorage and saw street people eating from dumpsters—still an unusual sight in pre-Reagan America—it didn't take them long to start sharing beans and soup with less fortunate neighbors. Their grassroots operation, Bean's Cafe, soon moved into permanent quarters and has since grown into one of the nation's largest and best.

Winter is long and mean in Alaska, even in the relatively mild latitudes of Anchorage. You can see it even in the summertime, in the thin, fragile-looking trees, and in the buildings that appear hunkered down with only tiny windows set in sturdy walls. It's no place to be homeless, yet people who work with poor folks here know that hundreds of people make it through the winter in snow caves and ramshackle huts, shivering and burning an awful lot of firewood. Some are unemployed oil-patch workers; others are hippie types who came to the Far North in search of independence and maybe a grubstake. Many are alcoholics. Alaska lures pioneers and more than a handful of misfits, and a lot of them end up at Bean's, looking for a meal and getting more, including a ration of dignity, self-respect, and a hand up and out of the troubles that put them on the street.

The Bellews quickly graduated from a rolling soup kitchen on a pickup truck to a concrete-block building in downtown Anchorage. Fire safety laws imposed a seventy-nine-person limit on occupancy, however, and before long hungry diners were forming long lines outside even in the dead of an Anchorage winter. Approaching the legislature when the state was flush with oil money during the early 1980s, Bean's got a $600,000 grant to construct the large, well-equipped building and high-tech food-service kitchen that now serves three to four hundred people daily, breakfast on weekdays and a main-meal lunch every day, 365 days a year, for a total of some 350,000 meals served last year.

They're hearty meals, too, rib-stickers intended to provide all the nutrition a hungry person needs for Arctic days. During an autumn visit in 1993, I sat with Bean's social service coordinator, Barbara Bennett, a busy woman who was nursing a severe case of laryngitis, and filled up from a tin platter heavily loaded with a slab of hot pollock and a bun, spicy macaroni and cheese, green beans, salad, prunes and figs, white cake—and the institution's trademark, a large, steaming bowl of bean soup. "It may be the only meal some of them get today," Bennett croaked, gesturing around the large room packed with several hundred hungry people.

Feeding hungry people is only a part of Bean's mission, however. When lunch is over, Bean's doesn't run its visitors out of the building, as many soup kitchens do. The doors are unlocked throughout the day, keeping the warm and welcoming room available as a day shelter for anyone—no questions asked—who walks in and is willing to obey its basic rules of behavior. Perhaps most important, through Bennett and a handful of volunteer assistants, Bean's offers simple, pragmatic services, shorn of social-work jargon and brought down to a fundamental "How can we help you?" Through asking this question and applying common sense to the responses, Bean's helps some fifteen hundred people each year to deal with their most basic needs: a safe place to store important papers or medications. First aid. A spot in a literacy class. Or bus fare to a job interview.

Like most creative grassroots programs, Bean's gets by on a spare staff (fourteen employees) and a modest budget ($500,000 a year), looking to volunteers to get the job done and community resources, ranging from corporate donations to small gifts from everyday citizens, to help keep the larder stocked. Even the state Fish and Game Department gets into the act, providing frozen venison in the form of road-killed moose, a protein source that is not insignificant on the northern frontier.

Bean's also shines in fund-raising and community publicity efforts. In its popular annual Bean-a-Fit drive, citizens of Anchorage host bean suppers at their homes and sell bags of bean soup mix (each year featuring a different recipe) for $3 apiece.

---

No one is starving on the Standing Rock Sioux Reservation on the barren prairie south of Bismarck, North Dakota. People aren't anywhere near clinical malnutrition, hollow-eyed and swollen-bellied, like the babies in Somalia. In fact, Charles (Red) Gates, the American Indian advocate who directs the reservation's federal Food Distribution Program, has a wall full of plaques and trophies honoring his national reputation as an effective hunger fighter who has been personally responsible for keeping food on the tables of thousands of Lakota Sioux families. But when Gates talks about keeping hunger at bay on the reservation, the sadness in his eyes shines right through his purple sunglasses. He knows that the federal commodities program he administers—along with food stamps, the Department of Agriculture's surplus food grants to women, infants, and children (WIC), and school breakfast and lunch programs—is all that ensures that the Standing Rock Sioux have enough to eat.

"Like the other Lakota Sioux reservations, we have close to ninety percent unemployment here," he said, shaking his head. "In the twenty-four years I've worked for the tribe, I've seen things go from bad to worse. So many of our people are so dependent on welfare, they think they're stuck there. I don't."

It was a near thing for him too, Gates says. As a young man, he followed the path of many other modern-day Sioux. "I got married young. I got into heavy alcohol. My wife and I had five kids before I was twenty-five." But somehow he got turned around, landing a job with the U.S. government and later, nearly a quarter of a century ago, taking over the reservation's food distribution program. Over the years he's developed renown as a spokesman for American Indian nutrition programs, rising to the level of president of the National Association of Food Distribution Programs on Indian Reservations. The coalition has successfully pressured the Department of Agriculture to change its practice of merely dumping surplus commodities on the reservations to at least marginally supplying nutritional needs.

There's nothing really new about the program at Fort Yates. As on many Indian reservations, the old commodities distribution program continues very much as it did before the Food Stamp Act of 1973 replaced it for poor people in much of America. On the reservations, a monthly food allocation remains an alternative to food stamps for those who choose it, and about half of Standing Rock's recipient families do. Some two thousand people from 720 households report to the program's gray warehouse on a dusty street in tiny Fort Yates for boxes of groceries each month. More families receive their shipments by truck to drop points closer to their homes on the two-and-a-half-million-acre reservation.

Why do so many prefer to receive the commodities themselves rather than food stamps? For a variety of reasons, Gates says. Grocery shopping is limited to one small supermarket and one or two convenience stores, where prices are high. The commodities allocation offers good value, even if the food is uninspiring. A single person's monthly load—seventy-five to eighty pounds of assorted items, mostly nonperishables and canned goods—is valued by the federal government at $37.50 but is actually worth two to three times that much on the open market.

Moreover, the paperwork is minimal. An applicant who brings in sufficient proof of income must fill out a single two-sided sheet—a far cry from the fourteen-page application for food stamps—and a decision is reached promptly rather than one's simply being put on a waiting list. And the atmosphere at the warehouse is friendly and supportive, in contrast with widespread reports of food stamp administrators who treat clients with sullen hostility. Shoppers simply walk up to a service window where the month's choices are listed, ranging from apple, grapefruit, pineapple, orange, or grape juice to lentils, pinto beans, or Great Northern beans to canned tuna, chicken, or beef. "The tuna is pretty good," says Gates. "The beef? It's horrible. But some people can make good things out of it."

Once the recipient makes out a list (elderly folks are allowed to jump ahead in line) and the computer spits out an invoice, the crew behind the long counter, with the efficiency of long practice, quickly assembles the order and carries it out to the customer's car. "For a family of four, the food covers this whole counter," Gates adds. In addition to food, the program distributes information on nutrition and health, (for example, brochures on preventing heart disease), and classes in diet and nutrition are also offered. Following up on a recent bright idea, the program is running a recipe contest, with cash prizes and bright ribbons for the best new ideas for turning USDA canned goods into appetizing meals.

Gates goes to considerable lengths to ensure that the books are up to date and accurate and that things run smoothly. Signs prohibit anyone under the influence of drugs or alcohol from coming onto the premises, sternly warning, LAW & ORDER WILL BE CALLED. Even smoking is forbidden in the warehouse.

So when Red Gates sits back in his office and looks out over his domain, he does so with justifiable pride. But at the same time, he knows it's not enough, and he doesn't have a magic wand. What can be done to relieve poverty at Standing Rock, or for that matter, on all the nation's Indian reservations? Bold leadership would help, he says, confiding that he wishes the reservation's tribal council were less conservative about trying new ideas for economic development, such as making use of the tribe's growing buffalo herd both for meat and as a tourist attraction. He wishes there were some way to end the turf battles that make it difficult for the reservation's various food distribution programs and those for the elderly to work together, since their concerns and their clientele often overlap. Remembering with obvious nostalgia the large garden his great-grandmother used to grow, he'd like to see the reservation launch a community gardening project.

Economic development, however, is central. Tribal colleges like

Standing Rock College at Fort Yates have recently made a big difference in offering teenagers on the reservation the opportunity to get an education. But when these students graduate, they face the choice of leaving the reservation to find jobs or staying home and finding none. Lakota culture being what it is, the majority stay.

"Four years ago," Gates recalled, "the state of North Dakota held a poverty conference. The farm crisis was going on, people were leaving the state, and they were finding all these people on welfare. They were really excited about that. So they asked me to speak at their conference, and I told them, 'What your group is talking about—we've faced it all our lives.' "

## *Inch by Inch: Community Gardening*

America's sorriest record on ensuring a fair shot for all its people has to be on the Indian reservations, although the competition for this ugly trophy is keen, with strong arguments for the title coming in from black, white, and Hispanic communities as well. To a considerable extent, we've demonstrated equal opportunity and affirmative action in the casual way we've screwed poor people.

Here and there around the country, in places as diverse as the Mississippi Delta country, the Rio Grande Valley, Appalachia, Alaska, and the Dakotas, I've heard a surprising number of people say, with almost boastful anger, that theirs is the poorest county in the United States. I've never heard it said with any more credibility, though, than in Shannon County, South Dakota, the western third of the huge Pine Ridge Reservation, where some twenty thousand Oglala Lakota Sioux live at a level of poverty that's difficult to imagine in the United States.

Stretched across a swath of arid prairie south of the Badlands and east of the Black Hills, which are sacred to the Lakota, the reservation is larger than the entire state of Connecticut, yet it contains just one full-service grocery store and two convenience stores to serve all its residents. According to the 1990 U.S. Census, fully 63.4 percent of Shannon County's people live below the federal poverty line. Fourth- and fifth-generation welfare dependency is all but inevitable in an area with an incredible unemployment rate of 87 percent. With such staggering numbers, it's hard to believe that such an idealistic emotion as hope is ever found here.

Yet hope was almost electric one Sunday afternoon in the summer of 1993 at the commencement ceremonies at Oglala Lakota

College, where more than one hundred graduates wore eagle feathers in their hair and joined in a traditional powwow.

"Look at that beauty," said commencement speaker Russell Means, the American Indian activist, gesturing at the unusually green hills that surrounded the reservation this damp summer. "How can we be poor when we live in such beauty? Why are we poor, without enough to eat and enough homes?"

Means, whose daughter, Michelle Charging Crow, was a member of the graduating class, spoke of a wave of freedom spreading over the land in recent years and challenged the Lakota to relearn self-reliance. "Look at this land, our sacred Mother Earth. In the years you have been in college, the world has waked up to freedom. I challenge you to put into play the concept that we are a Lakota Nation. Freedom is our byword. Remember freedom."

Meanwhile, amid the poverty of tiny frame dwellings and mobile homes that dot the rolling, treeless plain, a few good people are trying to make a difference.

When Tom Cook decided to defy the draft in 1970, he couldn't have dreamed that he was inadvertently setting his life on a course that would lead him, some twenty years later, to the Dakota Badlands. Cook, a Mohawk Indian, grew up on his family's farm in upstate New York, where he was driving a tractor by the time he was eleven. When the draft call came, he said, "I figured it wasn't my war, and told them I wouldn't go." Sentenced to two years of community service, he spent the time developing and directing a community gardening project on the St. Regis Mohawk reservation.

After a few years working as a steelworker on high rises in New York City, as many Mohawks do, Cook moved West, marrying a Lakota woman, Loretta Afraid of Bear, and settling down on her family's property near Slim Butte, in poverty-ridden Shannon County, near the South Dakota–Nebraska border.

Nine years ago, realizing that food stamps and welfare grants left his family and virtually all of his neighbors struggling to feed themselves, he decided to start a gardening project for the Lakota, for whom community gardening had been a tradition in the past but had completely died out as the younger generation lost interest in the old ways.

With the help of a grant from the Bryn Mawr Church of Philadelphia, Cook purchased a tractor and a small truck. He tilled, plowed, and disked, and began gardening an acre of property where his wife's family—all fifteen of them—lived in a fifteen-by-thirty-foot log cabin. "The produce from the garden supports about thirty people for two or three months a year," he said.

As the years went by, Cook spread the gospel of family gardening throughout the reservation. He tills and plows land for gardens, buys seed and seedlings using limited grant money and donations, and offers gardening advice, although he finds it's rarely needed, since the reservation's older people still remember the basics from pre-War days when gardens were common, and they love to teach the younger folks how things are done.

Cook now claims responsibility for 196 gardens producing vegetables for more than a thousand people, and he says this stretches his time, energy, and money to the limit. He's received small grants, mostly from the Christian Relief Services' Running Strong for American Indian Youth program. Living from grant to grant leaves him forever uncertain whether he'll be able to finish out each season, much less buy another tractor and truck so he can expand his Johnny Appleseed vision to nearby Wounded Knee and Kyle.

"We have so many social problems, and they're all derived from dependency—inertia caused by dependency," he says. "I'm hoping with the revival of interest in gardening, there'll be a surge of interest in self-reliance."

---

Just a few miles north of Slim Butte on the Pine Ridge Reservation, an unlikely partnership between a group of Lakota Sioux and a college in Germany has given birth to an amazing sight: a large, prolific garden in the traditional circle shape of Lakota mythology, bearing vegetables and hope—with the help of modern farming techniques that have transformed what used to be a dry creek bed.

College students from Bonn, Germany, work here every summer alongside Lakota students from Oglala Lakota College. Their completely organic garden combines the most modern sustainable agriculture techniques with the ancient medicine wheel of Lakota tradition. The curriculum gives the German students the kind of practical experience that comes with getting dirt under their fingernails. At the same time it exposes them to a culture that many of them never heard of, says Professor Martin Baumgart, a German agronomist whose long black hair and swarthy complexion make him look more like a Sioux than some of his students. Just as important, he adds, the project is seeding the Lakota Nation with a core of trained organic gardeners who can go into the community and teach their neighbors to build food self-reliance and pride.

This unlikely partnership started in 1989, when a professor from Bonn's agricultural school came to the Pine Ridge Reservation for a four-week visit and met Leonard Little Finger, a member of the now-defunct Lakota Produce Growers Organization and an advocate for health and nutrition programs. The professor left with the conviction that the Lakota land, people, and religion were ideally suited for organic gardening. The next year he dispatched Baumgart, who had been finishing his doctorate in biological plant protection and grasshopper control in Benin, West Africa, to Pine Ridge to start the partnership and the garden.

In its second year the curriculum attracted sixteen Lakota and fourteen German students for a full-time fourteen-week course lasting from May through August. Students are expected to do field work both in the community garden and in individual plots along with classroom studies of organic farming techniques and Lakota culture. Using drip irrigation and innovative mulching techniques, the gardens are not merely instructional but experimental. They yield heavily, and the produce is donated to nutrition programs for elderly people on the reservation. This completes another cycle of the medicine wheel, this one linking students and the community.

Most important, Baumgart says, is the lesson people are learning. Of eight Lakota students in the 1991 course, seven started their own gardens the following year. One was marketing his produce off the reservation for a profit; and two of them, Jody Plenty Wounds and Steve Bear Eagle, joined Baumgart as teaching assistants. "It needs time, time to get the community involved," he said. "We want people who can take over and train their own students. I won't spend my life here, *ja*? But these people will, and they can take it over."

If it survives, that is. At a time when Baumgart would like to expand the project to add community gardens in several other parts of the reservation—at an estimated cost of $30,000 per garden per season to cover equipment and salaries—the program lost its funding in 1994. Baumgart and Leland Bear Heels of Oglala Lakota College were busy dealing with red tape and writing grant applications in an effort to keep alive the program and the hope it brings.

## *Access to Food*

There is no lack of food in this country, but access to it is a problem for a fair number of Americans, and not only reservation Indians and other people who live in regions too isolated to support gourmet shops and sprawling hypermarkets. In a vivid demonstration of the inverse relationship between big business and morality, most major supermarket chains abandoned the nation's inner cities during the 1970s and 1980s, leaving many urban dwellers in poorer neighborhoods the choice between shopping at ill-supplied and overpriced corner stores or making long, difficult treks to the suburbs.

In Knoxville, Tennessee, activists and transit authority executives put their heads together and came up with a solution to the problem so simple that it's hard to believe no one had thought of it before. It works like this: anyone who rides the K-Trans buses at any time may ask the driver for a Shop & Ride coupon. Stamped to validate a purchase of $10 or more at any of the region's Kroger, Food City, or Cox & Wright grocery stores or at Watson's department store, the coupon is valid for a free bus ride home. It's as simple as that. Worth up to $1.20, the coupon offers a small but significant boost to those who must rely on public transportation to get from the city to suburban markets.

Although the transit authority assumes that most people who use the program are poor, the coupons are available to all, "even if they make $100,000 a year," said David White, director of marketing for K-Trans. What's more, no one minds if someone picks up a coupon and passes it along to a friend.

The costs of the program are minimal. The transit authority prints the blue-and-orange coupons, collects used ones, and turns them over to the stores' management, which reimburses their full value. A total of 2,286 shoppers claimed free rides in March 1993, resulting in a $2,000-plus investment that the grocery operators consider well spent as a way to get shoppers into their stores. The transit authority gains riders, and the benefits to the people who use the coupons are obvious. "It's a win-win-win situation," White said.

In theory at least, Shop & Ride has been on the books since before anyone now involved with the program can recall. It may have originated as a device to get people into the downtown department stores during the early 1970s, when the rise of suburban malls was sucking the lifeblood out of downtown Knoxville. But by 1990, only Watson's was participating in the program, and only a few riders were taking advantage of it each month.

That all changed when several happy coincidences resurrected the program in its new form, with the focus primarily on groceries.

First, activists started agitating about poor access to groceries for inner-city residents. In the informal discussions that followed among city officials, advocates, the Knoxville Food Policy Council, and the transit authority, Kroger's regional manager Hunter McWilliams agreed to get the chain's nine Knoxville stores involved, and the program took off. During the first full month of participation, just 25 Kroger shoppers got free rides. But after being publicized by advertising on buses, in stores, and on radio and television, the number of Shop & Ride passengers rose to 1,100 within six months. A total of 1,640 Kroger shoppers got free rides in March 1993.

Shop & Ride couldn't have survived without cooperation among a range of corporate interests, advocates, and the transit authority, which adjusted bus routes and schedules to ensure that inner-city areas and supermarkets were linked with reasonably direct and frequent service. K-Trans has received some local publicity, and its officials have won awards from the American Public Transit Association for creative marketing. But an idea this simple and this effective deserves more exposure. There's no reason that every American city with a bus company and problems of access to food in the inner city can't do the same.

A few other cities have tried more direct approaches to regaining access to groceries. New Community Corporation, a major project aimed primarily at restoring decent housing and job opportunities in Newark after riots devastated its ghetto neighborhoods in the mid-1960s, was able to persuade Pathmark Corporation to open a full-scale supermarket in an inner-city neighborhood nearly twenty years after all the major chains had abandoned the community. That effort, however, took ten years, during which New Community's organizers had to assemble a real-estate package and negotiate a deal in which the nonprofit organizer was both developer and landlord of the $16 million complex. It includes a fast-food restaurant as well as a supermarket, and is now a major employer, helping to make a dent in the neighborhood's jobless rate.

## *Urban Gardens*

Planting gardens won't end hunger in America's cities. No one can credibly claim that it makes sense to turn ghetto dwellers into small farmers capable of feeding themselves, their families, and friends out of garden patches in vacant lots.

But some surprising things happen when people start working together to plant a few tomatoes, a row of squash, some spinach and peas, and maybe a patch of marigolds on lots where burnt-out houses have given way to weeds and junk and flattened beer cans. Plant a garden and you don't just get a few baskets of produce. You get visual proof that things are changing. Seeing signs of change, sometimes the people in a neighborhood go on from there and turn to painting and fixing a few things. Things like dilapidated houses—or recalcitrant city councils.

I saw this in 1990 on my first trip to Houston's inner city Third Ward, where a handful of small but thriving gardens had me humming David Mallett's ballad: "Inch by inch, row by row, gonna make this garden grow."

Houston is a big city—with over two million people, the fourth largest in the United States. There's a lot of sophistication and a lot of money around, despite the poverty that's too often associated with large Hispanic and black communities as well as the oil-based economy, which took a severe beating in the 1980s. It's a town with no zoning regulations at all, which means that the view changes quickly as you drive down the street. Well-to-do residential areas and commercial districts, dingy slums and glittering skyscrapers are startlingly juxtaposed. Together with the hot, humid weather (even in October, my glasses steamed over instantly when I stepped out of my air-conditioned car), the unprepared visitor might suspect that he's wandered into an alien landscape.

More appalling than the humidity, however, is the condition of some of Houston's neighborhoods. The Chamber of Commerce rarely refers visitors to the Third, Fourth, and Fifth Wards, the ghetto sections that ring downtown, where you'll see mile after mile of tiny frame houses with windows covered with boards, rooflines sagging in disrepair, drab gray siding that hasn't seen fresh paint in a decade. I'd seen some scruffy places in my travels, but never as widespread or consistent a zone of blight as this. How about Community Development or HUD money, I asked my guide, Ellen Mitchell of the city's Interfaith Hunger Coalition. Didn't the city do anything about housing blight? She just shook her head and frowned. "Houston never really took advantage of that."

Houston was built by oil money and boosted by go-go developers. They would build a neighborhood, sell the houses, and move on, allowing the free market to do its best—or its worst. The inner-city neighborhoods didn't make it, and they got no help from the city, not for housing renovation or for infrastructure. The streets are as cratered as the lunar surface, and many blocks aren't even served by city water—within sight of the city's modern downtown towers. Only the subtropical vegetation, shade trees, and occasional flower beds save these neighborhoods from looking worse than the South Bronx or parts of Chicago's South Side.

Counting blacks and Hispanics together, Houston has a majority of minorities, who are well represented in its city council. However, black and Hispanic council members have made little effort to form coalitions to help their neighborhoods. Even if they did, Mitchell said, "There's no money there." The council's apparent lack of interest is mirrored in the two daily newspapers, the *Houston Post* and *Houston Chronicle*, which at the time I was there assigned *no* reporters to cover social services or domestic hunger, homelessness, and poverty. After all, as Mitchell grimly points out, "The people here whose lives are working never see the people whose lives aren't, and they don't even have any way of knowing it happens."

Into that setting, more than fifteen years ago, came the Interfaith Hunger Coalition, a church-related group of volunteers that started out feeding people and quickly expanded its reach. It now operates one of the nation's best networks of neighborhood gardens.

Like many grassroots antipoverty efforts, the group began as a handful of churchgoers who were concerned about the increasing number of people showing up at rectory doors begging for something to eat. Staffed entirely by volunteers, the group opened a few food pantries. Much to everyone's amazement, about five thousand people were served in the first year. By the end of Reagan's second term in 1988, the organization's 2,200 volunteers operated 135 pantries and served more than 1.2 million meals a year.

That last number had dropped significantly, to about 800,000 meals, by late 1990. The drop reflected both good news and bad news. The good news was that Houston's economy was reviving, and a lot of unemployed people had gone back to work. The bad news, however, was that not enough volunteers were available as people got tired, burned out, and quit. The media lost interest in covering the same old story of hunger in the inner city—though it had never been very well covered when it was a new story. Even once-reliable sources of donations dried up as food drives faltered and grocery chains opened salvage stores to sell the food that they used to give away. "It's frustrating," Mitchell said. "But we need to keep plugging away; a little bit of hope survives that someday we're going to see some changes."

Funded by a $750,000 annual budget, the Hunger Coalition's food pantries are largely housed in participating churches. They get their supplies from the metropolitan food bank, individual contributions, and a major annual food drive publicized by local television stations. The group also runs a separate program in which one hundred volunteers visit frail, elderly, and housebound individuals monthly, bringing them not only a bag of food staples but companionship and advice. This effort is entirely funded by private contributions, counting on the generosity of residents who commit $20 a month, $240 a year, to support one elderly person. It has been a godsend for its five hundred recipients, but it's estimated that as many as eighty-five thousand elderly people in the Houston area could be eligible for similar aid if the donors were there.

In its newest and highest-profile program, the Hunger Coalition has undertaken to establish community gardens in every poor neighborhood in Houston. Started in 1987 by a single volunteer, within three years this program of self-help expanded to include twenty-five separate garden plots scattered throughout the city and suburbs. It is supervised by a full-time staff member, Dr. Bob Randall, who has quickly earned a national reputation as an expert on urban gardening.

The original idea was simply to offer poor people a way to supplement their limited food resources, but the gardens quickly lured a larger constituency. A fair number of people who take part in the program don't need the food but simply like to garden. They then donate the produce to food pantries for those who need it.

Gardening isn't easy in Houston, where the hard, clay soil requires that garden beds be built up above the ground and filled with imported earth. The climate compels gardeners to schedule two growing seasons, one in the spring and the other in the fall, taking a break during the most scalding months of summer, when the heat batters plants and people with equal fierceness. Technical assistance is thus particularly important, and the Hunger Coalition provides expert advice at all its garden plots.

Based on members' reports of how much was produced, Randall estimates that the project's gardens provided eighty-five thousand servings of vegetables for hungry Houston residents in 1989. And there are spinoff benefits besides. The arrival of the Fourth Ward Garden, a manicured oasis in the middle of a dilapidated slum, prompted surrounding homeowners, including even absentee landlords, to spruce up the neighborhood. Quite a few houses sported their first coats of new paint in many years. Inspired by the goings-on in the community garden, some neighbors have started small gardens of their own. Best of all, the people who live near the gardens developed a proprietary pride. "They watch them closely," Mitchell said. "We get *no* vandalism in here."

---

Another remarkable urban gardening effort is Sue Gunderson's Self-Reliance Center, an innovative organization operating out of a sturdy, mustard-colored stucco house just south of downtown Minneapolis, where community gardens grow both vegetables and political power.

Founded in 1973 in response to the energy crisis and rising fuel costs, the center started as a home-weatherization program aimed at helping the neighborhood's poor people save on utility bills. Energy advocacy remains one of its main projects. It became the Self-Reliance Center when it merged with a small food program in 1976, and since then has worked toward the twin goals of keeping residents fed and warm.

Workers in the energy program go out to more than three thousand poor households a year to conduct free energy audits and give weatherization advice. As part of a progressive political coalition, the group also lobbies the state legislature on energy issues. In 1990, for example, it got a law passed that forbids utilities to cut off service to anyone who can come up with just 10 percent of the amount owed.

In its food program, the Self-Reliance Center oversees sixteen garden plots all over Minneapolis. More than five hundred families, about half of them Hmong immigrants from Laos, now enjoy home-grown fare from the gardens, which has allowed them to cut their grocery budgets significantly.

The gardens yield more than just zucchini and bok choy. Gardeners harvested a memorable political lesson when city officials proposed paving over a large plot near a mostly Hmong public-housing project. Most of the immigrants don't speak English well, and in their native country, criticism of the government is not prudent. So they were reluctant to object when the Minneapolis Community Development Agency announced plans to cancel the garden's lease in order to build a fancy French bakery on the site as an economic development project.

Organized by the Self-Reliance Center, however, several Hmong were given a quick, thorough preparation and paraded before the Minneapolis city council. Their appearance made headlines. Afterward they flattered the head of the Community Development Agency so thoroughly to reporters that the media dubbed him "the father of community gardening in Minneapolis." He soon promised that the garden would never be replaced.

Another initiative the Self-Reliance Center dreamed up is the Intergenerational Gardening Project. Older, mostly white residents who had yard space but lacked the time or energy for gardening were set up as partners with a racially mixed group of young, poor people who were eager to get their hands in the soil but had neither space to do it in nor experience. These team efforts resulted in huge quantities of produce as well as unexpected relationships between people who otherwise would likely have eyed each other suspiciously if they had passed on the street.

---

Here and there around the nation, other creative grassroots advocates have come up with other approaches to urban gardening. The Seattle Food Committee/Food Resource Network, for instance, has created Lettuce Link, a publicity campaign to encourage each of the two thousand participants in the city's P-Patch community gardening program to plant an extra row of vegetables each summer, and to donate the produce from that row to the city's food pantries. Lettuce Link transports donations from the gardens to the pantries; and it encourages poor people to grow their own food, in the P-Patches or in their own back yards. In similar fashion, the Austin Community Garden in South Texas operates two major garden programs. The popular Sunshine Gardens rent garden plots to middle-class and more affluent hobby gardeners, who may share their bounty with the poor. The twenty-two Greenspot plots are available free to low-income people at schools, public-housing projects, and other public locations throughout the city.

Inch by inch, row by row, a lot of people are making gardens grow.

## *Back to the Farm*

Americans are losing the connection between the food we eat and the farms where it's grown. When I visit farm country, it always surprises me to see things growing and walking around in fields that seem more familiar wrapped in neat plastic packages in the grocery store. But activists worried about feeding hungry people and a growing number of out-of-work farmers have begun to notice that they have more in common than they thought. One place where this is happening is St. Louis, a large industrial city that's not often mentioned in the same sentence with agriculture.

With close to two million inhabitants in Missouri and Illinois and a still-thriving mix of heavy industry and a growing sector of information and service businesses, St. Louis looks more like a Rust Belt burg than a prairie town. But the people who live here are proud to consider their city the "Gateway to the Plains"—as symbolized by the Arch, a looming presence visible for miles—and there's a strong tendency to look West rather than back to the Northeast.

Like other midwestern cities of German heritage (Cincinnati, Milwaukee, Louisville), St. Louis doesn't look poverty-stricken. It lacks the broad swaths of run-down and abandoned neighborhoods that you find in Detroit or Newark or even right across the Mississippi in East St. Louis, one of America's most battered towns. St. Louis appears clean and stable, free of litter and graffiti, and there aren't many vacancies in its sturdy redbrick houses and apartment buildings. The diverse industrial base ensures relatively low unemployment. Still, as is typical of urban America in the closing decades of the century, many full-time jobs don't pay enough to lift a family above the poverty line, creating that oxymoronic category called working poor. Low-grade hunger—not starvation, but never having quite enough, especially at the end of the month—is endemic, and emergency feeding is a major need. It's estimated that two hundred thousand people, fully 10 percent of the metropolitan area's population, rely on food pantries or soup kitchens for at least some of their nutritional needs.

One outstanding organization, Hosea House, not only distributes some twenty thousand pounds of food to four thousand people each month, but it goes beyond mass feeding to seek ways to help people feed themselves. One such way involves a creative link between hungry city people and poor farmers.

Founded in 1977 as a nondenominational organization of church people concerned about the increasing number of homeless people on the street, Hosea House responded by holding fund-raising rummage sales, then quickly added a food pantry that soon grew to become the city's largest.

Rather than depend on charity to keep the pantry's shelves stocked, though, the organization under executive director Amanda Pulliam decided to try to connect farm and market for mutual benefit. The Rural-Urban Linkage Project, known as LINK, works like this: Hosea House contracts with two Missouri farms—one run by a couple in the town of Bourbon who grow organic crops, and the other owned by a poor, elderly farmer in the state's southeastern "bootheel" region—to provide produce for distribution in the food pantry.

By dealing with the growers themselves, Hosea House cuts out the intermediate levels of wholesaler and distributor to get food products at direct-from-the-farm prices. At the same time, the contracts guarantee a market, and a living, to the farmers. But that's only part of the benefit. Because the produce comes in fresh from the farm, its shelf life is vastly improved over the often stale and shopworn produce that groceries donate and food banks provide. What's more, Hosea House hires unemployed and homeless people (for minimum wage) to help harvest the crops, providing them some income. And finally, by purchasing more produce than the food pantry needs, Hosea House brings in a surplus that is sold for full retail price at a city farmers' market, earning enough extra cash to cover the harvesters' pay and other incidental expenses. Over the coming years, the group hopes to contract with enough additional farms and increase volume sufficiently to transform the food pantry into a community food cooperative.

In a separate but similar project, Hosea House organized about forty other St. Louis–area food pantries to pool their financial resources and, with this increased buying power, arranged with Tyson Foods to purchase chicken by the truckload for a price better than even supermarkets can negotiate.

Hosea House doesn't stop when people are fed. It also runs a labor pool that organizes and markets the skills of inner-city residents, and it offers other services as well: literacy classes, counseling, a free clothes closet. Moreover, it has emerged as a leader in a political network of food pantry operators.

"We did a survey a few years ago," Pulliam recalled. "Our clients told us, 'Yes, hunger is a problem, but what the hell are we going to do with the rest of our lives?' As clients came in, volunteered here, they'd chat over coffee and doughnuts and talk about *why* they were hungry. We put two and two together and realized that there's more we can do here."

A statewide survey by the Missouri Association for Social Welfare revealed that some 450,000 people in Missouri were hungry at some time each month. Of those, 40 percent live in the St. Louis area, and 57 percent of the total are children. Hosea House's own statistics showed that 72 percent of its clients had children under twelve. "That motivated us to do something for those children," Pulliam said. "They're the next generation of St. Louisians."

The real issues underlying hunger, in the opinion of hungry people themselves, are lack of affordable day care, jobs and training, education, and housing. This reality drives more and more groups like Hosea House to graduate from distributing food to creating programs like LINK, which not only feed people but create income for family farmers.

## Farmers' Harvests

Some politicians and commentators argue that hunger doesn't exist in America because there's little evidence of clinical malnutrition or the debilitating diseases associated with chronic hunger in the Third World. But that's easy for politicians and commentators to say: they don't go to bed hungry.

The exact number of hungry Americans eludes analysis, at least in part, because hunger is difficult to measure and almost as difficult to define. But the 1992 Broglio national poll, independent statewide studies, and a combination of nutritional surveys by the government and respected institutions like the Center for Hunger, Poverty and Nutrition Policy at Tufts University make clear that hunger is a gnawing social problem in America. Some studies indicate that as many as thirty million Americans—about one in every eight of our neighbors—go hungry at least once each month. As many as a million elderly Americans are said to be malnourished, with another five million at risk of hunger. Fully 30 percent of older people tell pollsters that they sometimes skip meals because they don't have enough to eat. According to rigorous surveys by the Food Research and Action Center during the early 1990s, at least five and a half million children under twelve in this country went hungry at least part of each month, and another six million were at risk of hunger. Some estimates range as high as twelve million young Americans (under eighteen) having to go hungry at times during 1994, and half a million chronically malnourished.

I contemplated these numbers as I drove in late summer up the beautiful highways along California's Central Coast into Monterey County, a garden spot known as "the nation's salad bowl" for all the lettuce it grows—not to mention artichokes, broccoli, and lately strawberries, which are now the region's number-one cash crop.

Farmers there were congratulating themselves on the harvest of 1992. That year Monterey, Santa Cruz, and San Benito Counties grew and sold 1.4 *billion* pounds of produce, ranking the region near the top of the nation's agricultural producers. (Scratch a farmer and you'll find a pessimist, of course; local growers were also clucking that the total amount of sales was up only 1.5 percent over the previous year, less than the rate of inflation.) That's a lot of lettuce and artichokes and strawberries, making it all the more egregious that poverty and the hunger it causes are particularly troublesome in the area. Making things worse, advocates say, is the fact that Monterey's primary businesses, agriculture and tourism, are both low-paying and seasonal, meaning that large numbers of poor people not only can't make a living wage when they've got work, but they generally can't get work year-round.

The situation keeps activists busy at places like F.O.O.D. Crops, a project of the Second Harvest Food Bank of the Central Coast. Food Organizations Organizing and Distributing Crops was founded by Tim Driscoll, a local strawberry farmer who, as a participant in a national program called Agricultural Leadership of America, happened to visit a food bank in Texas in 1989. He came home fired up with the idea of enlisting the region's food growers and shippers to contribute produce to food banks. By applying peer pressure to guarantee that every farmer contributed, the system would ensure that everyone participated and that no one would have to bear an excessive part of the load. Area food banks, meanwhile, established a simple but efficient system to coordinate donations, divide them equitably among emergency providers, and ensure that transportation was available.

In 1990, the first year of the operation, local growers donated a total of 250,000 pounds of food for distribution to the region's hungry people. By 1992, donations grew to *2 million* pounds.

F.O.O.D. Crops operates out of a tiny brown trailer attached to the back end of the Watsonville food bank, in a flat expanse of broccoli fields that seem to extend as far as the eye can see. Using a toll-free number, producers telephone F.O.O.D. Crops as soon as they have a surplus available for donation. (The afternoon I was there, farmer Dave Johnson called in to offer a hundred boxes of carrots.) A worker immediately keys the details into a computer database, which keeps track of the totals and is also programmed to print out quarterly reports for the growers to document tax deductions. Donations are divided among the four regional food banks—Second Harvest of the Central Coast, Monterey County, California Gray Bears, and Community Pantry of Hollister—which pick up the produce and distribute it to community food pantries and soup kitchens.

The program initially took its chances on the timing of donations but has since evolved an effective new system. A total of thirty-six growers have agreed to donate a thousand pounds of fresh, usable produce every third week throughout the March-through-September growing season. The group is thus guaranteed twelve thousand pounds every week, though the take often rises to sixty thousand pounds at the peak of the season.

This generosity yields an occasional embarrassment of riches when a food bank receives more perishables (lettuce, for instance) than it can easily dispose of. At this point, sharing with other area food banks begins. The national Second Harvest network, as a matter of policy, doesn't let food banks trade surpluses with each other, but it doesn't object if they "share" their bounty among themselves. Last year, for example, the food banks in Monterey frequently gave quantities of salad produce to Fresno, which shared its surplus of fruit later on.

The basic program is working so well that it is already being replicated. It's clearly cost-effective, operating with a staff of one full-time and one part-time worker and a $45,000 annual budget. Its ideas are worth copying, and other groups are planning to do just that—not only in nearby Fresno, but across the country in Dade County, Florida. There, the Farm Bureau was looking into a similar venture, having learned about F.O.O.D. Crops from an article in *Packer* magazine, an agribusiness trade publication.

## *A Lesson from the Ancients*

Taking advantage of modern agricultural technology while looking to ancient tradition to find lessons for today: this is the theme of Native Seeds/SEARCH in Tucson, Ariz., an organization committed to rediscovering ancient food crops of the Pima Indian tribes of the Sonoran Desert country along the border between Arizona and Mexico. Native Seeds/SEARCH's scientists scour the high desert country from northern Mexico through southern California,

Arizona, and New Mexico in search of seeds, then preserve and propagate them. The seeds and technical advice are given free to residents of the O'odham Indian Reservation in southern Arizona, who are encouraged to grow the crops and use them in a healthful diet.

The O'odham people (whose tribal name is pronounced, approximately, by coughing gently while saying "Och! Oddam") have suffered severe health problems, including endemic diabetes, because of poor diet composed largely of fatty government commodities and fast food. Now they have a chance to enjoy a better diet, one they can grow themselves at little cost. Program director Mahina Drees says some native foods, including cholla buds, prickly-pear pods, and mesquite flowers, have been shown to help control diabetes by regulating the body's metabolism of glucose. Other nutritious crops, particularly tepary beans and corn, are high-protein staples that are much more healthful than the high-fat, high-starch foods that make up the typical diet on the reservations.

Through mail-order catalogs, Native Seeds/SEARCH also sells its unusual seeds at full cost to garden hobbyists all over the country, providing a source of revenue that helps support the program and its work with the O'odham. It's just one more example of a nonprofit organization that feeds people *and* changes their lives.

That's the point, of course: "Teaching people to fish" gives them the tools to change their lives, and the self-reliance they gain is better for them and better for the community they live in. Simply feeding people will keep them from starving, but it goes on ad infinitum. Turning welfare recipients into self-reliant individuals is a policy path with an eventual end—a positive end that satisfies everyone.

# 2

# People Need Shelter

THE CHIPS AND SALSA ARE TASTY AT THE IMPROBably named Carlos O'Brien's restaurant in Phoenix, and the servers are just as chipper and friendly as you'd expect at an Anglo-style Mexican spot that specializes in Margaritas the size of birdbaths.

Our server, a young woman whose badge bore the name TORY, had an especially attractive smile, and it sparkled as she listed the day's lunch specials.

"We paid for that smile," confided my companion, Suzanne Viehmann.

Eh?

Tory is a participant in The Bridge, one of the best transitional housing programs for homeless families I've run across anywhere. Viehmann, the director of the program, set up the lunch at Carlos O'Brien's so she could show Tory off. A once-homeless mother of two who'd ended up living in a Salvation Army shelter, Tory got counseling, an apartment, and a few thousand dollars' worth of dental repair work through The Bridge. Things were looking better in her life, she said between the burritos and the tamales, than they had for a long, long time.

"They gave me a lot of support," she said, flashing that expensive smile. "I finished school, and every time I wanted to whine about something, they let me do it."

Like the guys I met at Cafe 458 in Atlanta, Tory was lucky enough to find her way into a program that embodies a fundamental secret of turning lives around: it has to happen through one-on-one listening to people, listening to them long enough to understand what they really need. This is another premise that recurs: You can't rebuild people's lives on an assembly line.

The Bridge rebuilds lives with a flourish. Surprisingly simple in its outlines, it's an alliance of a dozen Phoenix-area churches, each of which agrees to raise $400 a month to cover the rent for a specific homeless family, like Tory's, for one to two years. But that's not all. In addition to cash, each church also commits ten volunteers to coach the family during that period, giving them support and friendship to back up the more traditional case management that each family gets from a Bridge social worker. Former director Marlene Bjornsrud told me that The Bridge uses the word *coach* consciously: A coach shows people how to do a job but doesn't do it for them. A coach helps people determine their potential and then lets them reach for their goals on their own. It's all aimed at helping the individual identify and work out the problems that got her on the street in the first place. This is not a short-term project; it takes three months of counseling before a formerly homeless parent is ready even to begin addressing underlying problems.

In a significant variation on most transitional housing programs, Bridge families aren't segregated away from the community in an institutional setting reserved for homeless people. Rather, they're moved into nine units scattered through the thoroughly middle-class La Mirada Apartments, a three-hundred-unit adobe-style complex with shady, manicured lawns, laundry rooms, and swimming pools. Bridge families aren't singled out as "special" or "different," and their neighbors generally don't even realize who they are.

After four years of operation, The Bridge is starting to establish an unquestionable record of success, with 84 percent of its participants returned to self-sufficiency: living in their own adequate housing and holding full-time jobs. One, an animal lover, had hoped to find work as a veterinary technician but, learning that this trade pays just $5 an hour in the Phoenix area, got a job as a dog groomer instead. With growing skills based on the experience, she has a reasonable hope of earning $30,000 next year. Another Bridge graduate is an electronics technician with the Federal Aviation Administration. Others are working well above minimum wage as respiratory technicians, practical nurses, even house cleaners—a line of work that some might consider menial but that in Phoenix's more affluent suburbs pays an attractive $15 an hour or more.

The program works, but its weakest element is the structural limit imposed by the number of churches and civic organizations willing to take on the long-term responsibility for giving a homeless family financial and moral support. With about a dozen sponsors in the picture and only nine apartment units available in La Mirada, the group has been able to move just twenty-eight families off the streets since 1991.

---

However, another outstanding nonprofit program, also in Phoenix, has found a way to tap a substantial source of federal housing money to operate a similar kind of program. Committed to providing what it calls a "continuum of care" for homeless families, from emergency shelters to transitional housing to self-sufficiency and homes of their own, the Homeward Bound program has built an enviable record in just four years, winning praise from Henry Cisneros, secretary of Housing and Urban Development, and President Clinton.

Founded as an independent nonprofit organization in 1990 by a group of local housing advocates, including Monsignor Ed Ryle of the Catholic Archdiocese of Phoenix, Homeward Bound was designed to fill the gap between emergency shelters and market-rate housing. At that time, the bad news of the real estate crash in the region became good news for activists for low-cost housing. As a huge number of foreclosed single-family houses reverted to HUD, advocates invoked the rarely used Single Family Property Disposition–Homeless Initiative rule of the Cranston-Gonzales Act, which requires that local offices of HUD, on demand, inventory all residential property every October and set aside 10 percent of it for use by nonprofit programs for homeless people. (This set-aside is widely available, but relatively few communities take advantage of it. It was particularly appealing in Phoenix because of the large pool of foreclosed property.)

In Phoenix's collapsed real estate market, 10 percent of all foreclosures amounted to a lot of houses. Homeward Bound soon built an inventory of 125 houses for which it pays $1 a year under five-year leases. Mostly single-family units but including some condominiums, they now house about five hundred homeless people (mostly in single-parent families) as they undergo case management, counseling, and skills training aimed at getting them back into the community.

Homeward Bound has built on this windfall with a public-private partnership akin to the Bridge's system of church sponsorship. Donors are sought within the community to provide both money ($3,300 a year) and volunteer support for each homeless family. Sponsors may be private individuals or corporations (both McDonnell-Douglas Corporation and the Phoenix Suns basketball team are on the list), and they may contribute either cash donations or volunteer help or both. Volunteers are carefully screened and trained before beginning contact with homeless families, and they work in concert with professional social workers.

To qualify for entry into the program, families must be homeless and earn less than 50 percent of the median income in Maricopa County; they are expected to be "clean and sober," having completed drug and alcohol treatment if necessary and free of substance-abuse problems for six months. As the adults find employment, they are expected to pay 30 percent of their adjusted gross income—equivalent to what they'd pay for rent—in program service fees.

Homeward Bound succeeds because it makes a firm and continuing commitment to the people it serves. Families spend an average of one year in "transition" as they go through counseling and rehabilitation, then may remain in Homeward Bound's housing for up to two more years as "graduates" while they accumulate the wherewithal to become homeowners or self-sufficient renters themselves. Even at that point they may remain in contact with social workers for up to two more years to ensure that they don't slip back into the difficulties that led to their homelessness. "Close, ongoing contact makes the difference," says Pamela Martin, the organization's director.

As of early 1994, Homeward Bound has brought sixty-seven families through its program, with an overall success rate of 84 percent—a figure that is constantly improving and approaches 95 percent among recent participants. It provides more than thirteen thousand "bed-nights per month" for individuals who would otherwise be in emergency shelters or worse.

Homeward Bound and The Bridge both demonstrate another principle that's common to many of the most effective grassroots programs: They've learned the importance of turning to their communities for support, both financial and through the goodwill of volunteers. This is not a trivial matter, given the scope of the problem and the willingness of many Americans to lend a hand, as long as someone shows us what to do and persuades us that it will make a difference.

## *Who's Homeless?*

The stories of people like Tory and her family reveal that there's more to homelessness than the standard image of street drunks and aggressive panhandlers, an image that many would willingly exclude from the discriminatory definition of "deserving poor."

Although estimates vary depending on the political persuasion of the observer, there's little dispute that somewhere between 1.3 million and 3 million Americans—enough to populate a large city—are homeless as defined by the McKinney Act, which provides funds for housing and job-training programs: lacking a fixed permanent nighttime residence or living in a temporary shelter, welfare hotel, or any public or private place not designed as a sleeping accommodation for human beings. Another 8 million live in overcrowded or dangerously substandard housing, at risk of becoming homeless at the whim of a relative or friend, landlord or building inspector.

While nearly half of the homeless population is made up of single men, fully 40 percent of America's homeless are families, and a quarter are children. One-fourth to one-third are thought to be mentally ill, with an equal (and significantly overlapping) number chronic alcohol and drug abusers. Without even getting into the contentious issue of such individuals' right to services, it's worth noting that the majority of homeless Americans are neither mentally ill nor substance abusers.

Issued in 1994, a federal report called "Priority: Home!" estimates that six hundred thousand Americans are homeless on any given night, and that seven million were homeless at least once during the second half of the 1980s. A disproportionate share of the homeless, about a third, are veterans and minorities. The homeless population is mainly made up of people under age forty with badly worn family ties, no steady employment, and a higher than average incidence of drug and alcohol problems as well as mental illness. The report traces homelessness to two main causes: poverty and chronic disability, including mental illness, substance abuse, AIDS, and tuberculosis.

"Homelessness is not just a housing problem," said Henry

Cisneros, chairman of the task force that came up with the federal report, "but a condition that can result from poverty, substance abuse, a lack of affordable housing, or the collapse of institutions that once cared for persons with mental and physical disabilities."

The most effective grassroots initiatives against homelessness attack it from two directions: Programs like The Bridge and Homeward Bound, which move homeless people and families into long-term transitional situations, and emergency shelter programs, which focus on short-term, immediate needs but, again, deal with homeless people as individuals and look beyond providing a bed for tonight to ask what can be done to make tomorrow different. Managing by objectives—setting goals and plotting the most direct and pragmatic path to them—is as important a factor in the most successful grassroots programs as it is in the most successful businesses.

## *Boarding Houses for the 1990s*

Boarding houses were a fact of daily life for working and middle-class people during much of our nation's history. But with rising expectations following World War II, single-room housing with community bathing and dining fell into disrepute. When the last of the old single-room-occupancy (SRO) hotels started to disappear from most American cities, the casualties of gentrification in the 1970s and 1980s, few advocates for poor people were sorry to see them go. Generally overpriced and roach-infested hovels run by slumlords, and often harboring drug dealing and worse, SRO hotels were equated with the worst aspects of low-cost urban housing.

But that was before the dramatic increase in street homelessness during the Reagan years created a new perspective. When the options are sleeping on a street grate or huddling fearfully in an armory shelter, a tiny but private hotel room with a toilet down the hall starts to look surprisingly appealing.

Then came Lakefront SRO, run by a group of Chicagoans who, as creative people often do, turned the conventional wisdom on its head. Defying the assumption that single-room occupancy hotels are necessarily fleabags or hotbeds of crime and prostitution, Lakefront operates modern SROs that provide hundreds of people with permanent places to live. By mobilizing grants and loans and a nonprofit approach, it makes them available at a price that poor people can afford.

Lakefront SRO started small, back in 1985, when a group of emergency-shelter operators in Chicago's yeasty and multi-ethnic Uptown neighborhood noticed a sudden, dramatic increase in the numbers of homeless people. It didn't take them long to discern that the problem was directly related to the disappearance of the neighborhood's traditional SRO hotels. Some were being "gentrified," converted into expensive apartments that the former residents couldn't afford. Others were lost to abandonment when property owners simply walked away. The same thing had been happening in many urban areas, as a study by the Jewish Council on Urban Affairs revealed back in the 1970s. Though much of the criticism of the sleazy side of the SRO business was thoroughly justified, advocates increasingly realized that well-run SROs could be an attractive alternative for people with very little money, and they were a big step up from living on the street.

For Lakefront SRO, it took a specific neighborhood problem to transform a group of concerned citizens into a nonprofit agency with a practical, effective program. Residents of the old Moreland Hotel, a dilapidated SRO with a dubious reputation, feared for their future when the owner, as other landlords had done, literally threw his keys on the street and abandoned the property. They contacted Legal Aid, which got in touch with the Lakefront organizers. With an eventual $2 million in city, foundation, and federal housing money, the group gutted and renovated the three-story building as a modern hotel. It reopened in 1989, renamed the Harold Washington SRO in honor of the city's late mayor. In addition to providing seventy safe, clean rooms for single adults, the Washington SRO also includes retail storefront space along busy North Sheridan Road—room enough for the organization's offices, with extra square footage to rent to commercial establishments to help support Lakefront's budget.

The idea worked so well that Lakefront SRO quickly moved to purchase and rehabilitate two more nearby SROs in the same neighborhood, the Malden Arms and a hotel for women only, the Miriam Apartments. By late 1994, with the opening of the Delmar, the Major Jenkins Hotel (named after a popular Lakefront resident), and Carleton Terrace, a gothic structure so imposing that its neighbors on shady Magnolia Street call it Dracula's Castle, Lakefront will have created 615 units of affordable housing in its immediate neighborhood. Rents vary according to tenants' incomes and to the specific financing requirements of each building. They can range up to 30 percent of the resident's income, in most cases from $90 to $250 a month. The group is now turning its sights to other Chicago neighborhoods, hoping to replicate its success in the larger, poorer West or South Side.

Lakefront has standardized manuals and information packages in order to respond to requests for technical assistance from other nonprofits interested in starting similar housing projects. The group's work is known throughout the country; I've run into organizations taking a close look at the Lakefront model as far away as New York City and Anchorage, Alaska.

Creating low-cost housing by renovating existing SROS is the organization's essential principle. Staffer Janet Spector Bishop says, however, that that's only half the secret of its success. The rest of the formula combines the bricks and mortar with full-time social services available to every resident. Lakefront calls it "blended management," with social workers and building managers working together to keep a close eye on residents and try to anticipate their needs. Social services are never forced on the residents; the programs are strictly optional. But because they're available in a friendly, supportive, nonthreatening setting, they get used.

"They make you feel like a person, not like some animal that you kick to the curb. If a guy wants to get his life together, he can do it here," said fifty-nine-year-old Richard Binion, who shuttled between homeless shelters and abandoned buildings for three years before moving into the Delmar SRO when it opened in May 1994. Once a scene of drug dealing and prostitution, the refurbished structure contains 163 neat rooms equipped with donated furniture.

Residential rules provide for eviction in cases of nonpayment of rent or disruptive behavior, but these stern measures are rarely needed. According to Lakefront's statistics, residents tend to stay. At the Washington SRO, for instance, just fourteen of the seventy occupants moved out during 1992, and only two of those were evicted or denied lease renewal. Two died; the rest moved on to other housing as working, taxpaying citizens.

That's a happy ending, Bishop said, but it's by no means a requirement. "What's a success story here? Two different stories are equally valid. One comes in, and over time, with the help of social services, is able to stabilize their life, follow the rules, make a life in the building, and never have to leave. The other comes in, uses us as a safe haven to get job training, rebuild their life, and hooray for them. If they get a good job and move on, that's a success story too."

## *Holistic Housing*

It's a long way from Chicago's Uptown, with its streets full of Vietnamese and Hispanic groceries and shops, to the seemingly slower-moving scenes of the Delta country in southern Mississippi. But poverty is pretty much the same everywhere, and a state effort has drawn a bead on its problems with an aim surprisingly similar to Lakefront's.

Mississippi is a state of considerable beauty, with rolling fields and pine forests, but a closer look reveals the stubble of worn-out cotton fields and many tiny, dilapidated dwellings along lengthy stretches of road where even the mobile homes that some folks use as permanent housing are ramshackle and in need of paint.

Mississippi's Special Initiative Programs (SIPS) hold real hope for change. Just being established when I passed this way in 1992, SIPS creatively link public and private sectors to build quality housing for poor people. Like Lakefront's hotels in Chicago, each development offers both low-cost housing and a range of social services. The rehabilitative programs aim to help residents make their stay in subsidized housing temporary as they lift themselves toward self-reliance and independence.

Linda Perry is executive director of V'BURG Inc., a nonprofit housing organization that became the state's partner in the Vicksburg SIP, one of two pilot projects. She says the idea for SIPS came out of the work of former governor Ray Mabus's 1989 Task Force on Housing, which found that quality low-cost housing simply wasn't available in Mississippi, and that the private sector had no apparent interest in building more.

Making it happen in cash-poor Mississippi required bringing together public money, grants, and donations from many sources. The state made the first move, coughing up $900,000 in HUD's federal Community Development Block Grant money to build low-income housing. The project also gets $357,000 from the city of Vicksburg for construction, plus $30,000 in in-kind services; $30,000 from the Warren County government; and $80,000 worth of heating and air-conditioning equipment from Entergy Corporation, the parent company of Mississippi Power & Light. When I saw Perry last, she was surrounded by stacks of papers on her dining room table in suburban Jackson, trying to figure out where to find another $230,000 to finish and furnish the houses built by the Vicksburg program.

In Metcalfe, Mississippi, just north of Greenville, a $1.5 million SIP has four components. Eight old military barracks are being redeveloped as a twenty-four-unit apartment complex with an education and development center attached. A two-year residential program will set up individual case management objectives based on each resident's specific needs and goals. Participants may continue their education and receive employment training, ranging from adult literacy and GED qualification to community college classes. On-site day care and transportation services are provided. Screening for physical and psychological disorders; arts, cultural, recreational, social, and civic activities; and counseling designed to deter adolescent pregnancy, drug and alcohol abuse, and gang membership are also available.

The Vicksburg SIP is building thirteen new single-family houses and a Family Training Center, primarily for single-parent families. Among the programs offered on the site will be licensed developmental child care for preschoolers and after-school activities for older children; a career development program for parents, including community college education and job training; and comprehensive family support services by more than two dozen state and local agencies to deal with issues such as primary health care, food, income, and rent assistance, and transportation, and to provide counseling in subjects like budgeting, nutrition, and parenting.

Perry argues that programs like those being tried in Metcalfe and Vicksburg would work well for any transitional residential group with common interests or concerns, such as mentally or physically handicapped people, ex-prisoners, even college students. "This model has strong implications for any group that wants to create a sense of community and combine housing with various human services." The approach seeks to bring group members into the mainstream by including them in general programs rather than segregating and isolating them, even for seemingly benign purposes.

SIP programs are not low-budget, Perry concedes. Even modest housing in a mild climate takes considerable money to build, and it takes more money to support families in transition. But, she says, "We've got to learn to apply resources, to bite the bullet to cure social and human ills. It's going to take a commitment."

Again, the key is the holistic approach. Program operators

aren't satisfied to put a roof over people's heads and declare all their other problems are somebody else's job. Restoring the lives of homeless people requires addressing *all* the problems that separate them from the community.

## *The Mr. Goodwrench Principle*

"Pay me now, or pay me later"—the dictum that Mr. Goodwrench offers motorists on television is equally instructive for campaigners in the fight against poverty. It makes far more sense to try to prevent people from becoming homeless in the first place than to pour our energies into stopgap measures. The Martin Luther King Center in Tacoma, Washington, aims to do just that: to stop homelessness before it starts.

Tacoma is a much smaller city than neighboring Seattle (about 150,000 compared with the larger city's 510,000), but its citizens do not think of it as a suburb. Until around 1900 the cities were closer in size and were quite competitive, but decisions to route major rail links to Seattle made its growth much faster. Nevertheless, Tacoma strives to keep up with its sister city. It has its own port, and its taxpayers eagerly invested in the construction of the Tacoma Dome to lure sports and civic events from Seattle's larger Kingdome. But whereas Seattle has coffee bars and bistros, Tacoma is blue-collar and proud of it. It enjoys its rowdy reputation, even if the effluent from the mills sometimes leaves the city reeking.

Tacoma was harder hit than Seattle by the shift away from heavy industry in the Pacific Northwest in the 1970s and 1980s. The port shrunk, a smelter and a boat factory closed, and real wages in the community increased only 27 percent between 1980 and 1988, while average rents rose 77 percent. That's the kind of simple arithmetic that left a lot of Americans across the country wondering where to find the economic development that they kept reading about in the newspapers.

Most of Tacoma's poverty is centered in the Hilltop neighborhood, which lies along a ridge east of downtown, away from the water. It's not an in-your-face slum, not with its trim, sizable houses with large yards in neighborhoods that don't seem at all unpleasant—at least not until a closer look reveals peeling paint and a surprising number of boarded-up windows and vacant lots.

Hilltop has felt waves of immigration as each newly arriving ethnic group gets its start here—the latest coming from rural

Cambodia, a group with the particular handicap of being from a preliterate culture, historically unfamiliar with reading and writing, not to mention urban life. Smaller groups of other Asians who haven't yet moved into the mainstream, American Indians, and a relatively few blacks and poor whites make up the balance of Tacoma's poor people. Though relatively recent, drugs, gangs, and crime are growing problems.

In this setting the Martin Luther King Center is working to fight homelessness, but it makes a practice of reaching out to do just about anything that the neighborhood needs to have done.

The center started in 1977 as a small organization of three local churches providing recreational programs for neighborhood children. That proved simple enough, but it didn't take long to see that the people of Hilltop needed more than swimming competitions and basketball games. As the former executive director, Maureen Howard, explains, the center wrote a broader agenda: "It would be a place where people would work together across the old barriers of race, age, gender, religion, class, skill, and disability. The work would meet critical social needs; workers would be fairly compensated; and management would be participatory. We would try to listen to and learn from the people we wanted to help. We would use that experience to advocate for justice."

The first social need was obvious: homelessness. Taking advantage of every funding opportunity it could find, the center began to attack homelessness on every front, from providing emergency shelter to establishing transitional housing programs for people working their way off the streets to strategies aimed at preventing people from slipping into homelessness. Within five years it found ways to finance and open four emergency shelters and two transitional housing complexes. It also offers a number of advocacy and support services as well as an unusual prevention program called the Housing Exchange.

This program applies the Mr. Goodwrench principle with a vengeance. It pays now, not later by giving people the means they need to avoid the catastrophes that lead to homelessness. Chris Phelps dreamed up the program after working with newly homeless people for a year. During that time he became increasingly frustrated because there seemed to be no way to intervene before people lost their homes, rather, programs for the homeless focused on offering them social services after they were already on the streets. Under Phelps's direction, a corps of staff and volunteers began making an aggressive effort to identify families who couldn't pay their rent, or for whatever reason were about to become homeless. The program aims to provide such families with resources before they are ever evicted. Emergency financial assistance might be offered (as cash flow permits), or sometimes information on tenants' rights and dealing with landlords or on access to social service programs will avert the crisis. "We're problem solvers," Phelps said. "We don't just give them a telephone number to call, but real help."

When people have already become homeless, the King Center has a collection of additional services to help them. Its G Street Shelter provides emergency housing for thirteen families with children. The attractive two- and three-bedroom cedar town houses nestling into the hillside neighborhood look more like a pricey apartment complex than low-cost housing. "If you make it look right, people respect it and keep it that way," Maureen Howard said. Because homeless children have problems separate from those of their parents, the G Street Shelter has on its staff a full-time children's advocate, Sara Chehraz, who devotes all her energy to the forty or more children living in the shelter on any given day.

Another King Center shelter, Mandela House, is a six-unit apartment building for single homeless women and mothers with babies. It rose, phoenix-like, from the burned-out shell of a gutted house that the center's staffers persuaded the city to give the group—along with money to rebuild it—rather than tear it down and leaving the lot vacant. An adjacent duplex that was initially purchased for office space was also later turned to emergency housing.

The King Center tries to scatter emergency and transitional housing throughout the community rather than concentrating it in a ghetto for homeless people. The Last Chance Shelter in downtown Tacoma, named after the storefront saloon that formerly occupied the premises, offers another example of how to do a lot with a little. It is a dormitory-style men's shelter with seventy-five beds lined up in three closely spaced rows of double bunks, with a bathroom and shower on one side and a small dining area at the back. It's sparkling clean, with a brightly colored tile floor waxed to a mirror shine, and resident manager Joey Neild said the residents keep it that way. Despite the close quarters and the relatively small staff (three workers during the early evening and two after 10:00 P.M.), it's a safe place, where fights, assaults, and robbery are unknown. The shelter's success is a matter of caring people being there, said

Neild. The staffers—all formerly street people themselves—like their jobs and treat the residents with respect. The shelter also houses weekly physical, dental, and psychological clinics for homeless people.

For homeless families needing intervention on many levels, the King Center's Sojourner Housing provides long-term, intensive case management. Social worker Michelle Johnson keeps contact with families "as close as they need," sticking with them for up to a year, or until their situation is stable. "The goal is for them to be in a position not to need us anymore," she said. "The key is to help them establish goals and get out of the feeling that tomorrow is their only concern."

Besides its housing facilities, the King Center boasts a variety of other approaches to the problem of homelessness. Its Outreach Project, for instance, hires formerly homeless workers to get out on the streets to find mentally ill homeless people and, in one-on-one sessions, gain their confidence and persuade them to apply for Supplemental Security Income (SSI) and other benefits. The project has been so effective that the Social Security Administration—which is known for its reluctance to let go of one dime that it doesn't have to—denies only 5 percent of SSI applications submitted through the King Center program, in contrast with a 70 percent denial rate nationwide.

Still another King Center activity, the Homeless Veterans Reintegration Project, uses Department of Labor money to find and assist the former servicemen, many of them mentally ill, who abound on the fringes of the many military bases in the Puget Sound area. Director Earlie Reynolds, a navy veteran of jungle warfare in Vietnam, works closely with these men. After getting cleaned up and adequately clothed, the veterans receive extended counseling to help them reclaim their lives. The process seems to be working: Reynolds placed twenty-one men in jobs in a single month in the winter of 1992, including a man who had been on the streets for more than three years.

## *The Challenge of Mentally Ill Homeless People*

The front lines of the fight against homelessness are on the streets, where the primary issue isn't whether the nation's street people number in the tens or hundreds of thousands or even millions. There the immediate objective is to keep people alive, and healthy, and fed and clothed, and after that, maybe, move them along into transitional programs.

People who work with the homeless often repeat with frustration the standard remark that a person who isn't mentally ill when he comes to street life will probably become so within a month or two. But even someone who has a significant disconnection with reality usually understands that it's more comfortable to be warm than cold, which is why you'll see a lot of homeless people out and around—and organizations to serve them—in places like southern California. In Los Angeles, for instance, the Downtown Women's Center treats mentally ill homeless people with dignity, and does it without wasting a lot of money. Operated by women for women, it occupies two cheerful and well-kept buildings that make an unexpected bright spot on dismal Skid Row, a gritty underworld only a short walk east from downtown.

Its day center, in a new building replacing one damaged in the Whittier earthquake of 1986, is painted in multicolored pastels with a huge wraparound mural featuring caricatures of regular visitors. It's filled with good art and furniture and looks so far from institutional that a visitor might mistake it for a trendy boutique or bistro, in the unlikely event that a visitor in search of such pleasures would stray into this neighborhood.

Former director Jill Halverson, who wrinkles her nose at the thought of the starchy, fatty foods that most rescue missions dole out on tin trays, prefers to serve residents nutritious hot lunches with plenty of vegetables. The center is open from nine to five daily, including weekends. Showers, beds for naps, a large-screen television, and a mail drop are available, along with other services a homeless woman might need, including medical and psychiatric care.

The adjacent forty-eight-room shelter provides permanent housing, not just a temporary way station. Each large, private room has a lighted entry that resembles a cozy front porch, complete with mailbox. The furnishings are simple and spare, with every surface made of formica or tile for easy cleaning, yet the pleasant combination of pastels and earth tones makes the decor anything but drab. The rooms have colorful framed prints, wall-size bulletin boards that allow residents to personalize their surroundings, and full-length mirrors, a way to gently nudge them to think about their appearance. Although the center has a communal kitchen that residents can use, every room has a small refrigerator for storing snacks.

Since almost every occupant is mentally ill, all qualify for SSI benefits. The center plays a strong advocacy role in making sure that they get these benefits, along with Medi-Cal, the state's medical insurance. The center requests $155 of each recipient's $755 monthly stipend as rent, which covers the building maintenance and leaves the recipient $600 a month for her other expenses.

Halverson has been working on Skid Row for twenty years, much of that time with male alcoholics. She decided to change focus and start the Downtown Women's Center in 1977 after she met and befriended Rose Arzola, an alcoholic, schizophrenic woman who lived in a parking lot and kept all her belongings in a shopping cart. Arzola, sixty-three, one of the center's first residents, had been sober for eight years and in treatment for her schizophrenia for three years when I met her in 1993. She smiled shyly and didn't have much to say, but she's told friends that she's happy now. And, Halverson said, "She's no longer hearing voices." In this business, small victories like this are sweet. Halverson says she sometimes despairs of moving these women out of poverty. Aside from the ravages of mental illness, the legacy of generational poverty, with grandmothers, mothers, and children caught in a cycle of welfare dependency, sometimes seems impossible to break.

Her clientele at both the day center and the shelter continues to increase as waves of immigrants from Central America and Asia crowd into the cheap housing on Skid Row and force poorer women—many of them black, many of them single mothers, most of them addicted to crack—onto the streets. So Halverson does what she can to give them a chance without insisting too strongly on unrealistic short-range goals. "They have to overcome several generations of nobody having work and having no role models. We try to take care of immediate needs and very basic behavior modification, like speaking in a normal tone instead of hollering, being on time, and sharing chores; but it's hard to get someone to the place where they can work for a salary when they can't show up on time to wash the dishes. We're really starting at step one. It's frightening what has happened to some of our communities—generations of living on welfare, no work, and then you lay drugs on top of that."

The life isn't easy. Mattie Lewis, who once made a decent living as a live-in housekeeper in Beverly Hills, told me of finding herself out of work after an operation and a nervous breakdown. She ended up in a single-room occupancy hotel whose management was so lax that, one night in January, she slipped out of her unheated cubicle to an all-night movie theater to stay warm. When she returned, the manager had changed the lock to her room, forcing her to a city congregate shelter. She eventually found her way to the Downtown Women's Shelter, and she says she never wants to leave: "All my friends are here, and I can sleep in." With her life stabilized for now, she is beginning to get her mind around the idea that she can work again.

In 1990 the Downtown Women's Center published a book of poems written by some of the women for whom it has provided refuge. This is Carol Webster's celebration of her home:

*Jill's Hotel is an oasis in Hell*
*The forgotten women doomed to the streets*
*Jill's Hotel is a heaven where they can rest and be clean.*
*The crimes of the street are locked out and forgotten.*
*No dirty motel of roaches and rodents*
*The pastel colors are more like a blossom*
*The rooms are comfortable like some vacation retreat.*
*To feel cared about makes us feel real good about ourselves*
*And makes us know that we are not forgotten.*
*The living room is comfortable,*
*Makes it more like a home*
*To some, for so long the only home*
*They have known.*
*In a dipsi dervi world we feel nice and secure*
*To those that made it possible*
*I want you to know*
*That you are greatly appreciated.*
*And Jill's loving kindness will not be forgotten.*

## *Restoring Homeless Families*

It's only a few miles on the freeway from Skid Row to the Boyle Heights neighborhood of East Los Angeles. The poor, mostly Hispanic neighborhood has seen better days, but it still musters neat lawns and flower gardens to contrast with spots of peeling paint, battered cars, and blotchy graffiti scrawls. A pastel blue bungalow on a hilltop is home to the House of Ruth, a place of hope for homeless women and children, who find both temporary shelter and a day care center, along with a well-planned array of support services aimed at giving residents the tools to rebuild their lives.

The House of Ruth began as a charitable effort by four sisters of the Carondelet order, who brought homeless women and children into their home and gave them beds, meals, and caring support. This effort gradually developed into a structured case management system, while the sisters' work evolved into a nonsectarian, nonprofit organization. It boasts a remarkable record of success. Director Judy Cole says all of the women who have come through its temporary (two-month) shelter and moved into the follow-up counseling and training program at Casa Guadalupe for six to eight months have found permanent housing and either located jobs or are in continuing education or training programs. "They've at least got momentum in their lives again."

The center's money management program requires residents to deposit all their earnings from benefits and part-time work. They may draw out up to 20 percent for pocket money but must save the rest toward rent and a deposit on an apartment. Job training through other community agencies focuses on attainable goals like secretarial, sewing, and housekeeping skills, although one resident successfully completed a course training to be a laboratory technician in anesthesiology. "We refer them to resources, we help them get on track, the kids in school, the mother to parenting classes, ESL classes, whatever they need," Cole said. "You have to take care of *everything*. If you just get the benefits taken care of without noticing that she's being abused, for example, you haven't done enough."

As with most grassroots initiatives, the numbers, though encouraging, are small. The House of Ruth wins victories by devoting considerable individual attention to each family, which pays off for the families but limits the population that can be served. With two case managers on the staff, the agency can only accommodate six families at a time, four in the House of Ruth and two in Casa Guadalupe. Over four years, this translates to about eighty families. For those families the program has made a world of difference—the difference between homelessness and poverty and a productive place in the community. For policymakers, it underscores yet again the lesson that if a self-reliance initiative is to work, it must have the luxury of time and resources to devote one-on-one to individuals. It's a job that can't be done by mass production on an assembly line.

---

There's a similar lesson on the other side of the country, in the eastern Pennsylvania steel towns of the Lehigh Valley, where the mansions of nineteenth-century industrial barons and sturdy, clean, freshly painted Victorian dwellings create urban streetscapes that don't show the worst signs of urban blight and decay. A diversifying economy and relative proximity to New York City bless the area with a relatively low unemployment rate. But there's a hidden poverty here, including a significant element of working poor, that makes homelessness a real and growing problem.

Two elements have combined to make things worse in recent years, inspiring new efforts to deal with family homelessness. First, local advocates say, the completion of Interstate 78 has brought New York City within commuting range, making it possible for people who work in the city to live in the Lehigh Valley. The effect was a sudden, sharp increase in rents and property values that pushed many low-income working people out of their homes. Second, a lack of affordable day care makes it difficult or impossible for wives to supplement family income with jobs, or for single mothers to work at all. As a result, deep, pinching poverty strikes at a few in a community where it has a low profile and can easily be ignored.

No one is ignoring poverty, however, at the Sixth Street Shelter in Allentown. Before 1985 the region had only two shelters, one open only to women and children and the other strictly for men. Absurdly, intact homeless families were forced to break up to get into the shelters. To address this problem, a nonprofit group bought three adjoining buildings in an older section of two- and three-story turn-of-the-century structures near downtown. Bootstrap financing allowed the group to start up quickly with limited capital: Initially apartments were rented out in two of the buildings, and the income was used to pay for a seven-unit shelter in the third. After two years, with the help of a state grant, the mortgages were paid off and all three buildings opened as shelters. Later acquiring another building around the corner, the agency increased its capacity to accommodate twenty-five families in two separate programs.

Fourteen units are used for short-term shelter. Here homeless families stay for a usual maximum of two months, giving them sufficient time to weather a crisis and find permanent housing. This program typically houses eighty to ninety families a year and currently has sixty-three families on its waiting list.

Residents in the other eleven units, mostly single mothers and their children, may stay for as long as two years while the parents go through a focused, individualized program of job training or education. As at the House of Ruth, the long-term approach at the Sixth Street Shelter is to work closely with people and stay with them until the job is done. When I passed through in 1991, of the eleven heads of household in the program, one was in nursing school, one was in training to be a nursing assistant, four were in cosmetology school, two were in business school, and one was working on getting her general equivalency diploma.

The Sixth Street Shelter works by methodically assembling support and educational services to help people beat the problems that keep them poor. Budget counseling is mandatory, so that families will learn to use their financial resources wisely and save. Residents also get training in "good tenant behavior" to enable them to defuse landlord-tenant problems before they occur. A weekly support group is disguised as an arts and crafts program, in which residents are painlessly exposed to peer counseling and friendly support in a warm, nonthreatening setting. Moreover, residents are introduced to a wide network of social services and community support such as food pantries and utility aid, familiarizing themselves with ways to meet these needs *before* they move back into the community. Finally, a full-time student liaison works with residents of the shelter and local schools in an effort to keep children in their home schools during their stay in the shelter and to work with school officials to help ease problems in the schools that these at-risk students face. This counselor continues to visit the families regularly for three months after they move into their own housing, to ensure that they get help before small financial or family problems grow out of control.

## *Homeless Men: The Bottom of the Barrel*

Women and children, particularly children, are a relatively easy product for grassroots warriors against hunger and poverty to sell. The Food Research and Action Center elected in 1992 to focus its national advocacy efforts on a Campaign Against Childhood Hunger rather than hunger in general, believing that it would be easy to drum up support, and contributions, by evoking the image of hungry children.

It's quite a bit harder to squeeze much concern out of the average citizen on behalf of an unshaven, shaky wino or derelict rattling a paper cup in your face and demanding change. But adults go hungry and homeless too, and some of the greatest grassroots heroes in America are those who understand that change doesn't just mean pocket money but making things different.

One such hero is Kent Beittel, a rail-thin man of intense electricity, whose trim beard and wavy, shoulder-length hair contrast with his blazer and red "power" tie. A former Methodist minister who has also worked as a midwife, Beittel claims that he has been working on the streets for twenty-two years and never held a job that he didn't invent.

He presides over the Open Shelter, a barracks-like institution in a former warehouse building just across the Scioto River from the Ohio state capitol and the skyline of bustling Columbus.

"Treat people with courtesy and respect. That's the undergirding dilemma of this whole thing," said Beittel, whose words flow so fast and right that it's challenging for a reporter to keep up.

An example: The first thing Beittel did when he took over the shelter in February 1984 was to fire all fourteen security guards. A shelter, he says, is not a jail, and surrounding homeless men with goons bearing guns does not send the proper message. "What I do is design social service mechanisms that people are actually willing to use, in the face of a social service mechanism that people are not willing or can't use. Almost everyone who has dealt with life on the street or with the social service structure assumes that there are only two kinds of poor in this country: ineffective crooks and lazy bums. Most of the social service field is based on that assumption, and it is *wrong*. Most programs are set up to find out whether there is such a thing as a 'deserving poor person.' I resist that, fairly vocally. The result here is that the programmatic assumptions are based on a simple need: assuring shelter with peace. Sleeping safely with your eyes closed.

"The assumption is, no one aspires to live in an old warehouse. In the focus of everybody here, people vindicate the wisdom of Charlie Brown, the best social service planner in the universe, who said, 'It's hard on a face to get laughed into.' From a recipient's perspective, most of the system is a demonstration that one of the ultimate rewards of being classed as 'deserving poor' is having your face laughed into. When people come to a shelter, they are keenly aware of their perceived lack of value."

A shelter must be fair and consistent—blatantly consistent. "This is more important than being 'nice.' It's not important to be lovable, but it is important to be trustworthy." Beittel likes to tell about a staff member who gave one of the residents a quarter to use the pay telephone. When Beittel found out, he insisted that the staffer bring in quarters for the rest of the one hundred residents the next day to underline the point that everyone is treated alike.

"In everything we do, we try to generate predictability. Everything is done as much by rote as possible. We open on schedule, we close on schedule, and it's all posted. Our policies are clear, and they are posted. The policies are written, and they are shared with everyone when they come here, and they are discussed to make sure there are no questions. The whole place is based on predictability. Doctors, lawyers, meal schedules are all done in the same way every day. This is all based on the assumption that we are dealing with adults and that some standard of conduct is expected of adults, and if one doesn't practice adulthood, to the best of his ability, one separates oneself from the group for clearly delineated periods, directly related to the severity of the disruption." Consistent standards are important because the Open Shelter allows clients to walk in twenty-four hours a day and requires no prescreening. People aren't judged on the basis of reputation or past behavior but on how they behave after they arrive. An effective shelter needs to satisfy two somewhat contradictory needs: It must find ways to help people stay as long as they need to stay, but it also must get people to leave as quickly as they are ready to get off the street and back to a self-reliant lifestyle.

How does Beittel propose to break the cycle of poverty?

Over twenty years of working with homeless people, he has learned that people who manage to stay alive on the streets despite the roadblocks in their way are not losers but survivors. "Our premise is, anyone who's on the street and alive has something going for him. Otherwise he would have died." But homeless people have little incentive to plan beyond the next immediate crisis. "A person who's homeless is . . . dealing with where to sleep tonight, where to eat his next meal, where to hide his property. That sort of shrinks planning to the next few hours. So we need to be about helping people readjust their planning sequence while at the same time taking care of tonight."

Beittel's shelter solves these dilemmas by combining them. If a homeless person wants the predictability of a guaranteed bed and shelter, he must contract for it by working on a specific plan to move on to something better. "Are they leaving for employment? Are they leaving when they save enough to fix their transmission so they can go on to Dallas, as was their original plan? By helping us work toward their leaving, we'll help stabilize their situation." If a homeless person is unwilling to come up with a specific plan, he'll be allowed to stay if there's room, but only at the risk of having to go back on the streets if the shelter fills with people more willing to work on their problems.

"So, in short, homeless people can make 'reservations' at the Open Shelter by agreeing to participate in a plan that will stabilize their lives. If they're not willing to do that, they're still welcome to stay, but they have to participate in whatever is left over, first come, first served. The key is *willing*. There are some persons who aren't immediately capable of stipulating how they will leave. Our contract with them is, 'We will help bring you to terms with what it will take to help you leave.' "

The policy works. Although the Open Shelter is one of the few anywhere with no fixed maximum length of stay, the average resident stays only a month, and the return rate is just 7 percent.

Contrary to the conventional wisdom about congregate shelters, Beittel says theft is rare and violence among residents uncommon.

How can this be?

"Two ways," Beittel says. "One is directly tied to the issue of consistency and fairness. There's no way that a staff of four people can control the behavior of one hundred eighty at meals and a hundred in the shelter; the one hundred eighty have to give the four permission to shape the environment because they know it is in their best interest if it works that way. It's truly as simple as that.

"That's the *nice* half," he added with a crafty smile. "The other half is, I run this place like a gang. I've been on the street for twenty-two years, and I know about turf battles. We deal with disruptions on a turf model. Specifically, this place is private property. It's a very important thing for people to know this. When people tell me they're going to sue me or they're good friends with the president of the city council, I hand them my business card and say, 'Be sure to spell my name right.'

"The big thing is that these people are adults. All we do is remind them of the consequences of their own activities. Funders and social service providers do not understand the difference between the existence of a service and its availability." Beittel cites an excellent local drug treatment program with a national reputation. It has ten beds and a waiting list two years long. It works great, but who ever gets to use it?

Above all, the Open Shelter tries to make programs accessible. Beittel brings in physicians, lawyers, and a dentist for regularly scheduled visits. He is especially pleased with a Columbus Bar Association program for which he claims a 100 percent success rate, as he defines it: People come in and talk with a volunteer lawyer, who helps them determine whether they have legal redress for their problems, in which case they get legal aid, or whether they have simply, as he puts it, "been screwed." "In the latter case, the lawyer can give him a look straight in the eye and say, 'You've got a choice. You can spend a lot of time walking in your own shit, feeling miserable, stuck in the same place; or you can drop it and move forward. Either way, use it for a springboard into your future.'

"This is not a home for people who are homeless. It is an attempt to provide a springboard from which people leave. It belongs to us, not them. Our rewards are about *leaving*. Then you deal with how to do it. You have to empower the homeless people, but then agencies charge them rent and make them pay to use the phone. If we want them to leave, why do we take their damn money? Residents here make twenty-four hundred outgoing phone calls a month. That's something about staying connected. We have a message service that we take seriously, and we have a grievance procedure that works.

"I'm not a saint, not a minister, not someone who treats everyone as children of God. Some of the biggest jerks I know are poor, and some of the biggest jerks I know are rich. This is not a messianic, 'Oh, the poor.' It's a pragmatic, 'Let's get people out of here.' "

## *Putting It All Together in Nashville*

Kent Beittel is a maverick and a bit of a loner, with strong opinions that he's not afraid to put into action. He's the kind of guy who gets things done. Sometimes, though, people seem to function best in teams, joining their efforts with others'. Nashville, Tennessee, offers a good example of how folks fighting poverty in a midsize town can win by working together.

Living costs are relatively low in Tennessee, as they are in much of the South; but wages are low, too, and social service benefits are limited, so the region's many unskilled workers are caught in the familiar pinch of the working poor, toiling full-time without making enough to support a family. Additional elements turn Nashville into a virtual magnet for the poor and near-poor: Six major interstate highways converge here, and the lure of the country music industry makes the city an eastern version of Los Angeles, the end of the road and the center of unfulfilled hopes and dreams.

On the positive side, Tennessee boasts a reputation for tolerance, and with a relatively low minority population (16 percent statewide, mostly concentrated in Memphis), Nashville escaped much of the social upheaval of the civil rights movement and white flight.

Nashville's population is heavily Protestant (in addition to being the nation's country music capital, it is a center for religious publishing), but it is a mainstream, socially conscious if not progressive Protestantism, and the spirit of reaching out to help less fortunate people seems deeply ingrained in the city's way of life. Even in this age of backlash, for instance, a *Nashville Banner* poll in 1992 found that 80 percent of residents said they "feel compassion" for poor and homeless people.

Father Charlie Strobel, an inner-city parish priest who runs Nashville's Room in the Inn, has turned such compassion into action. He met with me in the summer of 1992, and came straight from saying mass at Holy Name Church, doffing his religious vestments to reveal a bright green-and-yellow jogging outfit. Strobel is tall, thin, and athletic, with a shock of sandy hair that falls across his forehead. Quick and articulate, he is committed to doing something for the hundreds of homeless people who pass through Nashville every year.

As the pastor of an urban church, Strobel moved early into what he calls a ministry to the homeless. By 1983, when the first Reagan recession swelled the rolls of hungry people in Nashville and across the nation, he opened one of Nashville's first soup kitchens, Loaves and Fishes, in his church's basement.

A couple of years later, during an unseasonably cold spell in the winter of 1986–87, Strobel noticed that several families had started spending the night in their cars in the church parking lot. They would run their engines occasionally, just long enough to warm the car a little. When morning came, they'd approach the rectory and ask for money for gasoline.

Unable to sleep at night while people were suffering on his doorstep, Strobel decided to convert the church cafeteria into an impromptu shelter. With the help of volunteers who took turns supervising the quarters overnight, it was kept open from around Thanksgiving through the arrival of milder weather at Easter.

The following summer, Strobel fretted about what the next winter would bring, leading him to the idea that eventually grew into Room in the Inn. He invited several neighboring churches to band together with Holy Name to break what would be a heavy burden for one church into smaller pieces that would be relatively easy to handle as a shared responsibility. Each church agreed to open a room to shelter homeless people and to provide volunteers for one night of the week. This would guarantee safe shelter every night without placing an impossible workload on any one institution. The number of participating churches grew from 6 to 31 during the winter of 1987–88 and has continued to grow every year since then until now 126 churches and synagogues in the Nashville area are participating. Based in an old warehouse building near downtown, Room in the Inn is the hub of the winter shelter program lasting from the beginning of November to the end of March, which in 1992–93 served more than twenty-three hundred homeless individuals.

The program works like this. Each day, the twelve to fourteen churches whose turn it is to provide shelter that night are listed on a large board. Homeless people seeking shelter report to Room in the Inn, where their names are entered into a computer system that assigns them randomly to a church. Each church provides transportation from Room in the Inn to its shelter, where volunteers offer a hot evening meal and breakfast and a warm, safe place to sleep. Those waiting for rides can take advantage of television, snacks, and showers provided for them at Room in the Inn.

Room in the Inn doesn't do a single job, stop, and declare that the rest is up to someone else. Over the years other programs have spun off to address the problem of homelessness in Nashville. Matthew 25 is a single-room-occupancy transitional housing complex where homeless men with jobs can live while they get their lives together and save enough money to move into their own housing.

Another of its programs, Crossroads, assembles groups of up to a dozen homeless men for an intense three-month program of structured attention that ranges from drug and alcohol counseling to stress management, budgeting, and job-seeking skills.

Strobel is particularly excited about Room in the Inn's latest program, the Guest House, an aggressive effort to salvage street drunks. Started as a pilot program by the Metropolitan Court System, the Guest House was supposed to run for just a month, but it was such a success that Strobel kept it going even though he didn't have the slightest idea where he'd find the money to finance it. The Guest House is simply a rough-and-ready alternative to incarceration. When Metro police pick up a homeless drunk (man or woman) over eighteen who is guilty of no crime other than public drunkenness, they may elect to deliver him to the Guest House instead of the city jail's drunk tank. Run by volunteers and the residents themselves, the Guest House is not a treatment or rehab center (which require special licensing and medical staff) but simply a safe, clean place where drunks can sober up in a supportive atmosphere and then begin participating in a structured daily life environment where Alcoholics Anonymous and drug and alcohol counseling are available to those who want them. Living communally in a former Salvation Army building next door to Room in the Inn, the group included a number of residents whose personal calendars listed not weeks but months of sober living, one day at a time; and it was beginning to turn its success stories back into the community in the form of sober, employed men.

---

Room in the Inn isn't the only effective, innovative initiative against poverty in Nashville. Too many good organizations accomplish much and then lose funding, but two of the Tennessee capital's best grassroots organizations—the Downtown Clinic for the Homeless and the related Downtown Service Center—started life as nonprofit groups funded by private grants; they quickly became such an integral part of community life that local government agreed to take over their funding when their grants ran out. The Metropolitan Health Department supports both organizations, and related services, at a budget of more than $1.1 million a year, and officials call it money well spent.

The Downtown Clinic is a full-service primary-care center and emergency medical treatment clinic with a strong mental-illness component that is operated as a free service to Nashville's homeless people. Dr. Larry Madlock, the director, an enthusiastic practicing physician (and a dead ringer for *60 Minutes*'s Ed Bradley), runs a small but busy shop with the help of a part-time psychiatric resident, two registered nurses, three mental health social workers, and three therapists. The staff sees an average of thirty medical and twenty-five mental health cases a day.

The clinic's glossy white-and-peach walls are spotless, and the pale gray tile floors are buffed so shiny that they look like glass. Madlock demands such care as a sign of respect to his patients. But he won't be satisfied until the Health Department comes up with medical fixtures and equipment to replace the prewar antiques that now equip the place, and until someone finds funds to extend the clinic's weekday hours into evenings and weekends.

The Downtown Clinic has come up with a novel way to get needed health care to wary, sometimes paranoid street people. Its Mobile Outreach Team, a tight-knit group that includes a mental health social worker, a nurse, and a paramedic, operates a roving van that patrols the city's downtown neighborhoods like an old-time police car on the beat. The crew, widely known on Nashville's streets, stop to chat, and when they do, they unobtrusively offer every imaginable health service, from Band-Aids and a friendly ear to serious counseling time. By going out on the streets, they make friends for the Downtown Clinic and build the trust that's needed to get people in for care, tests, and education.

Just around the corner and down the block from the clinic, the Downtown Service Center is a day center for the community's homeless people, who have no place else to go but the streets after they leave the city's shelters and Room in the Inn churches in the mornings. The Service Center fills basic needs, providing clean restrooms, private showers, secure lockers, and washing machines and dryers. There is a large lounge area with couches, games, and television, as well as an enclosed recreation area out back in the fresh air. A separate area with lots of toys is reserved for mothers with children, and no one complains if a kid takes a toy or two home at the end of the day.

But covering the immediate needs of homeless people is only part of the Service Center's job. Its computerized records system builds a database about Nashville's street people and makes it easy to keep track of eligibility for food stamps, unemployment insurance, and SSI. People can apply for these services and more, such as drug, alcohol, and mental health counseling, right on the premises. Determination of SSI eligibility, a notorious bureaucratic maze in most cities, is streamlined here, with a Social Security worker and a psychologist visiting on a regular schedule to interview, evaluate, and process applications all at once. The expedited procedure has cut the waiting time for benefits from the usual ninety days to only two or three weeks. What's more, 80 percent of clients are approved, contrasted with 30 percent of all SSI applications, according to chief social worker Liz Sullivan.

Once a participant is getting SSI, Social Security, or other benefits, he is urged to enroll in the representative payee program. With permission, social worker Zel Morris opens regular checking accounts for each individual at a downtown bank, then works with him to develop budgeting skills and a savings plan. Initially, Morris writes checks to cover each person's rent and bills and allots him a personal allowance, with the understanding that as soon as possible he'll start handling this business on his own.

Finally, the Service Center has a full-time "job developer" who trolls the Nashville business community, setting up interviews and networking between area employers and the center's employable, drug-and-alcohol-free clients. Next on the agenda is a computerized job bank, a computer database that will serve as a citywide clearinghouse to keep track of all employable homeless people and all appropriate job openings, making matches when the right person and the right job converge.

The center operates seven days a week, every day of the year. "They don't get holidays," city homeless services director Ken McKnight says. "Why should we?"

That's a Nashville attitude. Also characteristic of Nashville is the innovative way a consortium of civic thinkers puts it all together. An old house in a shady, middle-class residential neighborhood just out the highway from Vanderbilt houses the Council of Community Services, a local institution remarkable for its farsightedness. Way back in 1923, progressive community leaders founded the council in order to plan the city's responses to social problems as they arose. The council was to work in concert with the newly formed United Way, which would pay for the programs it oversaw. The organizations the council established were no more radical than you'd expect in a medium-size southern city; council staffer Bill Friskics-Warren dryly describes the group in those days as "very mainstream." Nevertheless, this process built a stable array of community services that left few gaps, even before the Depression and World War II. The assumption underlying the early history of social services in the city, that these jobs must be done, continues to unite Nashville's service community today.

Among the council's many projects are a thick directory of all community services; a clearinghouse for the metropolitan area's Christmas charities; the Young Leaders Council, a training program to get upwardly mobile young Tennesseans excited about being involved in volunteer social service projects; a metropolitan Council on Aging; a Victim-Offender Reconciliation Program; a home-visit treatment team aimed at keeping mentally ill people independent and in their homes; and Book 'Em!, which enlists volunteers to donate books and read to children in schools in low-income areas. Two especially noteworthy ventures are the Coalition for the Homeless and Thresholds.

The council established the Homeless Coalition in 1983, the same year Charlie Strobel opened his church's basement to street people, in response to sharp increases in homelessness related to the recession of the early 1980s and the Reagan administration's cuts in services. Reasoning that knowledge was power and that detailed demographic information about the city's homeless people would be critical to addressing the problem competently, coalition staffers began to make careful censuses of Nashville's street population twice a year. These efforts have won national attention from activists for the homeless, and they didn't yield meaningless studies but models for action. The Downtown Clinic for the Homeless was founded with grants from the Robert Wood Johnson Foundation and the Pew Charitable Trust based on the findings of early surveys. The need for alternatives to the city's large congregate shelters, also explored in the surveys, gave policy justification and support for the development of Room in the Inn. With 120 members from 72 local agencies, the coalition represents almost all of Nashville's nonprofit and local government organizations and boasts considerable clout with the Metropolitan Council and the mayor.

Thresholds is perhaps the most original of the programs supervised by the Council of Community Services. Backed by a large grant from the Robert Wood Johnson Foundation ($300,000 for two years), it aims to provide homeless families guaranteed federal rent subsidies for five years. As many as seventy homeless families will receive intensive health care and social service case management throughout the period, with most of it brought to them rather than their being required to find time and transportation to get to an agency. The project was just getting under way when I visited Nashville in 1992. Organizers had posed a challenge for themselves by initially selecting extremely dysfunctional families wracked by problems with drugs, alcohol, and abuse to take part in the program. Even so, says Friskics-Warren, the forty chosen families quickly began showing marked progress. If grassroots action can salvage these worst-case families, it can handle just about any punch poverty can throw at our communities.

# 3

# People Need Decent Housing

WHERE DO ALL THE HOMELESS PEOPLE COME from? How did we suddenly shift from a nation in which almost everyone had some kind of a roof, however ramshackle, over his head to one in which millions of people have no roof at all?

You'll see it argued that this is all the fault of well-meaning bureaucrats who emptied out the old warehouse-style mental hospitals in a flurry of deinstitutionalization during the 1970s. There's some truth in that, particularly since this decision was quickly followed in the early 1980s by a massive refusal by federal, state, and local governments to follow through with the money for community-based treatment programs for the newly liberated individuals. But contrary to myth, mentally ill people released from institutions form only a drop in the oversize bucket of homelessness. Moreover, the widespread assertion that homelessness is merely the legacy of a generation of welfare programs doesn't bear close scrutiny. The real explanation is much simpler. Housing prices rose dramatically during the 1980s, but salaries didn't. At the same time, government declined to do anything to fill the widening gap between income and rental or mortgage costs.

In the postwar Housing Act, Congress established as a fundamental principle that every American family should have a decent place to live. Thirty years later, this goal has long since been forgotten. The numbers tell a tale that's too appalling to ignore.

According to studies by the Center for Budget and Policy Priorities and the MIT-Harvard Joint Center for Housing Studies, the median income of renters in the United States increased by 97 percent between 1970 and 1983, but the cost of the average rental rose 192 percent. Worse, the supply of the most affordable housing was the quickest to disappear, forcing working-poor families to set aside an increasingly large share of their income every month for housing, at the expense of spending for food and clothing.

Although the U.S. Department of Housing and Urban Development accepts the benchmark estimate that a family's rent or house payment should make up no more than 30 percent of its income, HUD studies show that the actual share of income devoted to rent by poor families has risen far beyond that. In 1986, the General Accounting Office found that the number of low-income families paying more than 30 percent of income for rent increased from 54 percent of households in 1975 to 64 percent in 1983. Among the poorest families of all—those whose incomes were 50 percent or more below the median in their communities—fully six million, exactly half the total, were paying more than 50 percent of their income toward housing in 1983, while nearly a quarter of all blacks and Hispanics, regardless of income, were paying more than 60 percent for housing. The nation's private housing industry was failing to provide adequate housing for poor people and had no incentive to do so.

"Housing in this state is substandard, inadequate—and people are paying way over fifty percent of their income to get it, which in turn is denying people access to education, health, and other benefits," said Linda Perry, director of V'BURG Inc., the Mississippi nonprofit housing corporation we examined in the last chapter. "To break the cycle of poverty, we need to address housing first. And if we use housing as an entrée, it's the nonprofit sector that has the desire to make it work and the willingness to put the profits back in rather than building a development and getting out. We need a whole new industry of housing providers—productive, but also human service oriented—to build housing."

How can we address the longer-term challenge of making decent, low-cost permanent housing available to all Americans? As I traveled across the country, I found creative people chipping away at the problem with varied strategies: nonprofit renovation and housing development programs; community development banking; and such oddball but exciting ventures as ultra-low-cost houses being built by teams of volunteers—including the people who will live in them—that are replacing hovels in places like isolated Sand Mountain, Alabama, and the achingly poor border country of

Texas's Rio Grande Valley. Home repair and weatherization programs effectively stave off the dilapidation and decay that turns once-livable houses into boarded-up hulks, and efforts to make residences accessible to wheelchair users and people with other disabilities are keeping people independent and productive in homes that they'd otherwise have to leave. Here and there, moreover, a few visionaries are throwing out the old rules in search of completely different approaches to the way we house ourselves and our communities.

One of the best-known programs, Habitat for Humanity—President Jimmy Carter's favorite charity—has built thousands of modest houses despite a self-defeating philosophy that declines to take advantage of government housing money.

The organization's new headquarters in a modest neighborhood in Americus, Georgia, looks a lot like a modern town house development. There's a reason for that: it was planned that way. "If we ever outgrow this building and need another headquarters, we can easily turn this one into housing for people," explains Mark Lassman-Eul, Habitat's training director, who gave me a tour on a mild spring day in 1992.

Habitat is a worldwide program that started with a simple idea and that recently turned over to a Georgia family the twenty thousandth housing unit it has brought about around the globe.

Habitat, which by its example has inspired many more similar but independent low-income housing programs around the country, links cash and voluntarism from affluent supporters with the sweat and skills of low-income beneficiaries. Together, volunteers and recipients build decent, low-cost housing in a consciously Christian ministry that, as its founder and president Millard Fuller says, bears witness by work, not evangelism.

Although Habitat funds a few projects directly, most of them overseas, it primarily spreads its efforts through affiliation, lending its name and expertise to independent, local nonprofit groups that adopt, and sometimes considerably adapt, the Habitat model to suit local housing needs and opportunities.

Fuller, an Alabama attorney and entrepreneur who became a millionaire while still in his twenties, gave it up and started over in midlife, joining forces during the 1970s with the Baptist biblical scholar Clarence Jordan at Koinonia Farms, a biracial experiment in communal living near Americus. Jordan and Fuller hit it off at once, and before long they came up with the idea of helping poor people get into decent homes through what they called "partnership housing." Well-to-do people would donate cash, and they would labor alongside poor people who'd contribute "sweat equity" to build a small house, then repay the debt with no interest and no profit over the next seven to twenty years. All proceeds from the repayment would go into a Fund for Humanity, a revolving fund used to finance additional houses. The idea hit a responsive chord with church people in the region, not to mention ill-housed poor people, and it didn't take long for more than forty new homes to spring up around Koinonia and in Americus.

Fuller and his wife next tried their ideas in Mbandaka, Zaire, in Central Africa, then returned home and formally incorporated Habitat for Humanity in 1976. It grew, slowly at first, never departing from its essential principles. But grow it did, and publicity started to trickle in, especially after Fuller published a book, *Love in the Mortar Joints*. By the end of the decade, Habitat's related programs had grown to about fifty in the United States and another fifteen or twenty overseas, and organizers aggressively sought national attention with such media events as a seven-hundred-mile walk from Americus to Indianapolis. Then, in 1984, the group got a major media break when former president Jimmy Carter, a neighbor of the group's headquarters from nearby Plains, put on his blue jeans, grabbed a hammer, and went to work on a Habitat project on New York City's Lower East Side. Growth accelerated; one hundred U.S. affiliates had signed on by 1985, and the number continued to spiral to more than eight hundred (and another hundred overseas) by 1993.

If Habitat is a franchise operation, it's a casual one. Affiliates are largely autonomous, and they are expected to raise their own funds. They must be nonprofit, with a board of directors representative of the community; must agree to charge no interest (adhering to a fundamentalist interpretation of a biblical injunction); and must accept no federal funds. Habitat supplies, in addition to the credibility that comes with the use of its name, its well-tried planning procedures, house designs, and considerable technical assistance. However, local groups are not required to follow the model precisely as long as they adhere to the organization's general principles.

The specific criteria for eligibility to acquire a Habitat-built house can vary somewhat, too, apart from these basics: the family must be in need, its current housing must be inadequate, and it must have exhausted all other alternatives. The family must have some limited ability to pay a monthly housing bill, although the amount may be very small. And it must be willing to participate as a partner in the building or renovating of the house, whether through sweat equity in the form of actual physical labor or by working at other needed tasks for the Habitat affiliate.

Habitat holds the median cost of houses built by its U.S. affiliates to about $35,000, varying widely depending on housing costs in the local area. Labor costs, of course, are essentially zero. Every Habitat community is a little different, but the neighborhood surrounding the organization's headquarters in Americus is probably typical in its average appearance. The houses are small, but they're well-kept and almost suburban in appearance, with pastel clapboard and manicured lawns dotted here and there with a tricycle or inflatable swimming pool. It has the well-kept look of a community where the homeowners feel pride.

## *Rebuilding Housing, Rebuilding Communities*

Habitat's opposition to accepting federal money isn't widespread. Most community development programs eagerly take funds wherever they can get them, knowing that dollars translate into boards and bricks and nails and labor.

Habitat's more fundamental principles, however, do translate well to other groups, and just about every local low-cost housing program incorporates at least the basics. Above all, they involve the people they serve as planners and builders and board members, not as mere recipients of charity. This ingredient is an essential element of success, although there's a significant difference between *involving* the recipients as teammates and workers and the simplistic belief that you'll find in some liberal quarters that no successful program can be imported from outside the neighborhood or ethnic group. People who are serious about changing their neighborhood, or their town or their country, take help where they can get it without asking too many questions, as long as it comes with sincerity and avoids the kind of smarmy paternalism that diminishes the luster of what might otherwise be sweet charity. Effective grassroots activists are pragmatic people, who may be idealistic but are seldom stupid.

There's nothing stupid about the New Community Corporation

of Newark, New Jersey, for example, where community activists and outsiders working together have converted a large swath of a city whose name is all but synonymous with urban decay into a clean, safe enclave of new apartments, and businesses.

When a crew of Irish Catholic priests built towering St. Joseph's Church in Newark's Central Ward from old ballast stones more than a century ago, they could never have dreamed that it would someday become the home of an exceptional organization serving the inner city with model low-cost housing programs, day care facilities, services for homeless people, and even a health club and a restaurant serving New American cuisine. The church closed years ago when its largely white congregation moved more or less en masse to the suburbs. But it gained new life when the New Community Corporation formed virtually spontaneously, in the aftermath of Newark's 1967 riots, when residents and neighbors said "Enough!"

Looking over acres of slum territory and blocks of burnt-out houses, the group's founders, including parishioners of nearby Queen of the Angels Church and their pastor, Father William Linder, concluded that housing—followed in short order by job creation and training—was the community's most acute need. The effort was frustrating at first, but over the ensuing two decades, by leveraging long-term financing from the state Housing and Mortgage Finance Agency and the federal Economic Development Authority and Department of Commerce, New Community eventually collected more than $130 million in federal money and private loans. That was sufficient to develop ten housing complexes in the Central Ward, which provide more than twenty-four hundred apartment units with six thousand residents—one-eighth as many units in inner-city Newark alone as Habitat for Humanity has built all over the world. These are not blighted cut-rate projects for mass housing but solid, well-built, well-kept buildings that now form what local real estate experts candidly call a "buffer area" facilitating the private development and gentrification of much adjoining property. City officials estimate that New Community developments over twenty years have created more than four thousand construction jobs, added $30 million in wages to Newark's economy, and restored $2.3 million in annual tax revenue to the city treasury. These numbers alone are enough to start turning a city around.

But New Community doesn't stop with housing. As discussed in Chapter 1, the supermarket it developed to serve the inner city is now a major employer for the neighborhood. Pursuing other job opportunities and training for residents, New Community also operates a no-fee employment counseling and placement agency that has found jobs for an average of more than a thousand people a year as well as a local federal credit union, a network of affordable day care centers that also provide parenting training and counseling for teenage parents, and an extended-care facility for ailing older people. Within the old church building—completely renovated with a $3 million federal grant—a commercial health spa and fine restaurant create more jobs in addition to offering much-needed community services.

---

It goes too far to say that examples of nonprofit organizations that are changing the physical and social landscapes of our cities abound in the United States. Here and there, however, certain grassroots groups stand out with a variety of similar-but-different approaches that are resurrecting their communities.

Consider West Garfield Park neighborhood in Chicago. Hit hard, like Newark, by riots during the middle 1960s and blasted by white flight and the neglect by absentee slumlords that followed, this stretch of Chicago's West Side for a long time seemed without hope. But hope was there, as solid as the tall shade trees and still sturdy houses that line its streets. And from a very small beginning in 1979 has grown another of America's most exemplary community development corporations.

Sponsored by Bethel Lutheran Church, Bethel New Life began with a budget of just $5,000 and two volunteers audacious enough to think they could take on a devastated community's need for decent housing. They started with just one building, an abandoned triplex purchased from the U.S. Department of Housing and Urban Development for just $275. With the labor of volunteers, they restored the house, then went on to restore another, and then another, until suddenly they realized that years had passed and, amazingly, the neighborhood was coming back. The group went on to develop more than 850 housing units in West Garfield Park, returning an estimated $37 million to the tax rolls, creating hundreds of jobs, and recapturing that priceless intangible that comes when even a few houses on an inner-city block get turned around.

Bethel New Life has restored far more than just a few houses.

In one project alone, the Westside Isaiah Plan, the group pulled together a multimillion-dollar package through the joint effort of local banks, government, and twenty area churches to build 250 new town houses.

If Bethel New Life had done nothing more than renovate a healthy share of its neighborhood's once sound housing stock, that would be credit enough. But like New Community in Newark, it didn't stop there. It planted scores of programs and projects in West Garfield Park. The group's rainbow logo hangs over its Mother Hen Day Care Center, while the abandoned hulk of old St. Anne's Hospital, resurrected as the Beth-Anne Campus, is now a community and cultural center. Bethel New Life's Employment and Training Center places an average of five hundred residents a year in full-time jobs at an average cost of only $275 per placement. After scouting prospective jobs through interviews with local and regional employers, the staff then sets up or contracts for specific training courses to prepare neighborhood residents to fill the jobs. CNA Insurance, for example, opens many job slots to local folks and sends in trainers to give them the skills they'll need to take and keep those jobs.

Seeking to move welfare recipients, some of whom have never held jobs, back into the mainstream, the Self-Sufficiency Program and Families with a Future offer welfare mothers and mothers-to-be counseling and training that leads to work. Not coincidentally, the programs have reduced the neighborhood's infant mortality rate from thirty-three to seventeen deaths per thousand between 1985 and 1989.

Bethel New Life itself has added more than 350 jobs to the local economy and hired residents to fill them. Its Recycling Center and Material Recovery Facility, for instance, provides thirty-five jobs, along with putting cash back into the neighborhood economy to the tune of the $9,000 a week that it pays out for cans, glass, and newspapers.

Besides all these projects, the group operates a health center and adult day care center, engages in partnerships with local schools, and more, mobilizing a staff of four hundred and a $9.4 million annual budget to make it all happen. This giant step beyond volunteers renovating a three-family house worth $275 stems from a combination of realism and idealism, says Mary Nelson, a co-founder and now president, and from "applying the bottom line of the marketplace to visionary goals. We have miles to go before the dream becomes a reality for all the people of West Garfield Park. But Bethel New Life is charting the course, one step at a time."

---

In Anchorage, Alaska, where the winters are so long that the national Christmas in April program, in which volunteers descend on designated neighborhoods bearing hammers and saws for home repairs, has to be deferred until the end of May, the nonprofit Anchorage Neighborhood Housing Services (ANHS) has figured out still more ways to get low-cost housing built. Founded in 1982 with the goal of redeveloping decent housing in Spenard, one of Anchorage's oldest and poorest neighborhoods, ANHS has become a model for competent, commonsense housing programs for poor and moderate-income people.

It works primarily in two separate but related areas. First, its housing counseling programs give prospective and current homeowners the information to make intelligent housing decisions. Then, its affordable-housing programs—like the ones we've seen in Newark, Chicago, and elsewhere—leverage government and private money to generate additional loans to finance low-cost housing.

The group's counseling programs provide people with the tools they need to become homeowners, says the group's chief housing counselor, Nancy Cruz. The prepurchase counseling program, for example, is a quarterly five-hour class for first-time home buyers, an A to Z course that covers everything from consumer debt and how mortgages work to helping each family calculate what size monthly payment it can afford. Other programs include crisis counseling to help keep people in their homes through a financial or other emergency, including referrals to banks and government agencies for help and, when all else fails, cash loans. Finally, rental counseling classes give formerly homeless people useful tips about tenants' rights and responsibilities and ways to cope with the bad credit and reference backgrounds that make it tough for a person who's had recent personal problems to get into a decent apartment.

On the bricks-and-mortar side, ANHS runs a broad array of housing renovation and repair programs. It writes loans of up to $3,500 at 5 percent interest for three years for exterior improvements visible from the street, which are a key element in boosting neighborhood pride. Its residential loans in neighborhoods targeted for help may range up to $65,000 for interior and exterior renovation, with terms depending on financial need and other specifics. And its Business Development Loan Fund, designed to attract new businesses and improve existing commercial ventures in the Spenard neighborhood, complements other financing services with flexible investments ranging from $10,000 to $300,000. On a smaller scale, seasonal projects such as Paint the Town, Neighbors Making a Difference, and Christmas in May mobilize volunteer labor, contributions, and the expertise of local building trade unions to sweep through the community and provide painting and house-repairs assistance, particularly to elderly and handicapped homeowners who aren't able to do the work themselves.

One of ANHS's most innovative programs, Mutual Housing, has provided low-income Anchorage residents more than eight hundred units of affordable housing through an unusual approach to homeownership. Two town house complexes, Village Commons and Turnagain Circle, work somewhat like urban cooperative apartments. New residents pay a onetime, refundable deposit of $1,500 to become members, plus monthly rent of $460 to $680 for one to three bedroom units—well below the market rate in Anchorage and eligible for federal Section Eight rental subsidies. Every resident is also expected to contribute to the complex's management through active participation in its Resident Council.

The organization also operates six town house complexes as traditional rental properties, and late in 1993 it opened the Loussac-Sogn SRO in downtown Anchorage. The city's only nonprofit single-room-occupancy hotel operates in a renovated historic building on principles similar to those of Chicago's Lakefront SROs, discussed in the previous chapter. Fifty-two units, eighteen of them reserved for mentally ill homeless clients, rent at low monthly rates and feature counseling services on the premises. Commercial retail space on the ground floor, leased at competitive prices, helps subsidize the cost of operating the SRO.

From home repairs to SRO rooms to town houses, ANHS has made a major difference in the quality of life for people in its Arctic town. The lessons it has to teach deserve a hearing all over the Lower Forty-eight.

## *Housing Partnerships*

Similar principles, of course, are being brought to bear all over the country. Get government or private grant money, and use creative financing to make it go as far as possible to build sound, decent housing. Take out the profit motive to hold down costs. And, in the best examples, make the people who will live in the houses partners in their construction and management.

Examples abound. One good one, in south Florida's sugarcane country, where immigrant cane cutters commonly live in Third World conditions, is found at the Holy Cross Catholic Church in Indiantown, which established a not-for-profit housing association that stretched a $225,000 federal housing grant to build a sixty-unit housing complex. New Hope Community offers low-cost rentals to working-poor and welfare families through Section Eight and related federal programs. This complex shatters the myth that poor families won't take care of subsidized housing. The colorful stucco duplexes with their lovingly landscaped yards could be Suburbia Town, Anywhere, U.S.A., and they stand in striking contrast to the expensive hovels in the region's ubiquitous apartment tracts owned and operated by absentee slumlords.

## *Self-Reliance in Rural America*

As you drive south from San Antonio, the soft green contours of the Texas hill country turn flat, dry, and harsh until you reach the Rio Grande, a surprisingly narrow stream that winds snakelike across arid plains turned agricultural by irrigation.

From May through October, a bounty of crops springs from the desert, creating low-wage, low-skill employment. Thousands of stoop laborers start here, at the southern end of the migrant labor stream, then follow the harvest north through the summer, returning home in the fall to weather the following months without any income.

I wish I had a dollar for every grassroots worker who's told me that his own county or town or neighborhood is the nation's poorest. I've heard similar claims, all credible, in the Arkansas and Mississippi Delta country, the Florida sugarcane country, urban inner-cities, Appalachian hollows, Native American lands in the Southwest—and now comes Hidalgo County, Texas, to contend for the title nobody wants.

By any standard, the flat, dry land of the valley, with feathery mesquite trees shimmering silver under a huge blue bowl of sky, houses some of the nation's poorest people. There's money here too; you can see it in the malls and office buildings in the town of

McAllen. But most of it is in the hands of relatively few Anglos, the people who own the farms and the small businesses that serve them. Little trickles down to the sixty thousand Americans of Mexican descent who live in the region, where the typical income for a farm laborer is $5,000 a year. Most of them live in one or another of 366 settlements called colonias.

A colonia is something like a suburban subdivision, and yet it's nothing like a suburban subdivision. A developer assembles small (fifty-by-one-hundred-foot) lots laid out on open land scored with a neat grid of streets. Sometimes the streets are even paved with a thin coat of blacktop. But a buyer purchases only the undeveloped lot, without a house or utility connections. Most lots have no running water. None has sewage hookups. Urban services, from garbage collection to police protection, are all but unknown. Texas real estate law deals residents another unfair hand. An individual buys a colonia lot under the terms of what is called a "contract for deed"—essentially, an installment plan, meaning that he does not take possession of the title until the full amount, including interest, is paid off in full. A scrub lot with no services can sell for up to $12,000. The terms of a typical loan—ten years at 14 percent annual interest—cost a farmworker $150 to $200 a month. Although developers are forgiving about delinquent payments (particularly during the months when a family travels north to work on midwestern farms), this is a mixed blessing. In a situation that can only be described as legal larceny, the interest on deferred installments is required in additional payments tacked onto the end of the loan, even if all delinquent payments are made up.

Since rental property is practically nonexistent in the valley, and extremely expensive when it can be found, it's not surprising that farmworkers spend all they have to purchase land, then have nothing left to build a house on the property once it's paid for. With admirable creativity, they manage to make do. Because of the almost complete absence of anything like zoning authorities or building inspectors, no objections are made to families living in shacks the size of packing crates pieced together from scrap wood or galvanized iron, without toilets or running water.

But times are changing in the valley, at least a little. Habitat for Humanity is building a few houses, and isolated groups of nuns and priests are at work here and there for housing and social justice. The community efforts of the Industrial Areas Foundation and other institutions have made great strides to break the grip of the Anglo minority on local and regional politics. The people are in control now, and changes are coming as fast as they can when money is anything but abundant. All the goodwill in the world is of limited value, however, when people have no resources.

Operating out of a sun-baked concrete-block union hall surrounded by dusty farm fields in tiny San Juan, Proyecto Azteca ("The Aztec Project") is a small effort to start to change that, too. Founded by the United Farm Workers Union, the nonprofit organization is governed by a board composed of UFW officials but explicitly independent of the union and operating on its own minimal budget. Its purpose is to create reasonably priced housing for farmworkers and their families, adamantly insisting that farmworkers don't want to live in decrepit hovels but will improve their living standards if they have fair access to means and resources.

This bears repeating: whether the subject is housing or jobs or food or training, the assumption that Americans want charity or will accept it if they have the alternative of doing for themselves simply doesn't hold up. Poor, disabled, discriminated against, or beaten down, people still get back up and go back to work as soon as they have a chance. This lesson keeps coming up again and again.

With the help of professional volunteers, Proyecto Azteca's board members drew up plans for a small, one-family house that anyone who can handle a hammer and saw can build with a little supervision and very little cash. Selected families are invited to build houses from these plans on colonia lots. They're given zero-percent financing to pay off their contract for deed on the lot, giving them a fresh start. The house is erected with the requirement that one family member—male or female, parent or sturdy teenager—take part in the construction crew. The "self-help" component not only reduces labor costs, but it also gives one member of the family an employable skill and the ability to handle maintenance and home repairs. The houses are not actually built on the colonia lot itself but at the UFW hall, where a supervisor paid with federal funds channeled through another Texas nonprofit, Motivation Education & Training Inc. of Cleveland, Texas, oversees a team of seven workers on a construction assembly line. When the house is up, it's trucked to the family's lot for finishing touches.

Using loans and grants from private, state, and federal sources,

Proyecto Azteca got off to a slow but hopeful start in 1992, with one house finished and six more funded and under construction during its first six months of work, and with financing at least tentatively available for a total of thirty-nine.

To qualify for a house, a family must earn between $300 and $800 a month, whether from work or welfare. The houses, which contain three small bedrooms, a large living room, a bath, and a kitchen area in a 720-square-foot, one-story frame structure, typically cost $12,500 each to build. With a lot cost of $6,000 and an interest-free loan, house payments range from $75 to $100 a month with a twenty-year term. The repayment period can be extended if necessary to hold monthly payments below $100, a sum that even a family of migrant farmworkers can manage.

In addition to new construction, Proyecto Azteca has also acquired eleven existing houses, some in need of renovation, from the Resolution Trust Corporation, the agency overseeing the cleanup of the savings and loan mess. These houses are reserved for a Rent to Own program, under which families move in, learn home-repair skills and do their own rehabilitation, then pay $150 a month rent for fifteen years to earn full title and ownership.

How do these new approaches play out in real people's lives? I stopped in for a visit in the summer of 1992 at the house being constructed for Isaac and Gloria Castillo, who live in a colonia the residents call Eldora but that the bank prefers to list as Barr No. 4, after the Anglo developer who sold the lots. In the front of the tiny lot a rough-hewn wooden building, no larger than ten by twelve feet but extended somewhat by an open-air patio under a galvanized iron roof, is now home to the Castillos and their three children. Even a fresh coat of startling blue paint and a plaque on the door bearing religious figures and the family name don't hide the reality that the shack is barely habitable.

Behind it, however, workers were slapping bright turquoise and magenta paint on a trim frame house that was soon to be the Castillos' new home. From the wrought iron coach lamp beside the door to glossy birch kitchen cabinets and modern plumbing (attached to a new septic system), the house, though small, is almost in another world. "Bueno! Bueno!" Isaac Castillo kept repeating, bowing and smiling and managing to bridge the language gap to say how he felt.

Decent housing should be available for all, up and down the Rio

Grande Valley. By dotting the landscape with affordable homes, Proyecto Azteca hopes to show how it can be done.

---

If there's hope in independent innovation, there's hope on Sand Mountain, way down at the tail end of Appalachia's spine. This northeastern corner of Alabama is considerably different from the stereotypical Deep South Alabama most of us imagine, in many ways it has more in common with the mountain culture than the South. Dominated by small farms, the population is almost entirely white, and uniformly poor. It's heavily Protestant, with strong family ties and a fierce loyalty to neighbors and kin. People here tend to reject welfare and handouts, preferring to stick together and do whatever they can to help out less fortunate neighbors.

Geographically, Sand Mountain is more like a huge ridge than a mountain. It's a *long* ridge, stretching forty miles and spanning some twenty miles across, rising between the towns of Scottsboro and Fort Payne. Close to the borders of Alabama, Georgia, and Tennessee, its residents who have televisions usually watch broadcasting and read newspapers from Chattanooga, Tennessee, rather than Birmingham. Although it's rural and agricultural in nature, growing cabbage, squash, and Irish potatoes, locals claim that Sand Mountain is the most densely populated rural area in the United States. And despite its relatively heavy population, Sand Mountain has no local government; it is haphazardly administered by town officials in the lowlands, who rarely bother to deliver to the mountain even the minimal services available in the rural South.

Into this setting came the Sand Mountain Parishes a quarter of a century ago, in the late 1960s. Realizing that their congregations of fifteen to a hundred parishioners were too tiny to do their community much good individually, the pastors of seventeen Methodist churches in the area banded together to form a joint community service organization. Like so many other grassroots groups that started in the giving spirit of traditional Christian charity, Sand Mountain Parishes began with basic emergency services, then evolved a wider vision intended to bolster self-sufficiency rather than continually providing emergency food and clothing to the same recipients year after year.

So, for example, what started as a food pantry grew into

Gardens of Plenty, furnishing seed and fertilizer to sixteen hundred families who grow their own produce, then turn a share of it back to the parishes for redistribution to people who have even less.

Then in 1992 the group turned an abandoned church building into a cannery, equipped with industrial-size equipment donated by a community action agency in rural Kentucky and a well-to-do parish in suburban Baltimore.

The cannery clanked into action in the summer of 1992, turning into useful, nonperishable canned goods the produce donated by Sand Mountain's gardeners or gleaned by volunteers who picked over fields where usable produce was left behind after mechanical harvesters had trundled on to the next field. The bounty goes to hungry people in soup kitchens and food pantries not only on Sand Mountain but all over Alabama.

The cannery pays a triple reward, says the Reverend Dorsey Walker, director of Sand Mountain Parishes. It increases the efficiency of the gleaning program by getting produce into cans quickly, before it goes to waste. It creates jobs for unemployed people, who are hired at decent wages to run the canning machines. And, he hopes, it will form the basis for a cooperative of local farmers who'll grow and process high-quality organic products for national sale through mail order.

But it is in this realm of low-cost housing that Sand Mountain offers the best story of all.

It starts with low-cost solar power, a subject that caught Walker's interest more than a decade ago when he attended a workshop given by Bill Dow, a pediatrician from North Carolina who gave up medicine to travel around the Southeast preaching the benefits of solar power and showing people how to attach greenhouses to their homes to grow produce and provide supplemental heat. Walker liked that idea so much that, over the years that followed, he worked with the local vocational-agricultural school to build or help neighbors build hundreds of solar greenhouses, ovens, and vegetable dryers.

Then, in 1991, they moved on to something even better: In less than twelve months' time, with volunteers and financing from the member churches, Sand Mountain Parishes built eleven solar-powered houses for families that would otherwise have been homeless. With the help of local architects and their own practical experience, Walker and his group came up with a simple plan for a 950-square-foot, one-story frame house that could be built by a crew of volunteers in just six days, at a total cost of only $12,000 for materials. Assuming a labor cost of $8,000 and land prices ranging up to $3,000, the houses can be erected for around $20,000 each. One church agrees to subsidize one house with cash and labor. When it is done, a selected family moves in and pays $75 a month, which goes back to the donor church in an arrangement that repays its incurred costs in just ten years.

This is remarkable mathematics, and even stipulating that the numbers come out best in rural areas and that solar heating works best where winter is mild and short, it's a concept that doesn't need to be limited to isolated mountain towns.

Walker, needless to say, is a long way from running out of ideas. In years to come, he hopes to train heretofore unemployable single mothers in the construction trades, then to turn them loose as a cooperative solar-house-building venture, making a good living by building houses that people can afford.

That's self-reliance.

## *Tenants' Rights and Local Housing Policy*

Landlord-tenant negotiations and arbitration and tenants' rights form another element in the challenge of ensuring that all Americans are adequately housed. Burlington, Vermont, forms a good case study for several reasons. Progressive in its politics, the city and the state are unusually ready to experiment with strong tenant-protection policies; and the economics of the community, an exurb and retirement magnet for both New York City and Boston, have caused intense housing pressures, raising rents and property values and, in an equation that turns up almost anywhere in the United States where housing demand exceeds supply, making things tough for poor people.

Burlington is an exceptionally pretty town of thirty-seven thousand, its clean streets shaded by mature deciduous trees and lined with Victorian houses, tucked into a broad valley between Lake Champlain and the foothills of the Green Mountains. It's one of those economically thriving communities, like Minnesota's Twin Cities and, in North Carolina, the Raleigh–Durham–Chapel Hill research triangle, that on casual inspection appear to have the problems of poverty and hunger whipped.

But looks, as they often are, can be deceiving. On the surface, the combination of a significant college influence—including the

University of Vermont, two other four-year colleges, and a community business college—and a vast IBM plant have created an apparent boom town, with a thriving downtown and a sophisticated commercial community. Unemployment is very low, and the local political scene, fueled by intellectuals and ex-hippies lured to the area by its colleges, scenic beauty, and sane lifestyle, has nurtured extremely progressive local government that started with socialist mayor Bernie Sanders's ten-vote victory in 1981 and continued under Mayor Peter Clavelle.

But Vermont is also known for tiny hardscrabble farms on rocky soil and families scratching to make a living on the farm or in the textile mills. The Green Mountain State never fully recovered from the loss of its major mills to the South during the 1950s. To this day, many of Vermont's blue-collar workers and their children have never regained the standard of living they enjoyed more than thirty years ago. By and large, the lost industrial jobs were replaced by minimum-wage work in the service economy, creating a large new segment of working poor people who depend on welfare to stretch their salaries. The rise of agribusiness displaced many small farmers, creating the ironic image of dairy farmers dependent on government commodities programs as their source of butter and cheese.

In this setting, the gentrification of Burlington's Victorian neighborhoods by émigrés from New York and Boston generated a white-hot housing market with a vacancy rate that actually dropped below 1 percent for a time, and that consistently remains at a tight 3 percent; a condition that's fine for landlords but very bad for tenants, particularly low-income ones. Further, although street homelessness is not widespread in Vermont's snowy winters, it does exist, and the near invisibility of homeless women and children (who typically double up with friends or family or even live in their cars) tempts local pols, however progressive, to downplay the size of the problem and the need to deal with it.

Thanks to Vermont's politics, much of the action on behalf of low-income tenants has taken place in City Hall and the capitol rather than in the streets. In Burlington, a project of the Chittenden Community Action Program, Vermont Tenants Inc. (VTI), has been a prime mover in the field of low-income housing. The group organizes tenants and lobbies on their behalf. It pushed hard for Vermont's first landlord-tenant law, a measure that despite the state's populist reputation was not enacted until 1986. VTI also organized tenants to push for low-income housing programs in Burlington, and it formed the Housing Strategy Group, a coalition of tenants, advocates, developers, and city officials that has met every three weeks for many years and has become an essential means for participants to communicate their sometimes conflicting needs and interests. VTI also provides direct services in the form of advice and counseling for both tenants and landlords, who are routinely sent educational materials about landlord-tenant rights and responsibilities. Landlords themselves have responded unexpectedly well to public workshops on their duties and obligations, suggesting that even people with vested interests in maintaining the status quo may be open to intelligent communication.

By involving developers and government officials with tenants and advocates, the process has yielded a surprising array of unusual local laws that could serve as national models. Burlington's Housing Replacement Ordinance, for instance, requires that any builder whose development results in the loss of a unit of housing must replace it with a new unit elsewhere in the city. The Condominium Conversion Ordinance protects tenants from being taken advantage of if a property owner decides to convert apartments into condominiums. Under this law, landlords must give tenants ample notice, help them relocate, and offer tenant groups first option to purchase the property and convert it into cooperative housing. A Housing Board of Review hears complaints from both landlords and tenants and seeks to mediate disputes; and a city apartment inspection fee ($19 per unit per year) builds a fund that helps pay building inspectors' salaries and also helps finance Vermont Tenants Inc. through a city allocation.

There's no question that Burlington's tough tenants' rights ordinances are controversial; landlords would certainly oppose them in a town any less open-minded than this one. But the laws do work, and they have gone a long way to ensure decent living conditions for poor people.

Another project developed by VTI, along with other advocacy groups and government organizations, is the Burlington Community Land Trust, which negotiated a combination of federal grant money and tax credits to set up a $26 million tenant takeover of the aging Northgate public-housing project, forestalling its conversion into high-priced condominiums.

The agency's emergency assistance program distributes private donations to help cover winter utility bills for people who have fallen through holes in the government safety net. VTI has lobbied for legislation to prevent winter cutoffs of utilities for nonpayment of bills and, so far unsuccessfully, to establish a cap on the cost of utilities for poor people.

Finally, the organization's housing program addresses households at risk of homelessness, going to bat for them with city, regional, and state authorities to find suitable transitional housing. The agency operates a family shelter in a refurbished firehouse and a nine-unit transitional housing complex that offers intense case management and counseling.

VTI's parent organization, the Community Action Program, attends to other wants of poor people, operating a full range of service programs: community gardens, income-tax assistance (with business students from Champlain College serving as volunteer counselors), and direct cash grants to those with essential needs not met by other programs—including providing lactobacillus milk to allergic children, or gasoline to people just beginning jobs who can't afford the fuel to get to work until they get that first paycheck. The group's food shelf, a combined soup kitchen and food pantry, serves one hundred meals a week and distributes five tons of groceries a month, and Project Self-Sufficiency offers job training and education to single mothers on welfare.

Like other effective antipoverty programs, whether the focus is housing, food, jobs, or training, the Burlington groups have spread their reach to cover an array of related needs, coming up with competent, innovative responses to individual situations and working closely with people in trouble until they've got the tools to solve their own problems.

## *New Technology in Low-Cost Housing*

Another approach toward making housing affordable is to cut costs by using natural energy sources or developing house designs that take advantage of the surrounding environment.

When young Quaker vegetarian newlyweds Steve and Elizabeth Willey decided to build a house on an isolated mountaintop in the Idaho panhandle some fifteen years ago, they came in for a shocking surprise: the Idaho Power Company wanted a cool $24,000 to run electricity to their cabin on Rapid Lightning Creek Road, a dozen miles north of Sandpoint.

"We didn't have it, and we couldn't get it," Steve recalled. But rather than giving up their dream, the Willeys responded creatively, erecting a windmill to drive an electric generator. Neighbors saw it, wanted one for themselves, and before long Steve was in business, making a few extra bucks by building windmill-powered systems for folks all along the scenic shores of Lake Pend Oreille.

He soon discovered, however, that wind power, though cheap, is an unpredictable source of energy in northern Idaho, and that solar power had more potential. Gathering a few friends in an informal cooperative, he taught himself the rudiments of photovoltaic power, bought parts and equipment, and started selling the equipment while preaching the gospel of energy self-sufficiency. Over the years he's built a mailing list of between ten and twenty thousand subscribers to his newsletter and catalog and has all the business he can handle. In the process he has become something of a national expert in the realm of economical, efficient solar power for homes.

To this day, no electric wires run into the Willeys' charming house, a free-form modern building made of wood, with a hexagonal extension and a multistory tower capped by the windmill, which rises through the pine trees that cloak the mountain. This is no spartan backwoods cabin but a large house filled with amenities. Its computers, televisions, microwave oven, and vibrating recliner are all powered by solar cells, wind power, and a rarely used backup generator fired by propane. Stored energy is channeled from heavy industrial batteries through an inverter system that converts battery power into alternating current.

The Willeys' experience demonstrates that it's not only nonprofit organizations that are waging the fight against poverty. Helping people who have little live for less can be both a good business practice and a moral one. Although Steve Willey emphasizes that his company primarily aims to make money, not uplift the poor, he's well aware of the economic implications of solar and wind power. Apart from the fact that a solar power system, once installed, provides a literally endless source of free electricity, solar- and stream-powered irrigation for agriculture could be a tremendous boon for rural poor people. Major utility companies speak of solar power as a dream unfulfilled, requiring $60,000 or more to set up a system sufficient to supply a typical suburban house. But Willey notes that the combination of insulation, application of passive solar principles, and use of low-energy appliances and lighting can cut the cost of equipment to a fraction of that. He installed a minimal system in a nearby mountain house for $1,500; most of the home systems he sells range from $6,000 to $9,000. When the electric bills stop coming, that turns into a mighty attractive investment.

---

Pliny Fisk III, a vibrant toothpick of a man with a crown of wild hair, lives and works on the cutting edge of "appropriate technology." Mirroring the lifestyle of the Willeys in Idaho, Fisk and his wife, Gail Vittori, live on a hilltop east of Austin, Texas, in a building largely made of local materials and powered by passive solar devices. Their twenty-year-old nonprofit organization, the Center for Maximum Potential Building Systems Inc., affectionately known as Max Pot, has won international applause for its innovations in the field of "appropriate technology," which is to contemporary technology as "sustainable agriculture" is to corporate agriculture. Pioneering small-scale building and development methods take advantage of available resources and put back into the environment as much as they take out.

Fisk, one of those delightfully intense people who spit out ideas like sparks, is an architect with background in ecological land planning and systems engineering. Fired by a passion to spread the word about appropriate technology, he and his first wife started a laboratory for students at the University of Texas in 1972. A year or two later, armed with a foundation grant, they started Max Pot to help the residents of Crystal City, Texas, find a new source of energy to replace the area's played-out natural gas.

In this small, largely Hispanic town near the Mexican border, Fisk developed the approach that continues to guide Max Pot: Define a community's natural and its human resources, and come up with a solution that takes advantage of both. The organization solves problems by choosing alternatives that tap natural resources without despoiling them, and it carries out the plans in a manner that enhances the local economy rather than damages it.

In Crystal City the solution Fisk proposed to the town's energy problems was in the form of simple, inexpensive solar heating devices that residents could make themselves (and sell) from gas water-heater tanks, burnt-out fluorescent light tubes, and metal printing plates. By the late 1970s the town was relying entirely on solar power to supply its energy needs. The wave of publicity that resulted from this audacious experiment launched Max Pot as one of the nation's best-known exponents of appropriate technology principles.

Fisk and Max Pot have since combined commercial work for individual clients with nonprofit technical assistance to governments and planners across the United States and around the world, earning both respect and awards. Max Pot was the only U.S. organization honored as an Exemplary Local Government program at the Earth Summit in Rio de Janeiro in June 1992. The United Nations also recognized Max Pot's Green Builder Program in Austin, a system under which all new housing is assigned a rating based on how effectively it uses local materials as well as the efficiency of its waste disposal system and its use of water and energy. Initially intended primarily to inform consumers, such sustainability ratings, as yet unique in the United States, may eventually be used to determine tax incentives or penalties for builders.

Max Pot has also advised the Russian Commonwealth of Independent States on sustainable development; helped plan the Habitat project in Vancouver, British Columbia, in 1976; and developed appropriate planning technologies throughout Central America and the Caribbean, including a prototype home for indigenous Miskito Indians in Nicaragua. Based largely on Max Pot's work, the American Institute of Architects devoted the agenda of its 1994 national convention entirely to appropriate technology and appointed Fisk to its planning committee.

In one of its best-known projects, Max Pot built a showcase farm in Laredo, Texas, demonstrating sustainable building, water, energy, food, and waste systems for the semiarid areas of the Southwest. Unfortunately, however, the project was allowed to lapse after a change of administration in the Texas Department of Agriculture.

Max Pot, however, is not about to lapse. Fisk has a dozen projects under way, and ideas for dozens more, ranging from designing computer software for community planning to drawing up a solid-waste disposal plan for the city of Houston and inventing a safe and inexpensive way to use sulfur in building cement. With organizations like Max Pot leading the way, we will find ways to cut housing costs that none of us can now imagine.

# 4

# People Need Education

THE PUBLIC SCHOOL SYSTEM IN LOUISVILLE, KENtucky, was a beat that hardened reporters who'd covered death and destruction would grovel and beg and even consider bribery to avoid. During my last years at the *Courier-Journal* the superintendent of schools was a smooth-talking, silver-haired gentleman named Dr. Donald W. Ingwerson, a skilled administrator and equally skilled politician, controlling a well-oiled publicity machine that spent a lot of time sorting out the good news and bad news about the schools and doing everything possible to keep the bad news under wraps.

Louisville's schools had been through very difficult times during the 1970s, before Ingwerson jumped onto what appeared to be a sinking ship in the early 1980s. The old independent city school district had declared bankruptcy and put itself out of business, forcing a merger that nobody really wanted with the suburban Jefferson County Public Schools in 1974. The metropolitan district that was thus formed ranked among the twenty largest in the nation, with more than a hundred thousand students in 150 schools and more than eleven thousand employees.

More significant, the new system came into being as a model case of de facto racial segregation. The student population of the old city schools had been about 30 percent black. The suburban schools, reflecting the communities they served, were more than 90 percent white. The federal courts, in the activist tradition of the time, were already scrutinizing the metropolitan area with an eye toward requiring that the separate city and county schools begin busing students across district lines to achieve racial balance. Such a precedent-shattering order would surely have gone all the way to the U.S. Supreme Court, but when the districts merged, the issue became moot. As a result, school officials didn't seriously contest the federal court order that busing begin throughout the new unified city-county district in the fall of 1975.

As it turned out, the busing plan went relatively smoothly, with a few rock-throwing incidents and relatively little white flight, with only the most ardent bigots proving willing to give up their homes and neighborhoods to flee across the county line to avoid integration. The system's administrative merger, however, was much more painful, under the scandal-ridden supervision of an administration that was certainly incompetent and possibly corrupt. Ingwerson was seen as something of a savior, and he did get things quickly organized, but the incessant bragging of his public relations operatives quickly wore on reporters, who got tired of hearing it and soon learned to routinely doubt anything they heard out of the school district's suburban headquarters building.

So when I got out of Louisville and away from the newspaper and started looking seriously for institutions that were really making a difference in the field of poverty, I had to overcome some hard-earned prejudices before accepting that the local school system in general and Ingwerson in particular had some remarkably good ideas. Viewed from outside bluegrass country, the Louisville schools have a substantial national reputation for innovation and creativity in poverty-related fields.

Moreover, the Jefferson County Public Schools stand very much alone. As Jonathan Kozol discovered in *Savage Inequalities* (which unfortunately missed Louisville's positive example in its scathing indictment of inner-city public education across America), one of the nation's greater scandals is the way that we've abandoned the education of our children in urban areas by declining to finance quality public education in our poorer communities or to insist on competent administration of inner-city public schools.

Louisville's schools escaped these savage inequalities largely by sheer chance. The sequence of events that forced the inner-city and suburban schools to merge into a single district with no racially identifiable schools made it politically impossible for the equation that Kozol discovered in most other cities to occur. Because the children of relatively affluent suburbanites were thrust into the same schools as inner-city families, and because the city schools were no longer racially identifiable, it became impossible for taxpayers to "triage" the school system. Rather, every school had to receive an equal share of the tax money, and no school could be neglected when competent administrators and teachers were assigned. Ingwerson understood this, and saw to it that every school received its equal share, a distribution that played itself out in student achievement test scores and the percentage of graduates who went on to college.

To his credit, Ingwerson also understood—and insisted that his administrators and staff understand—that the community of Louisville could only gain economically if its school system turned out graduates who could actually read, write, and do simple mathematics. This assumption, sadly, is not widely understood across the nation, as the grassroots organization Focus: HOPE learned in Detroit when it was forced to set up its own alternative school to reteach purported high school graduates basic literacy and math.

Patti Hearn, Ingwerson's administrative assistant, put it like this during a lengthy interview I had with her in 1991: "We have changed the philosophy of the school district to reflect that all kids can learn and that everyone in the community has a right to be educated—not just young people, but adults also. When you set that kind of goal, then you have to back up and say, 'What do we have to do to make this kind of thing happen?' Number one, kids can't learn until their families think that learning is important. Kids can't learn until they have adequate nutrition. And kids can't learn unless they see an end to the cycle of poverty that they are in."

This philosophy applies not only to education but to every aspect of the grassroots war against poverty, but it's particularly critical for educators. They are not outside the battle against poverty but on its front lines.

Poverty is not a trivial issue for the public schools in metropolitan Louisville, where 41 percent of the student population on the Kentucky side of the Ohio River comes from families that the federal government defines as at risk and eligible for nutrition assistance. Ingwerson wasn't just talking about idle theory—although he remained far out in front of most of his peers in public education—when he gave his standard speech warning that demographic trends suggest that public schools face ever-increasing numbers of children from families in poverty over coming decades.

Ingwerson, who had been superintendent of a showplace suburban school district in southern California, arrived in Louisville as a healer and peacemaker in 1981. The Louisville-area schools were lucky enough to have a superintendent who considered poverty important, and who was a strong enough administrator—with a cooperative school board and a relatively malleable teachers' union—to conceive major policy changes and make them stick. Curiously enough, despite the trauma of all the changes, the busing program had worked better than anyone expected by the early 1980s, prompting the educational demographer Harold (Bud) Hodgkinson, author of *Ready or Not, Here We Come*, a report on the future of American public education, to declare Jefferson County the most effectively desegregated large school district in the nation, with racially integrated schools prevailing in the ghettoes and in the suburbs. With the problems of race and segregation that have consumed the energy of so many school districts largely behind Louisville, the district—with new leadership and a new mandate—was ready to blaze new trails in education. Ingwerson called for a commitment to ensure that every student—and every adult—in the community would have equal access to education. He built strong coalitions with local government (from which schools in Kentucky are independent) and with industry, winning grants from General Electric, IBM, and other industries sufficient to place more computers per capita in Louisville-area schools than any other system in the nation. And, at the level of basics, Ingwerson implemented policies that kept poor kids in school, improved their grades, and ensured their good health. He reached out to their families, too. He put his power and prestige behind these programs, and he found the money to pay for them.

"It took vision and strong leadership to do these things," said the district's coordinator of community education, Georgia Eugene, a teacher with roots in the system so deep that she remembers teaching in Louisville's all-black schools before integration was the law of the land. "And it takes a willingness to take risks, on the part of the superintendent and the board."

The Jefferson County High School offers a good example of the Jefferson County Public Schools' innovative approaches to fighting poverty through education. It is a fully accredited, separate high school intended entirely for adults who dropped out of school but now want to complete their education, and for whom a general equivalency diploma is not enough. This centrally located school features flexible scheduling, "adult" relationships with students, and, most unusual, is open daily from 8:00 A.M. to 9:00 P.M., including many classes on Saturday. A student's full-time work schedule no longer prevents attending high school classes, thanks to its simple premise that a high school for working adults ought to make itself accessible to its students, rather than the other way around.

Another innovative program, one that predates Ingwerson but grew and won a national reputation during his administration, is the Teen-Age Parent Program (TAPP), started in 1970 in the old city school district to keep pregnant students and young mothers from dropping out. After struggling for years in a donated room at the YMCA, TAPP came into its own with Ingwerson's backing and the tireless efforts of principal Georgia Chaffee, who oversaw the program from the beginning. By the early 1980s it boasted a $2 million annual budget—80 percent from the school district and 20 percent, raised mostly by Chaffee, from the federal government and foundations. TAPP now occupies two school buildings, one in the central part of the county and one in the southern suburbs, serving eight hundred pregnant high school students, a handful as young as sixth-graders. This figure includes some two-thirds of the fifteen-hundred teenage girls who are pregnant in Jefferson County at any one time, according to estimates by the county board of health. It's a high proportion, given that not all teen pregnancies involve public school students and that the TAPP program, after all, is not mandatory. Pregnant teens have the right to remain in regular classes if they wish, although counselors strongly encourage them to enter TAPP because of its benefits.

It's a startling thing to find an entire school—a modern one-story building with big windows overlooking a green lawn and trees in suburban Fairdale, Kentucky, with science rooms, computers, and all the other elements of a typical high school—occupied entirely by pregnant young women, who sit at broad tables rather than desks, "because they don't fit into desks," laughed instructional supervisor John Shober.

Chaffee, who's been a principal for a quarter of a century, has strong ideas about how a school should be run. Men teachers wear coats and ties, women wear dresses. Teachers stand while lecturing, and the doors to the rest rooms don't read BOYS and GIRLS but LADIES and GENTLEMEN. But the teachers seem to like the program; every one of the 106 on staff asked to be assigned to TAPP, and the average tenure is more than nine years.

Besides traditional classes, TAPP students attend daily sessions on prenatal care and parenting. There's a medical clinic on the school grounds and an intake office for the federal nutrition program for Women, Infants and Children (WIC), so students don't have to give up valuable class time for a day at the doctor's or the social services office.

Nor does the school day begin and end in the classroom. Mrs. Chaffee's approach, developed over twenty years, includes a remarkable array of support services: weekly classes for the fathers-to-be, married or not (only about two dozen of the eight hundred girls, in fact, are married); support sessions for the grandparents, who are typically in their thirties and stunned by the notion that a third generation is on its way; counseling sessions, in groups and individually, by student advocates (who prefer that title to social workers), and clubs and support groups for teenage mothers-to-be who intend to give their babies up for adoption (a small minority) and for youngsters from abusive situations or who have considered suicide.

## *Family Literacy*

For too many teenage girls, getting pregnant and giving birth means dropping out of school and facing the probability of years on the welfare rolls. Louisville's schools, however—along with a few other innovative efforts—seek to reverse this unnecessary equation by making sure that young mothers stay in school and get the tools they need to become and stay self-reliant. Louisville's model Kenan Family Literacy Program is essentially similar to Kentucky's much-publicized PACE program, which in turn resembles HIPPY, a widespread initiative that I've seen in Kentucky and Arkansas, which in its turn is based on a model from Israel.

In all these cases, the simple but effective process works in the same basic fashion: The young mothers of infant children return to school in sessions designed specifically for their needs, and they bring their babies along. The mothers work as a group on GED qualifications during the morning, while workers in early childhood centers on the premises care for the kids. Mothers and children are reunited for lunch, followed by early childhood classes in the afternoon.

I visited a Kenan group at Schaffner Elementary School, a relatively new building on an urban edge of Louisville where blue-collar suburbs meet a predominantly black city neighborhood. (This school, by the way, also houses yet another unusual Jefferson County innovation—except for the parent-and-child classes, it is a "kindergarten school," that is, it's used entirely for kindergarten and preschool programs, with no older children in sight.)

Principal Amelia Tyra, an older woman with many years of experience but a youthful approach to new ideas (this attitude seemingly a prerequisite to be a principal in Jefferson County's innovative programs) explained that the Kenan groups are subdivided depending on the age of the child, to keep parents with similar problems together.

Tyra doesn't like the word *literacy* in the program's name and wishes that authorities would change it. When ABC-TV did a national news item on Schaffner, she said, the reporters called Kenan's adult students "poor and illiterate," a characterization that may have been accurate as far as "poor" is concerned but was a long stretch off base about the students' literacy. Most of the women in the program are working at eleventh- or twelfth-grade level, make excellent grades, and are quite proud of that. One recent graduate, for instance, ten years after dropping out of school and having three children, came back to the Kenan program, earned her GED, and went on to Jefferson Community College in Louisville, where she is taking classes in elementary education. She intends to become a teacher and is already working as a substitute at Schaffner, teaching young women with stories much like her own.

There's a message here, and the students are certainly hearing it. Tyra couldn't keep the twinkle out of her eyes when she told of a dilemma her students faced one spring. They had the chance to go on a system-wide field trip to Otter Creek Park, a lovely forest a few miles down the Ohio River from Louisville, but the trip conflicted with test week at Schaffner. Tyra gave students the choice, and the verdict was unanimous. "Forget it," the onetime dropouts said. "Education comes first."

I stopped by a class of eight mothers, most of them in their late twenties and early thirties—about the same age as Susan Henderson, their teacher. When I asked what it was like being back in school and how their attitudes had changed since they had left as teenagers, replies came flying back like summer lightning from all around the room:

"It's turned out to be fun."

"It was scary at first, but it's fun now."

"It's a new experience. You *want* to be back, after so many years."

"You try harder. When you get a second chance, you try a lot harder."

"It's difficult, because in your child's eyes, if you drop out, you'll have to explain it."

"The important thing is, you have to take the first step and do it."

These are not the stereotypical comments of welfare mothers who purportedly don't care. This program *works*. And best of all, the mothers said that going back to school with their children had borne unexpected rewards; having the time to spend learning with the child at school, unencumbered by the countless demands at home, opened new realms of communication and helped them know and love the kids more than ever.

## *From School to Community Center*

Schools are for all ages—or so officials in Louisville's system believe. A good example for any community is found in Louisville's DuValle Education Center. Once a middle school located on the border of the city's meanest public housing project, DuValle was targeted for closing in 1980. In a case of the continued tinkering that's required to maintain the school district's commitment to racial balance, the school board proposed closing it to distribute the increasingly black student body among several newer suburban middle schools in the same end of town. But DuValle's community saw the move as a slight, another in a string of perceived institutional affronts to the predominantly black West End of the city, which has seen increased disinvestment in stores and factory closings since World War II. Rather than ignore this, Ingwerson came up with a compromise: He stood fast on plans to close the school as a regular-classroom institution. But instead of selling the building on the open market, as the school district had done with many closed schools over the decade, he sent representatives, including longtime teachers who had the community's respect, to interview the neighborhood's formal and informal leaders to solicit their ideas.

They asked, "What do *you* think we should do with the school?" and they got good answers back: day care, early-childhood programs, recreation, job training, GED courses. School officials heard them out, and they delivered. Although DuValle is no longer a school, the sturdy, redbrick building is now a fully renovated community center, housing eleven Head Start units and six parent-and-child early childhood classes similar to the Kenan programs at Schaffner. It offers recreational programs, from billiards to gymnasium activities, which stay open until 10:00 P.M., giving neighborhood youngsters a safe area to play off the streets, one that is supervised not by high-paid school staff but by volunteers from the Boys and Girls Clubs. The building also holds GED classes, just as the neighbors asked, and a learning center for adults who may have graduated from high school but want to come back to sharpen specific skills, from clerical skills to computer techniques, to enhance their employability. DuValle's sewing classes serve a dual purpose: teaching employable skills and producing inexpensive, presentable clothing to wear to job interviews. An upholstery class teaches prospective workers how to use industrial sewing machines (a skill often requested by local factories hungry for skilled workers), as well as meeting a request of neighbors who wanted to learn to repair their own furniture. There's an evening pottery class, using donated equipment and volunteer teachers.

School doesn't have to end when the final bell rings for the kids at two o'clock. With very little fanfare and very little cost, this model institution provides safe recreation, education, and job training for people of all ages in a community with little else to offer. Why isn't this happening all over America? People who care might want to ask this question in their towns.

## *Getting Homeless People Back in School*

Innovation doesn't insulate programs from funding woes, not in the crazy world of creative attacks on poverty. One of DuValle's, and the nation's, most promising iniatives, Project Worth, has demonstrated its effectiveness many times over, yet it has remained in constant jeopardy of losing its funding as an experimental program under the Department of Labor's Employment Training Act. This shortsightedness is bipartisan, with the annual here-they-come-with-the-ax-again problem continuing unabated from the Bush administration into the Clinton regime.

Project Worth recruits homeless people from Louisville's congregate shelters and soup kitchens and offers them the chance to learn marketable skills, primarily in the building trades, while they pick up GED credits. In addition to classes, the program seeks to prevent the simple but troublesome problems that so frequently derail a homeless person's plans to get back on track. So, for example, the program provides daily transportation to class in vans and buses between DuValle and local homeless shelters, rather than simply handing out bus tokens and leaving the students on their own. For students with children, Project Worth provides on-premises day care in DuValle's early childhood program. And even after students complete training and get jobs, program workers stay in contact for at least thirteen more weeks to help out with, say, lunch money or day care assistance if unexpected problems develop.

One of twenty-five Department of Labor pilot programs in the U.S., only Project Worth was open to any homeless person in its community, a relatively challenging population. The others were limited to target groups such as single men or recovering alcoholics. One of only nine such programs refunded for a second year, it served more than 330 homeless people in 1992 and found jobs for almost all of them.

This program, too, works. It makes sense, and it makes a difference. And sure enough, again in 1994, the Department of Labor came around talking ominously about the "experiment" being over and the money running out. That same month, President Clinton also spoke of "ending welfare as we know it" and finding ways to get people off the dole and onto the payroll.

"When they came into office, we thought they were on our side," said Marlene Gordon, director of Project Worth. She was not smiling. Despite Project Worth's success, it fell afoul of a policy shift in the Clinton Labor Department aimed at "mainstreaming" job-training projects operated by nonprofit organizations using federal funds, returning control to the bureaucracy. This unfortunate policy direction runs counter to the evidence of the most effective nonprofit initiatives, in which experience suggests that the federal government would do well to extend support rather than withdrawing it. But arguments to reason failed to persuade Labor, and 1994 was to be Project Worth's last in its current form. Gordon said Project Worth hopes to convince Job Training Partnership Act officials to continue contracting with the school board program so it won't have to stop turning homeless people into productive workers.

## *People and the Schools*

Getting the public involved with community problems is one of the basic principles of most effective grassroots initiatives, and public education is no exception to this rule. One of the most promising approaches, with many local efforts all over the country, is Cities in Schools, based in Washington, D.C.

Working through local chapters, Cities in Schools builds partnerships between schools and the business community, with the goal of improving education by strengthening families. It grew from an informal organization of storefront alternative schools, called Young Life, established in Harlem during the 1960s by Bill Milliken, a young white man from Pittsburgh who moved to New York to work with poor communities to try to make a difference. Now there are independent, but related, Cities in Schools programs in three dozen cities, mostly in the Southeast but ranging as far afield as New York City, Chicago, Pennsylvania, and the Southwest.

I visited Cities in Schools in Charlotte, North Carolina, where Executive Director Cynthia Marshall explained how the concept works in North Carolina's largest city: Three-person teams of full-time Cities in Schools workers—a counselor, a social worker, and a psychologist, paid by a combination of public money and private contributions—are assigned to middle schools or junior high schools in low-income neighborhoods. Each school's counselors and teachers identify children who may be potential dropouts—six hundred kids each year in the Charlotte school system—and invite them into the program. Then the Cities in School team goes into action, even before the beginning of the school year, visiting the family and trying to figure out what social barriers are hurting the family, and thus the child. Whatever help the family needs, whether it's housing, clothing, food, benefits, or drug-and-alcohol counseling, the group brings appropriate services to bear, calling in private help if public programs aren't sufficient, and considering not just the student but the entire family, parents and children, as a unit.

Rebuilding a stable family by diagnosing its problems and writing a social prescription is strong medicine, but for Cities in Schools, it's just a beginning. In addition to the work of the full-time team of professionals, the program in Charlotte musters more than three hundred volunteers to work as tutors and mentors. Recruited by corporate members of the organization's board (which is top-heavy with blue-ribbon executives, CEOs, clergymen, and college presidents), the mentors range from IBM and Duke Power employees to enthusiastic students from nearby Davidson College. Their formal task is to meet with the youngsters once a week to help with schoolwork, but they invariably go beyond that to become "big brothers and sisters" to them. Middle school youngsters who participate in the program then take a turn as mentors themselves. With the slogan "each one teach one," they help elementary school pupils with their work, not incidentally gaining a sense of self-esteem from being looked up to and treated as somebody important.

The numbers tell the tale of this program's worth: Fully 95 percent of the youngsters in the program have earned promotion at the end of the term—a term that began with them being judged at risk of failure. And, in a school district where 6 percent of the student body drops out in each year of high school, and almost one out of four fails to graduate, the Cities in Schools kids don't drop out. Period.

Here's another truism: The best grassroots programs don't rest on their laurels. When you've won one battle, you go on to fight another. Charlotte Cities in Schools demonstrated that in 1992, when, in partnership with the school system and the Mayfield Memorial Baptist Church on Charlotte's predominantly black northwest side, the group opened an alternative high school. The fifty students in this voluntary program receive the full high school curriculum, and then add on a course of focused vocational training that goes far beyond traditional shop classes. Kids in the program learn skilled trades taught with the help of prospective employers, who fuel the engine by providing internships, meaningful summer jobs, and an inside track to permanent employment when they graduate. Now that's a promise guaranteed to keep a kid in school.

That's the whole idea behind Cities in Schools, a program pragmatic enough to win the support of corporate America. Its brochure prominently features a remark from no less an icon than Lee Iacocca: "All of us in the business world like a program that gets results. Cities in Schools gets results. Kids who were once dropouts or at great risk, are now graduating from high school and college. They are productive members of society."

## *Grassroots Education*

Grassroots education doesn't happen only in schools. It happens in storefronts, in youth clubs, and in church basements in neighborhoods like Chicago's blighted Lawndale, a bleak expanse within sight of the Windy City's towering skyline, where the Lawndale

Community Church appears almost as an oasis, with its fresh paint and bright marigolds and crowds of people coming and going.

Like much of the West Side of Chicago, Lawndale has undergone wrenching change in just a few decades. The Christian Development Corporation of the Lawndale Community Church is trying to wrench it back by identifying leaders among the neighborhood's young people and working with them to develop the potential with which they might be able to turn their community around.

The idea came from a seemingly unlikely source. Wayne Gordon, a young white graduate of Wheaton College, outside of Chicago, was barely old enough to vote when he became an evangelical Christian and felt a call, as he puts it, to minister to Chicago's black community and serve its poor people. Against the advice of just about everyone he knew, Gordon got a job as substitute teacher and volunteer football and wrestling coach at Farragut High School in Lawndale. When he took an apartment nearby, he became the only white person (and the only Farragut teacher of any race) in the neighborhood. Within days he was making friends with the toughest neighborhood kids—and teaching them Bible classes in his storefront apartment after school. Before long the youngsters, and their parents, had formed a nondenominational community church that aimed to focus as much on the everyday lives of its people as on their spiritual welfare.

Operating in a large, sparkling building that, back in the 1920s, housed the auto dealership where Al Capone purchased his cars, the Lawndale Community Church has a variety of ministries aimed at both serving people and nudging them toward self-sufficiency, with particular emphasis on Gordon's goal of developing "indigenous leaders." It starts with a smorgasbord of educational programs that seek to go beyond the basics available at Chicago's troubled public schools. A tutoring program, for instance, bolstered by ten donated Apple computers, offers kids three hours of homework help and intensive enrichment work every day after school and during summer vacation. Twenty-five high school students are enrolled in the Lawndale College Opportunity Program (LCOP), an after-school tutoring and role-model program with a major incentive: Every child who completes the program, stays in school, graduates, and goes to college will receive a $12,000 scholarship, endowed by an anonymous donor.

Gordon's indigenous leaders are already coming back to Lawndale, and they're making a difference. Two young doctors who grew up in the neighborhood and fought their way out have returned to open a medical clinic. Another, a welder, has opened a welding shop and is hiring and training his neighbors as employees. The church's housing ministry is hiring people from the neighborhood too, training them in construction trades as they rebuild dilapidated houses for resale at low cost. This gives Lawndale a double boost: they're not only renovating the community's stock of decent housing, but the group is also quietly buying up crack houses and the homes of drug dealers, offering undesirable neighbors a reason to take their money and leave.

---

A similar multiple-service organization on the multiracial and multiethnic West Side of Kansas City, the Guadalupe Center, has education as its primary goal. Tracing its roots back to a volunteer school and clinic established by the Catholic Diocese of Kansas City for Mexican immigrants in 1919, the center is one of the oldest service agencies in the country. It has been independently operated by Hispanic Americans as a private nonprofit organization since 1974.

With six separate facilities around the city, including an administrative center, alternative high school, senior center, health clinic, social service center, and youth recreation center, the Guadalupe Center offers comprehensive services covering health and social services, senior citizens and youth recreation. Its educational programs are available for all ages: a bilingual preschool, enrichment courses for elementary and high school students, parent-child classes, literacy instruction, courses in English as a second language, adult courses, GED classes, and job-training courses. And, to encourage young Hispanic American students to go to college, the center established the Greater Kansas City Hispanic Scholarship Fund, which distributes $60,000 a year in scholarships. The pattern that distinguishes the nation's most effective programs shows itself again here in Kansas City: The Guadalupe Center doesn't do just one job and leave the rest of the work to others; it grasps the scope of a problem and brings to bear a battery of initatives to overcome it.

The growing numbers of Mexican and Central American immigrants throughout the Midwest has prompted the growth of many programs like the Guadalupe Center that seek to build self-reliance in their communities through education.

## *Literacy: A Weapon to Fight Poverty*

Reading and writing are such fundamental tools of daily life, most of us rarely consider what a handicap illiteracy must be to someone struggling to make it on society's lower edge. But for youngsters shortchanged by inadequate schools, for new immigrants still trying to cope with English, and others who for whatever reason never mastered these skills, the connection between illiteracy and poverty is as obvious as the challenge of filling out an application form that they can't read or learning a skilled trade without understanding the manual.

Literacy South, based in Durham, North Carolina, is working hard to do something about that. Inspired by the premise that illiteracy and poverty go hand in hand, this model organization (funded by the Z. Smith Reynolds Foundation) acts something like a Johnny Appleseed for literacy training. It trains people who work for grassroots organizations to teach others how to teach literacy. These people go back to their communities and teach more people how to set up and run free literacy classes as volunteers.

Under a curriculum designed by executive director Hanna Fingeret, Literacy South makes it easy to learn to read by marshalling *relevant* reading materials that grab the attention of adults, including community organizing information and news. Originally organized to develop a network of literacy trainers in North Carolina alone, the group changed its name from North Carolina Center for Literacy Development after its leaders decided to expand their attention to the entire Southeast. But even Literacy South may be too narrow, as it has advised organizations as far away from Durham as Harlem in New York City.

---

Another attack on illiteracy comes from grassroots groups serving the waves of immigrants that have come flooding into the United States looking for work and a better life. One excellent example, based in the massive redbrick Live Stock Exchange Building that rises like a citadel in the middle of Omaha's sprawling stockyards, is the Nebraska Association of Farm Workers. This group lobbies for the rights of the Mexican immigrants who have moved into the state over the past decade, lured by the relatively high wages and frequently broken promises of a quality life and benefits for farm workers and packinghouse workers.

Founded in 1979 by a coalition of advocates concerned because Nebraska provided no social services for migrants and seasonal workers, the nonprofit association grew with Nebraska's Hispanic community, which increased 33 percent during the 1980s to number 17,000 of metropolitan Omaha's 650,000 people and 35,000 of the state's 1.5 million. The significance of this development, however, was largely lost on Nebraska's legislature and local officials. "It's an educational process," executive director Ella Ochoa said. "Many communities never saw a minority person, except for Omaha. There were lots of problems with police, medical care, discrimination in employment and housing. The state still has a long way to go before actually meeting these needs."

The association tries to fill the gap not only through basic social services programs but through education. It uses federal Labor Department grants to provide training in English as a second language, literacy training, and GED courses, and it has joined with local vocational colleges in Omaha and Scottsbluff to offer more advanced training. Individuals who complete the GED course move on to career assessment and job-search classes in On-the-Job Training (OJT). The association enlists employers to provide OJT opportunities and half of the worker's salary during training (the other half being supplemented with federal money), with a full-time job waiting at the end of training. A total of 135 people claimed good-paying full-time jobs through this route in 1992.

---

Approaches like these turn up all around the country, wherever grassroots advocates recognize that teaching people to read gives them a powerful tool for digging their way out of poverty. In New Orleans, for instance, the nation's fourth-largest utility company, Entergy Corporation, donated $80,000 worth of computers and software to the Orleans Parish Community Correctional Center, where education director Henry Helm uses them in a high-tech literacy-training program based on the hope that education might be one way to break the cycle that keeps repeat offenders coming back to jail.

Helm, who's seen quite a change since he retired at sixty-five as principal of New Orleans's Benjamin Franklin High School for gifted students not long before I met him in 1991, showed me a colorful room where twelve women inmates chattered quietly as they worked at a dozen beeping and whirring computers. The computer program lets wary new readers manipulate colorful symbols on the screen instead of using the keyboard. One of the women, Kathy, jailed on a prostitution charge and totally unable to read, had worked her way up to Chapter 11 in the basic reading course. By following along as the computer displayed a comic book–like narrative, its synthesized voice speaking into her earphones, she picked up vocabulary with unexpected ease. After just six months she reads with startling fluency, going through a section of text with articulate confidence. Better still, she not only reads but now uses the computer with an expert's casual skill. Other women who came to the program with more advanced reading ability have moved on to learn typing, computer programming, mathematics, even foreign languages through computer courses.

Weekday mornings, men prisoners who have volunteered for Sheriff Charles C. Foti's About Face program use the computers as part of a comprehensive, high-intensity boot camp course. They live separately from the other prisoners in a Marine Corps–style program that combines computerized education with strict, morale-building discipline.

On a Navajo reservation that straddles the Continental Divide near Thoreau, New Mexico, volunteers at the Gathering Place see learning to read as one of the most important ways that people can improve their lives. Literacy instructor Clara Begay said the Gathering Place has reached more than three thousand individuals through its three courses. The Pathway Program starts with remedial reading and goes on through GED qualification. The Mom the Teacher program, designed for mothers who receive WIC supplements, uses clear, easy-to-understand brochures about parenting as texts for reading instruction. Finally, Keepers of the Beautyway is a literacy class designed with sensitivity to the cultural needs of elderly Navajos brought up before public schooling was available on the reservation and who never learned to read.

In Greensboro, North Carolina, a different approach to literacy comes from the public library. With an unusual idea that would be exceptionally easy for other communities to replicate, the library, the business community, and local government joined hands to teach children and adults to read. The Community of Readers started, recalled librarian Steve Sumerford, a youngish, bearded veteran of the peace movement, when workers at the library's Southeast Branch, located in a poor, mostly black neighborhood, became concerned because the branch was doing poorly in terms of the traditional measure: circulation. "We're not the kind of branch where people walk out with stacks of Stephen King novels in their arms," Sumerford said.

So what's the logical move for a library that wants to build a clientele? Help people learn to read better, and show them that reading is fun. To get the community involved, though, rather than merely announcing reading classes, the librarians built a coalition involving public agencies like the school board, mental health department, and mayor's office as well as local businesses, which have a stake in an educated community. With this backing, the Community of Readers made its reading programs big local news. The library sponsored Families Reading Together workshops, providing reading materials suitable for parents and children to share. Children's librarian Lou Saunders has held dozens of Catch 'Em in the Cradle workshops at classes for pregnant teens, high schools, and meetings of civic groups, energizing young parents to enrich their kids' lives with books and reading from the start.

The library also trains literacy teachers in frequent workshops, and it has organized annual Young Writers' Conferences for more than six hundred Greensboro students, who compete for prizes for their stories, articles, and poems. Librarians donated duplicate copies and older library books to the city's Pathways shelter for homeless families, where they're used in teaching subjects ranging from family budgeting to nutrition.

The once nearly dormant Southeast Branch, proudly renamed the Vance H. Chavis Lifelong Learning Library, now buzzes with activity from opening time till closing as children and adults stream in and out with armloads of books. It *still* doesn't circulate a lot of Stephen King novels, but it has moved from the bottom to become one of the busiest libraries in the Greensboro system. And the city is not only no longer talking about budget cuts, but actually plans to expand the branch with a major building addition.

Schools, jails, Indian reservations, libraries—wherever people read or want to learn how, there's opportunity for literacy training. In inner-city Milwaukee, one ardent advocate produces a newspaper for adults who are learning to read. *The Key*, an eight-page monthly tabloid newspaper, widely distributed in Milwaukee's inner city, is specifically designed for adults, covering serious world, national, and local news in articles written for—but do not talk down to—people with less than full adult reading comprehension.

The newspaper is the brainchild of Suzanne Zipperer, who got the idea of preparing reading material for people with limited literacy when she taught English in Zimbabwe. When she returned to the United States in 1990, she got a job as a part-time literacy teacher at Journey House, a twenty-year-old nondenominational community center in a racially mixed neighborhood on Milwaukee's South Side, where she soon discovered that the reading materials available for adult students were, in a blunt word, "abysmal." Typical material fell into one of several categories: childish ("Dick and Jane" stories); naively patronizing ("Learn to read and all life's problems will be solved"); or demeaning ("You're poor, you should be ashamed of yourself, and you have too many children").

Considering alternatives, she had a bright idea: Make a newspaper just for adults learning to read. The paper covers the same subjects as the daily newspapers and television, but frames the stories in plain, simple English at a beginning reader's level. It was an idea whose time had come, and funders and community supporters bought in enthusiastically. The Milwaukee Area Technical College (MATC) coughed up $50,000 for the first year's funding, and the *Milwaukee Journal* agreed to print ten thousand copies a month without charge. *The Key* is distributed free at 125 libraries, MATC learning centers, and community organizations throughout the city, and it was an instant success, both among poor people and adult-literacy teachers.

"A student told me," Zipperer said, " 'This is the first time in my life that I can read a newspaper. It's my *own* newspaper. I take it home.' "

# 5

# People Need Healthy Children and Families

One clear path out of the permanent underclass and multigenerational poverty that afflicts the nation's inner cities and many of its rural areas lies in building the strength of the next generation. The key to this effort, in turn, may be found in helping families survive the shattering impact of poverty. This principle, as we've already seen in the model transitional housing programs like the Bridge and Homeward Bound in Phoenix, works at the grassroots level by identifying families in need and focusing on them a broad and comprehensive battery of services that social workers sometimes label with the buzzword "holistic."

If the ultimate solution to poverty for most Americans lies in work and wages, then each step along the way is based on getting people ready for work. As we've seen in earlier chapters, it's necessary to get people off the streets, fed and clothed, and in control of drug and alcohol habits. But there's still more to be done, as unfortunately in America today a person with the will to work may still be barred from earning a decent living if she doesn't have access to—or can't afford—quality care for her children while she's away at work, not to mention sufficient health insurance and health care. In this chapter, we'll make quick visits to some of the nation's best grassroots programs that are working to fill these gaps.

## *Filling the Gaps in Reno*

The Children's Cabinet, describing itself as the "central control tower" for problems involving children and their families in Reno, Nevada, came about in 1985 as the result of a businessman's dream, with the help of a family court judge and a caring community. When developer Mike Dermody, who wanted to do something significant to help local youngsters, and Judge Charles McGee, who saw the deep problems troubling many of Reno's families on his court docket, put their weight behind an effort to change things, the community's welfare establishment and nonprofit organizations listened.

They started with a simple but brilliant concept: Every major player in local nonprofit and government services for children and families would be a board member of the new organization, which would be called The Children's Cabinet because, like a cabinet, it brought the leaders of organizations together to work toward solving problems.

Starting with a simple intake process to ensure that youngsters coming into the social service system for any reason wouldn't fall between the cracks, it quickly evolved into a score of programs, operated with considerable efficiency thanks to the large number of community leaders with a stake in its success. Dermody personally paid the director's salary for the first year, grants came from government and private sources, and the organization drew its staff from employees of the various local agencies, assigned to the Cabinet on a rotating basis. Now boasting a staff of thirty-five (and countless volunteers) and an annual budget of about $2.25 million, the Cabinet is housed in an impressive complex of three white buildings in a modern industrial and commercial park on Reno's southeast side.

One of its most innovative programs, the Truancy Center, is located in a poor section of northeast Reno and is staffed by an employee of the public schools and a probation officer. When police or school attendance officers find a child playing hooky, they bring him to the center, where an intake worker immediately begins the process of setting up a supportive program for the youngster and his family, aimed not at punishing the child but at working on the problems that led to the truancy. During the first year of the program, school attendance jumped dramatically. Police say it's no coincidence that daytime burglaries and thefts from cars in Reno dropped 65 percent at the same time.

The Cabinet's consistent principle is to provide competent individual assessment, referrals, and counseling aimed at intervening in young people's problems before they become more serious. Its intensive Family Preservation program works in the same way, targeting families with problems that could otherwise lead eventually to the children being placed in foster care. The Reach for the Academic Difference program, known by the slangy acronym RAD, lines up students considered at risk with volunteer tutors who help them study during sessions at school. A wide variety of other programs include a gang prevention project, parenting education, an adolescent health care clinic, a shelter for homeless young people from infants through teenagers, and a teen center in Reno's poorest neighborhood that offers both recreation and educational opportunities where kids are and when they are there; no business-hours agenda but midnight basketball, if that's what the youngsters need in response to the perennial complaint "There's nothing for us to do."

## *Investing in Our Children*

Wyoming is a harsh land, with an austere beauty and darn few people. The nation's least populous state, it's a conservative place, with conservative politicians and people—and in the mid-1990s, quite a few of them are poor. The mining boom of the 1970s went bust in a crash that saw a peak of thirty-six thousand mining jobs drop to twelve thousand. Something similar happened with oil, leaving the pretty little town of Casper, one of the state's largest cities with only about fifty-five thousand people, with thousands of people living unemployed in its split-level homes. Because of the oil and mining bust, and the advanced decline of the family farm and ranch, Wyoming's already small population tumbled during the 1980s, losing 3 percent of its people (Casper lost 15 percent) during the decade.

You can drive for miles through Wyoming's desolate, rolling hills, with the Rockies on your left and the Plains on your right, hardly ever seeing a house or a sign of civilization, save for here and there a tiny farmhouse (some made of logs), a cluster of cattle, oil derricks (an occasional one still pumping), and now and then, unexpectedly, a huge coal-fired power plant in the middle of nowhere like the gigantic Dave Johnston Power Plant at East Glenrock, between Casper and Douglas, sending a towering plume of white smoke into a clear, blue sky.

Nutrition and Child Development Inc. fills the space that once housed a department store in a rambling shopping center on the south side of Casper, where the shady bowl of hills that embraces the city rises toward a range of jagged black peaks. NCD is a large, well-run day care center—and more. As one of Wyoming's three "sponsoring agencies" for the U.S. Department of Agriculture's Child Care Food Program, NCD distributes an average of $86,000 every month in federal Agriculture Department money to more than three hundred of the state's smaller day care centers, where it's used to feed eighteen hundred children a day. While there's nothing particularly unusual about this—every state has some similar umbrella organization to distribute federal money to feed poor children in day care centers—this thirteen-year-old program does an exceptional job of carrying out the federal mandate to accompany the money with nutrition education. It also offers a first-rate up-by-the-bootstraps model: By aggressively offering child care and management training to poor families so they can operate family day care centers, it creates jobs and increases the availability of affordable day care.

In addition to operating four Casper-area day care centers serving about two hundred children, NCD supervises more than three hundred other family centers. Its staff inspects the centers three times a year, providing operators with nutrition education and technical assistance to make sure every eligible child in day care receives healthy, well-balanced meals. NCD also provides the state-mandated training programs (eight credit hours per year of approved training) needed for day care providers to receive state licensing. Training is offered at periodic all-day workshops, as well as through correspondence courses, in a baker's dozen of topics such as Health and Safety in Child Care, Stimulating Children through Activities, Managing Your Child Care Business, and Children with Special Needs.

In another model program, NCD uses a small endowment fund to give $50 grants to family day care operators who need a little money for such necessities as toys or books for the children or classes to enhance their own skills. It also operates an afternoon and summer program for latchkey children, giving approximately one hundred children a safe place to go after school, plus field trips, assistance with homework, and transportation.

## *Affordable Day Care*

When adults go homeless, their children go with them. Twelve years ago, horrified to realize that increasing numbers of youngsters were moving into the dirty and dangerous flophouses of Los Angeles' Skid Row, Tanya Tull opened a safe and modern center, Para Los Niños (For the Children) to house and protect them while their parents were working or looking for work.

Parts of Los Angeles may still be Glitter City, but the city of the angels has changed a lot in the past twenty years, and not all of the changes are for the better. Heavy migration by low-income immigrants from Mexico, Central America, and Southeast Asia, and a massive shift away from the industrial economy—a change that came to southern California much later than it did in the Northeast and Midwest—coupled with the near demise of the aerospace industry, have set the scene for widespread poverty, with many unemployed and more underemployed. This is particularly harsh in a city where the average cost of housing (more than $600 for a one-bedroom apartment) is higher than anywhere in the country except San Francisco and New York City. Particularly in the aftermath of the riots following the Rodney King trial, Angelenos seem beset with multiple racial tensions and a fear of crime that transcends even the paranoia of New Yorkers. Adding still more spice to this stew is the huge population of homeless street people, many of them mentally ill, drawn to California by the combination of a mild climate and welfare benefits that are still generous in comparison with those of most other states.

The turquoise-and-yellow building, once a false eyelash factory, that houses Para Los Niños shines like a beacon on a drab block in an industrial area just east of L.A.'s downtown, in a neighborhood so poor that, of the 550 youngsters at the nearby Ninth Street Elementary School, all but one are eligible for free school lunches. While its primary purpose is to keep the children of Skid Row's families safe and bathe them with a warm flood of enrichment activities, the "hub of the wheel," director Patricia Tomlin says, is the associated social service center, where social workers intervene immediately to find food and shelter for new families that have none.

Para Los Niños's services include a food pantry; a weekly medical clinic (and immediate referrals, when necessary, to a community health clinic); classes in parenting; help with job and housing searches; the central service, a first-rate day care program for four hundred preschoolers a day; additional after-school day care for latchkey kids; and a teen program for eighty older kids, who are lured in by social activities and movies but stay for more serious stuff, including training for SATs and guidance on staying in the classroom and out of gangs.

---

Similar stories abound across the nation as communities recognize a problem and good people band together to address it. Atlanta's Summerhill community, for instance, is a poor neighborhood with a lot of problems and an exceptionally proud history. Atlanta's oldest black community, Summerhill was founded by freed slaves shortly after the end of the Civil War. It was a center for black business and commerce as well as stable residences, and by all accounts, its neighbors got along well with nearby racially mixed neighborhoods and the residents of its traditionally Jewish section.

But Summerhill, like a lot of other urban neighborhoods all over America, went into a steep decline during the 1950s and 1960s. A network of interstate highways crisscrossed the neighborhood and knocked out many houses and businesses, and so did Fulton County Stadium, the nearby home of the Atlanta Braves. "It all happened before the neighborhood had time to adjust, and the neighborhood was asked for no input," said Sonya Tinsley, director of the creative program, Summerhill One-to-One. "All the people who could afford to move, moved, and those who couldn't, stayed."

But an unexpected and happy thing occurred. Even though the neighborhood's decline meant that almost no one who could afford to move out was willing to stay, Atlanta's large middle-class black community, almost universally remembering childhood ties to Summerhill, retained a sense of loyalty. A neighborhood reunion brought back hordes of former residents for a day of picnicking and nostalgia that drew wide media attention. The reunion organizers suddenly realized that, if they could get that kind of crowd together, they ought to be able to mobilize a similar force to rebuild the community. They formed Summerhill Neighborhood Inc., an organization that takes the initiative through low-income housing and community development programs and a real-estate corporation. But unlike most organizations of this type, which work almost entirely in housing and community development, Summerhill Neighborhood Inc. added an additional target: the community's estimated five hundred schoolchildren.

Through its innovative Summerhill One-to-One, the organization provides four related programs for young people. Its youth group, Voices of Summerhill, organized by the youngsters themselves, meets every Saturday for activities such as discussion groups in which kids talk openly about their lives and the things that concern them. The after-school tutoring program offers help in math and reading. There's a mentoring program modeled on Big Brothers/Big Sisters. And finally, it sponsors a cluster of enrichment activities including sports teams, art classes, and dance classes. Two more programs are coming soon: An entrepreneurial training program, funded by a foundation in Washington, D.C., will nurture small-business projects for older youngsters who'd like to start their own businesses when they finish school. Another project will recruit neighborhood teenagers to volunteer in many community service activities, from tutoring younger kids to helping with housing rehabilitation. This "kills two birds with one stone," Tinsley said. It will get teenagers into worthwhile activities that expose them to good mentors and role models, at the same time providing the organization a ready source of willing hands. "We try to be a catalyst for creating a lot of outlets for kids," Tinsley said. "Not just a place to pass spare time, but to build these kids up."

Another proud southern town, Savannah, Georgia, perhaps best known for its genteel mansions and shady squares, is a little less than proud of its record of gang violence that would do justice to Los Angeles. While I was visiting there, the news media chronicled the life imprisonment without parole of a twenty-year-old gang leader and high school dropout, who had built a multimillion dollar drug empire run by a gang whose members were expected to earn initiation by killing someone.

In an industrial neighborhood on the not-so-historic side of this pretty but troubled town, executive director Sherry Murone of the Second Harvest Food Bank of Coastal Georgia brings a special spark to a small and unusual food bank. A former church secretary and single mother of three, she had never been inside the doors of a food bank before she was drafted as director in 1990. Unfettered by tradition and blessed with a board of directors willing to entertain creativity, she has come up with good ideas that other food banks would do well to copy.

The food bank's most hopeful program is intended for kids. It's a soup kitchen serving a hot dinner to latchkey children whose mothers are working to keep the family together but can't afford day care. Murone and food bank volunteer Elaine Erlich came up with the idea after a local food pantry was repeatedly victimized by burglars. The perpetrators turned out to be two preteen boys, who admitted that they broke into the pantry because they were hungry. Their mother, a crack abuser, never made dinner.

Murone and Erlich knew a lot of latchkey children and youngsters from malfunctional families weren't eating well, but in conversation with mothers at area soup kitchens, they realized that the rough, mostly male street-people environment of the usual soup kitchen was no place for youngsters. So they created a separate kitchen just for kids (and their moms). In addition to feeding youngsters after school, the three-hour program on weekday afternoons also provides play supervision, and there are always at least a few adult role models hanging around. It certainly beats the streets.

## Working Out of Welfare Dependency

There's been a backlash in America against poor people and people who don't look like "us." It's a backlash with respectability, and that's made it a little too easy for citizens who consider themselves open-minded to buy the line that we no longer need to help people down on their luck get through tough times.

Of course welfare as we know it is ill planned and badly administered and it needs to be changed. Aid to Families with Dependent Children (AFDC) is fundamentally flawed by its provisions that discourage the women who receive its benefits from forming two-parent families or from going back to work. But there's a big difference between *changing* welfare and *eliminating* it. In fact, even if all the nation's best grassroots initiatives against hunger and poverty were replicated within a single community—a happy circumstance that would dramatically change the lives of millions of Americans—we'd still need government to play a role in providing basic support for the poorest of the poor.

This is doubly true in light of another, separate public policy that's not often examined on the same stage as welfare: In order to keep the economy from overheating and inflation from getting out of control, the government, through its Federal Reserve, consciously tries to prevent the unemployment rate from going below 6 percent. That's not 6 percent of all workers, but 6 percent of the smaller pool defined as "in the labor force." If it's our policy to keep millions of workers off the job for the sake of the economy, and this is no secret, then there's no moral excuse for a policy that declines to support people who have no work.

AFDC specifically was based on the humane assumption that a mother with infant children and neither a husband nor a job deserved a hand, and through the Nutrition Program for Women, Infants and Children (WIC), a meal for herself and her babies. One putrescent symptom of how far the backlash against poor people has gone is that a lot of Americans who consider themselves middle-of-the-road no longer accept this assumption as valid.

In contrast to the government welfare programs with their disincentives, the most effective grassroots initiatives nudge their participants toward working out the problems that keep them in poverty and toward getting an education and a job. This is not a bad thing. The more difficult challenge of welfare reform, however, is whether a broad plan implemented through the political process and delivered through a federal bureaucracy can provide the kind of caring, focused, flexible, and one-on-one attention that seems to be the critical element of success for the most effective local efforts by nonprofit organizations and local government efforts that go beyond the ordinary.

## *One-Stop Shopping*

Welfare offices that send clients running out in tears offer a vivid demonstration of one serious problem with our current welfare system, but this unhappy event rarely occurs at one of the most humane welfare offices in the country: the Emergency Services Center of the Carroll County Department of Social Services in Maryland, in the rich, rolling farm country near the Pennsylvania border. As often seems to be the case, this gentle arrangement turned out not to be so much a matter of conscious policy as the result of the efforts of a single caring individual: Sylvia Cannon, a longtime social worker who—despite being outspoken and a bit of a maverick, characteristics that don't usually enhance a social worker's career—rose to become manager.

Cannon's agency demonstrates several of the most effective ways to deliver social services competently—concepts that ought to be widespread but, unfortunately, are not. For almost ten years, it has provided "one-stop shopping" for social service recipients, and it links government, nonprofit, and volunteer services in an effective partnership.

I was a bit disillusioned when I found my way to Cannon's office in an old distillery turned office building on the outskirts of

Westminster. From outside, it displayed all the warmth of a recruitment office for the Foreign Legion. Signs on the rickety wheelchair ramp caution women to walk up the ramp wearing high heels "at your own risk." The doors are locked, so visitors have to be buzzed in; when they get inside, bored-looking clerks behind bulletproof glass windows make them sign in and wait.

Once you make it into the inner sanctum, however, you will find good things happening here. Most of them, apparently, are being done by Cannon herself, who works sixty hours a week and is a constant source of ideas. Her bosses (the same bureaucrats who installed the buzzers and bulletproof glass) are smart enough to smile benignly and let Sylvia do whatever she wants to. Which is, simply, to put herself in the position of the person needing services and then visualize how her agency can most effectively help.

The "one-stop shopping" concept occurred to her early on, before 1980, when it struck her as foolish that a person who needed food stamps, AFDC, and Medicaid had to go to separate offices, fill out separate forms, and deal with separate social workers for each of these different but related services—a daunting job that often took weeks.

First, she got permission to devise a consolidated form (a version of it is now used statewide in Maryland) and to have a single caseworker assigned to each recipient rather than requiring the client to start anew at each stop along the line. This worked well, and it didn't take long to notice that, in addition, the first social worker a client met could ask a few more questions during the initial interview and find out what other services the recipient might need, then start the process of getting those services. After all, how complicated a concept is it to sit down with a person at the beginning of the process and cover all the bases at once? It may seem logical enough, but no one had bothered to think of it before.

Once Cannon thought of it, though, a lot of the area's nonprofit organizations serving poor people noticed what was going on, and they started suggesting additional ways to work together. Carroll County Food Sunday, the local, all-volunteer food bank, decided to prepare a supply of nonperishable food boxes—enough staples to feed a family of four for three days—and stock them in Cannon's office. That way, people in a crisis who didn't have the necessary paperwork to satisfy the food stamp bureaucrats could at least take home a box of food to tide them over.

Simple ideas? Of course! But no one had thought of them before, at least not in Carroll County, a fast-growing community in Baltimore's outer suburban ring, where homelessness and hunger exist but don't get a lot of attention. Now, thanks to Cannon, low-income Carroll County residents can come to one place, on one visit, and receive immediate assistance that lets them start to deal with problems of homelessness, housing, utility cutoffs, appliance breakdowns, food, clothing, emergency heat, household items, and medications.

The idea, says Cannon, is to spell out a continuum of available services and then look for the gaps in it. Once you've identified the gaps, find ways that the public and private sectors can work together to fill them. These don't have to be complicated strategies. Carroll County Food Sunday, for instance, worked out a simple deal with the local game warden. He confiscates illegally taken deer, the food bank gets venison. "We try to effect cures rather than treat symptoms" is a stock Cannon phrase. Another is "I'd rather hire attitude than aptitude." Her boss, Alex Jones, loves to tell visitors that Cannon puts in sixty-hour weeks, and she doesn't deny it; she just shrugs and says that when you need to write a grant because you don't know where the next dollar is coming from to fund a needed program, you can't get too picky about knocking off on a Saturday. And overtime doesn't seem to bother social workers whose morale is high because they see recipients doing well when the system works. Cannon's unit has eliminated some of the frustration and red tape that drives social workers nuts, and they respond with enthusiasm.

One-stop shopping is another of the basic principles that turns up independently in creative grassroots organizations, not just welfare offices. It represents the kind of goal-driven management that understands the importance of the simple question, How can we do this better?

## *Down and Out in New Orleans*

New Orleans is one of my favorite cities to visit, but a trip to its poorer precincts shows a different scene than the one that tourists see in the French Quarter or the Garden District. Like an overripe tropical fruit, the city is bright and looks pretty at a glance, but the colorful exterior hides a soft, rotten core. For many of its inhabitants, it is one of the poorest cities in America, and although Mayor Sidney Barthelemy, a former social worker, brought good intentions to his administration, the city's systemic problems seem to defy solution. It makes a useful, if disheartening, case study of the way that social factors pile up to make poverty for some people all but inevitable.

Although tourism has always been a factor in New Orleans's economy, the oil industry and the city's deepwater port traditionally played a much larger part in terms of dollars. Or they did, at least, before the oil depression of the late 1970s, which wasn't just damaging but terminal. Big Oil's regional headquarters (Amoco, Shell, and Gulf, among others) pulled back to Houston during the hard times and did not return. The Port of New Orleans, too, stands mostly idle now that the once-thriving banana shipping industry has died. What's left? Tourism, once an afterthought but now central to New Orleans's fortune. And the bad news for working people is that the tourism economy is a low-skill, low-wage economy without a lot of ladders up.

Other factors make matters worse still: White flight has created a mostly black, mostly poor urban area with pockets of white affluence, surrounded by thriving suburbs that are located in different parishes (counties) where they make no contribution to the city's tax base. State law forbids cities to levy business, occupational, or personal income taxes, and all property assessed at less than $75,000 is exempt from property taxation. This limits the city to a high and regressive sales tax as the primary revenue source for a tight, shrinking budget insufficient to finance needed services. The streets, particularly in poor neighborhoods, are cratered with potholes, and more than a thousand public housing units are vacant, their windows boarded up and doors padlocked, because local government can't afford to maintain them.

Furthermore, because the city's white population is largely Catholic and has traditionally sent its children to parochial schools, the New Orleans public school system has always been predominantly black, has never been well financed, and owns a frankly spotty record for wisely administering what little money it receives. The result shouldn't come as any great surprise: a population that's not only poor but poorly educated, offering little incentive to any high-tech industry that might consider moving in.

All these problems, moreover, exist in a state that ranks among the nation's worst in providing social services and welfare. The basic welfare grant for a single person in 1992 was $72 a month; for a mother with one child it increased to only $138. To make matters even worse, qualifying for welfare in Louisiana is prerequisite to eligibility for food stamps, AFDC, and most significant, Medicaid. A person who wants to work and finds a part-time job for less than minimum wage faces a stern requirement: Drop off welfare and lose all the benefits. Priced the cost of health insurance lately? It sounds like enough to make poor people and their advocates simply give up. Yet, in the midst of such morale-busting realities, a few grassroots warriors are out on the streets doing what they can to change things for the poorest of the poor.

Just a few blocks yet a whole world away from the elegant lawns and antebellum houses of New Orleans's Garden District, the Hope House program occupies a musty old house in the Irish Channel neighborhood, once home to blue-collar immigrants but now inhabited by desperately poor blacks, ripped by poverty, drugs, and crime and tallying a 50 percent unemployment rate. Directly across the street stretches the Dickensian vista of the St. Thomas houses, one of the nation's most vicious public housing complexes, where six hundred of the fifteen hundred units are boarded up, and where rats and junkies wander in and out of vacant, graffiti-covered red-brick buildings scattered indiscriminately among those that are still lived in.

Here Dominican sister Lilianne Flavin, a thin, graying Irish lass with a crooked smile, and Brother Don Everard, a Christian Brother who would require only a suit in place of his sport shirt and khakis to pass for a prosperous young businessman, work with a staff of ten who are a mixture of Catholic nuns and brothers and some folks hired from the community. They all differ from traditional social workers in one key aspect: They have decided to put their lives where their work is, in standard housing units in the St. Thomas project. "Social workers go home at five," Everard says. "We don't. This has made all the difference."

Hope House started a dozen years ago with just that idea in mind, Flavin said. Sister Laurie Schaaf, who taught upper-middle-class Catholic girls from affluent neighborhoods at the city's Mercy Academy, decided to demonstrate in a very direct fashion what the religion books meant in referring to the church as the mystical body of Christ, by taking her well-to-do charges to the projects, where they would meet black youngsters and discover how the other half lives. Their parents, Flavin recalled, "went bananas," and it didn't take long for the bishop to forbid using public housing projects as a living laboratory for religious education.

Schaaf, reasoning that she couldn't teach about the mystical body of Christ if she wasn't permitted to practice its precepts, gave up her teaching job, took an administrative position as the diocesan religious education coordinator, and moved into the St. Thomas project, where she set about getting to know the people. As the extent of their poverty became clear to her, she got more and more involved in community organizing around energy assistance and public housing issues, and eventually got permission to set up Hope House and direct it full-time.

The organization grew, adding programs as the residents demonstrated a desire and need for them: First came GED training, an obvious requirement for a community in which 70 percent of the residents never finished high school, and a huge number—perhaps a majority—are functionally illiterate, unable to read at sixth-grade level. Hope House also set up an emergency assistance program to help people in crises with cash for rent, food, or utility payments. The group raises $35,000 a year in cash and another $60,000 in food and clothing through rummage sales, a thrift shop, and contributions from area churches.

Finally, Hope House started a transitional housing program in a renovated six-family building that it rented from the city for a dollar a year. Families with potential for employment will move in, receiving free rent, utilities, and a telephone and, most important, assistance in working out an action plan with specific goals, including a strict family budget that sets aside 30 percent of their first earnings to build a nest egg to help them move on to independence as soon as they can.

Along with its efforts to turn poor people's lives around, Hope House tries in a modest way to turn around the attitudes of the middle class. Its Education for Justice workshops and seminars offer more affluent residents a chance to see the human side of poverty by meeting poor people and hearing firsthand about their fears and dreams. Anyone who's willing to stick it out through the week-long workshops is irrevocably changed. "At the end of the week," Flavin said, "their entire systems of prejudices—the belief that poor people are poor because they are lazy—are eliminated."

Added Everard, "When they hear people talking from experience, whether it's a welfare mother or an ex-con, to discover that these people are insightful, thinking human beings just blows people away."

## *Family Support Programs*

There's a reason why the Idaho Hunger Action Council was chosen by the Senate Select Committee on Hunger as one of the ten most effective grassroots groups in the nation in 1988 and has been a consistent finalist in World Hunger Year's Harry Chapin Self-Reliance Awards. It combines a record as one of the nation's top statewide coalitions of antihunger activists, and it rolls out more than its share of creative ways to help people beat hunger and poverty in their own lives.

Although the job of any statewide organization in Idaho is complicated by the state's sparse population, physical size, and the challenge of the roadless wilderness area separating its southern tier of towns from the northern panhandle, the council has accomplished more than seems likely for any one organization. It created a major food bank, the Idaho Foodbank Warehouse; mobilized a toll-free legislative hotline staffed by volunteers; and persuaded the state to streamline its lengthy and complicated application for public assistance. The council's lobbying and promotional efforts have boosted school breakfast and summer food programs for hungry children. All of this, however, is merely support to the council's self-reliance programs that are showing poor Idaho families how to pull themselves up by their bootstraps.

Any low-income member of the council, which now has chapters in Boise, Lewiston, and Idaho Falls, is eligible to take part in the Low-Income Family Training and Support (LIFTS) program. Participants receive education and training in just about any topic they request, from life skills and family budget training to dealing with back pain. Members attend monthly meetings that combine a session with a guest expert on a selected topic with recreation and fun to keep things light. LIFTS members are also eligible for the Gleaning Program, organized by the chapters themselves. Participating farms invite them to gather the surprising amount of produce that remains unharvested after mechanical pickers have passed through. The produce goes to the food bank, which exchanges it for shares of the food bank's wares.

---

It's many miles and a long cultural leap from rural Idaho to Hispanic neighborhoods in Washington, D.C., but low-income families everywhere have similar problems, and inventive people often come up with similar solutions. Dr. Ann Barnet, a pediatric hearing specialist who practiced at an inner-city hospital in the nation's capital, became worried about youngsters more than a decade ago. A horrible percentage of the toddlers she was seeing, she recalls, were not thriving. They continually needed medical treatment, and they seemed to leave their parents overwhelmed, either depressed and apparently uninterested in the child or else upset and angry.

Convinced that these children weren't getting the medical and family support they needed during the critical early childhood years, from birth to age three, she approached members of her church, the Church of the Savior, the unusual ecumenical Christian community that has no church building but puts its energies into establishing "missions" with specific purposes in the inner city.

After several years of "chewing on it," as she says, church members opened the Family Place in the mid-1980s, "a neighborhood drop-in center for the support of parents and young children" located in a deceptively stylish-looking section of Northwest Washington. It's not far from Embassy Row, but most of the once-elegant town houses and brownstones have been carved up into small apartments that house a community mostly made up of refugees from El Salvador, of whom 40 percent are single parents and few speak English or know much about the life, the culture, or the social service network in the United States.

Pregnant women and mothers of infants may come in at any time and find a warm, caring environment that aims to mirror the comfortable extended-family feeling that is so much a part of Hispanic life. There's day care for children while mothers attend groups ranging from classes on prenatal health to Alcoholics Anonymous sessions and lectures on domestic violence. Fathers are welcome too, of course, as is anyone, Hispanic or Anglo, regardless of race, religion, or ethnic background, and without regard to family income, immigrant status, or whatever. In practice, about 85 percent of clients are Hispanic and virtually all the rest are American blacks.

Although the ultimate goal is to strengthen families for the benefit of children, the Family Place also addresses short-term needs; breakfast and lunch are served daily, and emergency food packages are distributed, as are its other services, with no questions asked. Among its initiatives to lure needy people in, the Family Place operates a laundry in its basement, using washers and dryers donated by a supporter who owns a chain of Laundromats. Mothers are entitled to wash two loads a week free, provided that they attend prenatal or parenting classes while the machines are doing the diapers. "Maybe two percent of the people will take advantage of us. So be it," said program director Maria Elena Orrego. "One thing I say, if we have one box of espaghetti left and someone knocks on the door and says 'I need food,' they get the food. If two people knock on the door, we'll split it in two."

The center's open approach pays dividends in building trust. This is especially important with the organization's two main groups of clients. Because of previous bad experiences, Washington's blacks tend to be cynical about the social service system, and they respond well to being treated with respect for a change. The Salvadorans, in contrast, have recently come from a society in which social services are mostly unheard of and, where they exist, are not trusted. Their culture demands going to family, friends, and the church for help; the idea of a nonprofit agency is difficult for them to get used to. But the Family Place is building bridges, and people are starting to come across.

---

In Maryland, the low-income mothers of small children to age three are lucky enough to have a statewide network. Friends of the Family Inc., a creative nonprofit, operates independent, community-based Family Support Centers to bolster mothers and their children during these critical early years of child development.

Executive director Rosalie Streett's high-intensity style offers further evidence that one enthusiastic person can inspire an entire institution. She credits Frank Farrow, former director of the Maryland Social Services Administration and now a vice president of the Center for the Study of Social Policy, with the idea for Maryland's Family Support Centers, but it's clear that a lot of the credit goes to her, too.

Streett was director of health and parenting for the Children and Youth Project of Johns Hopkins Medical School—serving twenty thousand low-income pediatric patients a year—when he enlisted her in 1985. They got the Maryland General Assembly to allocate $297,000 to establish the first pilot centers, persuading the state to grant the money to a private agency, a then-unlikely move, because they came to the legislature with a detailed plan, and because the state was in the midst of a scandal, facing lawsuits over failures in its foster care program. The time was ripe for a preventive alternative aimed at strengthening families that might otherwise have to give their children up to foster care.

They received enough money for two centers but opened four anyway, taking the risk that they would have to lay off staff if they couldn't persuade the state to double their grant in the next year. Streett recalls sleepless nights spent worrying that she was gambling with her workers' lives, but the risk paid off, and the legislature increased the grant in the second year from $300,000 to $600,000. The organization also actively seeks private sector support, considering it important to be seen as a working public-private partnership and not merely another government program.

Maryland now has eleven centers, six in Baltimore, the rest spread through the state. Centers offer a full array of early childhood support, much like Washington's Family Place: classes in parenting skills, with day care for children while their parents are in class. Case management and counseling are provided by social workers whose caseloads aren't too heavy to make one-on-one talks practical. Overall, it's another demonstration of a warm, welcoming environment where parents and children can come and feel supported while they learn the skills they need to give their kids a good start in life.

---

Here's an attitude to cherish: "We're sort of the last holdout of idealism in Dallas," says Pam Schaefer, director of Trinity Ministry to the Poor. "We're small enough, intense enough, passionate enough, and yet we're for real." With a small staff, a lean budget, and a corps of 150 volunteers from church and civic groups all over Dallas, Trinity Ministry wields influence far beyond its size. Feeding eight thousand people a month, offering breakfast and lunch six days a week, it carries another 250 people a week in individualized case management aimed at solving the problems that keep them poor and homeless and has at least fifty people in job training and counseling on any given day. Reporter Jeff Weiss of the *Dallas Morning News* calls Trinity "the best operation in town" and routinely sends the poor and desperate people who call him for advice to Trinity Ministry for help. "Whatever people need, these people seem to be able to find ways to do something for them," he said.

Trinity Ministry started in 1981 as a program of Holy Trinity Catholic Church in Dallas, but it grew too big. Although its programs were financially self-sufficient, the church seemed to want both to control it and to get rid of it. The inevitable conflict led to a fairly messy public divorce, but the program is now independent and claims excellent support from just about all the local churches—including Holy Trinity. The organization provides almost every social service except overnight shelter in a busy, happy mélange of soup kitchen, food pantry, clothes closet, job-training programs, medical and psychiatric clinics, and family counseling services. It views all of these services as part of a holistic approach that works to get people and families back into the mainstream through sensitive but intense counseling and support from an individual social worker assigned to the family.

Trinity enlists the cooperation of clients by leveraging the services it provides, volunteer coordinator Margie Smith explained. A family can get a week's groceries from the food pantry, for example, but it must earn them by fulfilling certain responsibilities, whether by showing up for an AA meeting or helping serve in the soup kitchen.

Trinity's Family Stabilization Program takes the holistic approach to the limit, and it's paying off. Families, selected on the basis of need and their potential for rehabilitation, receive supportive assistance in every imaginable area, from housing and drug or alcohol problems to children's schooling. "We just commit to stick with them for one full year," Smith said. "They need advocates in almost every area. We look for families with a spark, in some way seeking to fight their battles, yet families that are dysfunctional and need the help." The program sets four basic goals: Keep the family together, get it into decent housing, find employment for at least one parent, and keep the kids in school.

"The thing we see so often, the Band-Aid approach or the quick fix that addresses only the symptoms, has got to stop," Schaefer said. "People's problems are so complex. We literally technically evaluate a family, trying first to determine what the problems are, then setting up a specific program to fix them. We try to be diagnosticians. We don't just give them $500 to pay the rent without finding out something about their job history and their life. If we can determine what the problems are that are causing the dysfunction, we can address them honestly and get the help they need. We find a person in crisis, stabilize them, and then they can start doing what they need to move toward self-sufficiency. Some people aren't going to be able to go very far, frankly; but they don't have to be sleeping on the street."

---

Emily Vargas Adams, who was a social worker in South America for many years, modeled CEDEN, the Family Resource Center for Development, Education and Nutrition (Centro de Recursos Familiares), on an organization in Colombia. When she came back home to Austin in 1979, she found poverty, health, and literacy problems of Third World scope on the heavily segregated black and Hispanic side of the city. She realized that an approach that worked in Colombia might work just as well on Austin's Spanish-speaking East Side.

Third World poverty? Fully 60 percent of the families CEDEN serves earn less than half the poverty level, which in Texas is low indeed—just $12,000 a year for a family of four. More than 20 percent of all the families in Austin, including plenty of Anglos, have poverty-level incomes, although the numbers are disproportionately high among blacks and Hispanics. The infant mortality rate for blacks in Austin is 19.5 per 1,000, among the highest in the nation, and the city has the highest pregnancy rate in Texas, which in turn ranks among the worst in the nation, for children seventeen and under.

CEDEN combats poverty with the many specific programs it has evolved over a decade. In one of the most effective, the Prenatal Education Program, workers visit poor pregnant women at home and refer them to clinics during pregnancy and at the time of delivery. Workers screen each childbirth and refer infant and mother to postnatal programs if necessary.

Sticking with these new families, CEDEN's Parent-Child Program workers continue frequent home visits with low-income mothers and their infants to help with advice on infant stimulation, child development, family health care, nutrition, injury prevention, and home improvement, all aimed at ensuring a healthy, nurturing environment for the child. "We help parents plan for their children," Adams said. "If you have a malnourished child, you can provide that child with good protein, vitamins and minerals, vegetables, fruits, and dairy products, but unless you provide infant stimulation at the same time, the child will fall back soon. The well-nourished but unstimulated child is still passive, tied into itself, and tends not to use the food well. Attention and affection are like another form of food." The program has shown excellent results, restoring malnourished, sick infants to normal or above-normal development within six to nine months.

Other CEDEN projects include a Saturday parent-child learning center, in which parents and children learn reading and arithmetic together. Its parent-and-child development program in a local school for pregnant girls and teen mothers got 90 percent of twenty-seven young mothers through school successfully in 1991. Every single one of them has avoided becoming pregnant again. A paternity project counsels the fathers in teen pregnancies. There's also family counseling and, for emergencies, a small food pantry.

## *Abused Women and Poverty*

One particularly ugly category of poverty involves battered and abused women—women who find themselves on the streets after leaving an abusive husband or boyfriend, sometimes carrying nothing but the clothes they wear.

The Abused Adult Resource Center in Bismarck, North Dakota, offers a particularly good example of how one community dealt with this tragedy. It began in the early 1970s when a group of caring individuals recognized that the community needed to deal with this problem. Initially, it operated as the Abused Women's Resource Closet, a half-joking reference to the size of its storefront headquarters. Its purpose was to provide a safe place for abused women to go, and it did that by volunteers opening their homes as "safe houses" that were available whenever there was a need. Even today, when the center has grown into a warm and cozy twenty-bed shelter in a large frame house that it purchased and renovated three years ago, twenty safe houses still operate as stopgap emergency havens for women and their children on the street without notice at night.

The Abused Adult Resource Center offers more than just shelter, however. Upholding the premise that people have a right to relationships in which they don't have to be afraid, says executive director Diane Zainhofsky, the center has evolved educational and counseling programs that are meant not only to care for battered women but to help them regain self-esteem and secure their legal rights. It also intervenes with programs intended to prevent abuse before it happens.

With a staff of twelve full-time workers and more than a hundred volunteers, the center operates programs in four areas. First, Safe Shelter incorporates both the shelter house and the safe houses. Women and their children are assigned pleasantly furnished rooms, and they are expected to take part in daily living activities that walk the line between giving them freedom and a sense of their personal rights and maintaining order in a community living situation. So, for instance, they may come and go to work and on errands but are expected to be in the shelter by seven so that they can spend time together during the evenings. Residents share chores, participate in weekly group sessions, and meet regularly with an assigned caseworker to set and work toward accomplishing specific goals. The typical resident stays six to eight weeks, and when she leaves for permanent housing, she takes along baskets of groceries and essentials donated by local churches and civic groups to help her get started.

In the Criminal Justice program, a trained worker helps women complete the paperwork and filing required to obtain protective orders directing abusive partners to leave them and their children alone. This program also keeps in touch with local police to ensure that they understand the issues of domestic violence and enforce current laws and regulations regarding warrants and protective orders.

A third area is concerned with kids. Children's and Adolescents' programs range from "good touch, bad touch" classes for second-graders to presentations on dating violence for teens in local high schools as well as counseling sessions for youngsters of the families in the shelter.

Finally, in the Crisis Intervention Center, workers and volunteers staff a hotline twenty-four hours, seven days a week, with a toll-free number for women to call if they have a problem. In Bismarck, workers will go out immediately to meet women and take them to safe shelters; callers from elsewhere in North Dakota are referred promptly to local programs.

Over the past three years the center has sheltered fifty to seventy families a year and served as many as eighteen thousand meals, primarily with food from local donations and the Fargo Food Bank. Roughly half of the shelter residents are American Indians, largely from the nearby Standing Rock Reservation at Fort Yates. And although the vast majority of abused partners are women, cases of abused men are not unknown, and the center helps them, too.

A poster in the Bismarck shelter tells a powerful story through a childish stick figure of a woman with a mottled face. "Listen to the children," its legend reads. "A four-year-old girl drew this picture of a woman with a black eye. She describes her picture with mature awareness of domestic violence: 'This is what happens to mommy when daddy is angry.'"

## *Health Programs*

Of all the cities where I've stopped along the road, it's hard to recall one that offers greater contrasts than Memphis. The largest city in Tennessee, and one of the largest in the Old South, it combines a magnolia-blossom southern gentility with the brassy noise of Beale Street and Rust Belt industrial decay. It's a city with severe problems. Income statistics list Memphis and Shelby County as the poorest metropolitan area in the United States, ranking behind such urban nightmares as Detroit and East St. Louis. The infant mortality rate is among the nation's highest, ranking worse than that of Washington, D.C., and its rate of violent crime is significantly higher than that in New York City.

Memphis is also historically one of the nation's most segregated cities, a situation that only got worse in the early 1970s, when a busing plan for city schools did not extend to the suburban school system, prompting massive and immediate white flight. A map of the region's census tracts now shows sharp racial divisions, with a ring of mostly black neighborhoods in the city almost fully encircling a white enclave in the stylish Midtown area near downtown that extends east along a narrow line of boulevards lined with the city's best shopping centers, restaurants, and boutiques. Outside the city limits, in the aptly named White Haven and Germantown, wealthy white subdivisions predominate, with the suburban black minority (about 20 percent) almost totally confined to the rural slums of Boxtown, in agricultural country south of the city along the east bank of the Mississippi.

Among political factors, the city was long under the strict control of the Boss Crump organization, a corrupt conservative Democratic machine that ran City Hall for at least three decades. Avoiding daily racial confrontation and allowing blacks to vote long before it was routine in the South, the Crump machine boasted a decent reputation for race relations, even though blacks were restricted to ghettos that received little or no city services. To this day, the condition of houses, streets, and public services in inner-city neighborhoods in Memphis appears more decrepit than in any other city I've visited save Houston. But the real story behind minority poverty here is not so much racism as economics. A collecting point for generations of poor blacks fleeing failed farms in the Delta in search of unavailable jobs, Memphis's poorer neighborhoods labor under a legacy of broken dreams. Even the city's limited industrial base has largely fled for the Third World, and what industry remains—soybean and other agricultural processing plants—is largely automated and offers little fulfilling employment. Virtually the only jobs available to unskilled workers are in fast food and services and the relatively low-paying hospital and health care industries.

And yet there's surprising hope about. The 1992 election of W. W. Arrington, the city's first black mayor, created a dizzying sense of empowerment. Perhaps even more important, a change in electoral procedures requires future city council members to be elected by district rather than at-large, a measure that generally improves services to a city's poorer neighborhoods.

What's more, something that might look silly from outside seemed to alter attitudes here. In midsummer of 1992 the city opened the Pyramid, a bizarre-looking coliseum and sports center in the shape of an Egyptian pyramid. While this might at first appear to be another case of modern-era smokestack chasing and money wasted on a sports arena that could better be spent on the infrastructure, it had an unexpected impact: By celebrating the classical Egyptian history of the city's name, it made public the city's historic connection with African heritage, giving the black majority a sense of ownership that's still rare in the South.

There's a lot of imaginative creation going on too, not least in the field of low-income health care, where Memphis stands out for an innovative model program established by Dr. Scott Morris, a charismatic idealist who decided in high school that he wanted to be an ordained Methodist minister and a physician and spend his life ministering to the health needs of poor people. His Church Health Center fills a major gap for working poor people, those who earn too much to qualify for Medicaid but not enough to pay for private medical insurance. This health insurance gap not only puts people who work but don't earn much money into a tough pinch, but it hurts the community by straining emergency rooms that are being used for primary care. The center's solution is to provide a competent, dignified medical, dental, and optometric walk-in clinic, with fees charged on a sliding scale based on ability to pay.

In addition to Morris's full-time medical service and the help of another doctor, a dentist, and three nurses, the center's staff is supplemented by more than two hundred physicians and sixty-five dentists from the Memphis area, who volunteer their services on a rotating basis, one evening or weekend shift every few months. Furthermore, one hundred area specialists have agreed to accept referrals from the clinic without charge, and more than four hundred community volunteers also help the clinic keep its programs operating at minimal cost. Its $1.1 million annual budget is funded by a combination of patient revenues and contributions from a consortium of 150 churches.

Morris also reaches out to the community with more creative ideas. His Lay Advisers corps is an Americanized version of the notion of "barefoot health care" that Morris discovered in Zimbabwe, where he once worked. Working with the ministers of the church consortium, Morris has identified nearly one hundred natural leaders, mostly older women active in their churches, and put them through an eight-week training session on community health care. They learn about such common public health issues as detecting diabetes and cancer, dealing with drug and alcohol abuse, and advising mothers-to-be about prenatal care. When they go back to their communities, they are not expected to act like health care professionals but simply to look out for neighbors who may need corrective or preventive health care and, as the natural-born busybodies that they are, encourage them to go get it.

In another Morris dream aborning, the Memphis Plan has recruited two hundred doctors and asked them to take on ten poor patients each as a pro bono contribution to the community. The organization then enlists two thousand poor people and negotiates with their employers to contribute a minimal $20 a month as "medical insurance." For this payment—which goes not to the doctors but to the Church Health Center—the employee is guaranteed free access to a specific doctor for all medical needs, while the center earns enough to administer the program. It all hangs together. Poor people get medical care at a fraction of the cost of commercial insurance or private treatment. The call for physicians to perform pro bono work is spread so widely across the community that none burns out. And the organization enjoys the backing of an ecumenical, multiracial cross-section of churches to assure its financial survival even during troubled times.

Poor people in Memphis who don't even have the low-end jobs needed to qualify them as working poor have another alternative at the Mid-South Family Health Care Center, a straightforward free medical clinic in an old but thoroughly rehabbed nursing home in one of the city's worst ghetto neighborhoods, a mixture of dilapidated redbrick housing projects and decaying single-family houses.

Director Yvonne Madlock (whose husband, Larry, is the medical director of the Downtown Clinic for the Homeless in Nashville, discussed in Chapter 2) says it's about all the clinic can do to keep up with the need. The only one of its kind in Memphis, it was started in 1989 and is funded by two hospitals, the regional Community Health Agency, and the University of Tennessee. Seeing more than a hundred patients a day, the clinic takes considerable pressure off hospital emergency rooms by giving people a better alternative for routine care, while it improves public health by providing primary and preventive care.

---

Across the country in southern California, the Senior Health and Peer Counseling Center has grown in fifteen years or so from a tiny beginning into a major force guarding the health of elderly people in Santa Monica and West Los Angeles. Founded in 1976 by five elderly people who saw a problem that affected others like themselves, it has continued its self-help orientation, using primarily elderly volunteers (with some social service professionals) to run its programs.

The five seniors, friends who shared a background in health care, decided that health services for the poor left a gap in treatment of the elderly, and they set out to fill it. With minimal funding from the city of Santa Monica, volunteers initially started doing blood pressure testing and health screening. It didn't take long for them to see that a lot of the elderly people who came to see them had serious problems that went beyond physical health. A large number were lonely, depressed, and suffering other mental health problems related to aging and solitary living. Out of this grew the program's second major component, peer counseling. Working out the process as they went, they trained older volunteers, age fifty-five and up, as counselors. Those being counseled are matched with volunteers who've been through similar problems, whether it's ill health or divorce or recent widowhood. Peer counselors, according to the manual, "are sensitive, compassionate people selected for their ability to evoke trust and response from their contemporaries seeking aid. They offer similar life experience, practical wisdom, and the valuable capacity to listen."

## *The Mentally Ill Homeless*

When Dr. Leonard Abel of Anchorage Community Mental Health Services used federal McKinney grant money to open Crossover House in Anchorage, Alaska, seven years ago, it seemed like a simple idea: Open a drop-in center offering homeless people such basic services as showers, a laundry, and telephones. It wouldn't be long before Abel's real target, the "psychiatrically disabled" individuals among them, lured in by the services, would volunteer for treatment. It wasn't quite that simple.

"The problem is, mentally ill homeless people don't say, 'I need help,'" said John Bajowski, a mental health professional who came to Alaska's bush country to work with Native Alaskans in 1985 and became the director of Crossover House five years later. Painstakingly building a workable approach, the staff has learned that reaching mentally ill homeless people requires more effort than simply building a program and assuming that they will come.

Now, six of the program's seven full-time staff spend days and evenings, seven days a week, out among Anchorage's homeless people. They go where the people are, whether it's the St. Francis Shelter, Bean's soup kitchen, the city's malls, the jail, the camps where the homeless fashion rough shelters in the snow or under tents of plastic sheeting, and even in the cafeteria at Nordstrom's department store, where twenty-five-cent coffee (the cheapest in town) lures folks who admire coffee and a warm place to sip it.

Gaining the confidence of these people is a slow process that may begin as tentatively as observing a schizophrenic street person who trusts no one, then gradually moving to casual greetings, conversation, and ultimately an invitation to drop in at Crossover House.

"We see treatment as the ultimate goal, but we keep it in perspective," Bajowski said. "We go at their pace. Once they are receptive to receiving treatment, we serve them right here" using the center's staff psychiatrist, clinician, and nurse to diagnose each individual, begin treatment, and refer them for any other medical problems that may need attention. "Once somebody gets to the point where he's willing to accept that they do have an illness and we aren't going to poison them or do anything against their will, *then* we can start with treatment and get them stabilized."

Crossover House also provides housing assistance, relying on federal mental health money to provide no-interest loans for rent. Two job-development workers lend a hand to anyone who's ready and willing to look for work.

This conservative approach doesn't pay off in large numbers. Of 2,982 individual contacts last fiscal year, just 55 were listed as "successfully engaged into services." But of those 55, nearly 40 percent have been moved into housing. And best of all, Bajowski says, he takes home at night the memories of some real success stories: The individual from the St. Francis Shelter who needed two and a half years to get into counseling but who's now resolved his physical and mental health problems and is working, and the man who was once so ill that he would stand up against the wall of the soup kitchen talking to himself—and then responding. He's now in treatment, and making progress.

When the well-intended but poorly conceived policy of deinstitutionalization turned thousands of mentally ill people out of state hospitals onto the streets of the nation's cities during the late 1970s, a network of community services was supposed to be waiting to support them. But it didn't materialize, because local and state governments generally declined to fund the services, leaving it up to nonprofit organizations and thoughtful individuals like Susan Dempsay to find ways to take up the slack.

Dempsay, a tall, stylish West Los Angeles housewife, never dreamed that she would be working with mentally ill people, much less homeless street people, until her son Mark, then just eighteen, had a schizophrenic breakdown during the late 1970s. Discovering that there was little or nothing in the way of supportive programs available outside of institutionalization, Dempsay and a group of parents she assembled vowed to create something. They formed a support group, and eventually, with the help of the Los Angeles County Mental Health Association, rounded up enough money to open Step Up on Second, a day center in Santa Monica where mentally ill people may go for comfort and respect, and take part in activities ranging from stress-management classes to poetry-writing sessions.

Step Up on Second supports mentally ill people with a program resting on three legs, Dempsay says: social, vocational, and educational programs. Initially, the founders expected to serve people much like their own children: the young, educated offspring of the neighborhood's relatively affluent families. It came as a considerable surprise when hordes of homeless people began turning up at the group's storefront office on a busy city street just a block from Santa Monica's pedestrian mall. Now, the clientele is largely homeless, a change that has prompted some of its original supporters to flee but has lured new volunteers, who keep a constant hum of activity in Step Up on Second's bright, warehouse-like room, where colorful banners fly overhead. The doors are open eight hours daily, weekdays, weekends, and holidays, and there's never a charge for its services, which include meals, showers, restrooms, and a telephone message and mail service.

Specific programs are aimed at helping mentally ill people live as normally as possible by teaching self-help skills, expression, and socialization. Case managers help Step Up "members" apply for benefits, get other necessary services, and locate affordable housing.

The organization also makes efforts to provide job training and help members find ways to support themselves, although Dempsay acknowledges that this is a particularly difficult barrier for some mentally ill people, who face other challenges before they're ready to consider employment seriously. Cuts in federal and state funds eliminated a major job-training program, but Step Up continues working at a lower level to hire homeless people to do small jobs in and around the center as a way to earn a little money while redeveloping work skills. The center operates a tie-vending cart and a hotdog wagon on Santa Monica's streets, providing a small income and, more important, work experience for its participants.

---

At about the same time, another response to homeless men and women came in Houston, where a private group of Christian businessmen founded The Shoulder in 1977. The Shoulder is a nonprofit drug- and alcohol-abuse rehabilitation center for indigent people who need treatment but have no way to pay for it. Using a combination of federal and state grants, foundation money, and private contributions (and some food for its excellent cafeteria from the Houston Food Bank and church collections), it houses up to 260 men and women substance abusers in a low white-brick building that was once home to Houston's Southeast Community Hospital.

Dr. James W. Bryant, executive director, estimated that 75 percent of The Shoulder's residents are homeless people, and the rest are "medically indigent," without money or insurance to pay for their treatment. The center walks a narrow line in imposing religion on its participants. Bryant describes it as a "nonprofit, Christian organization" in which residents are invited but not required to take advantage of chapel services, Bibles, and a regular chaplain. Spiritual counseling is also available on request for residents of non-Christian faiths, Bryant said, adding that many scientists and secular authorities nowadays recognize the need to address a spiritual element (such as the acknowledgment of a "higher power" in Alcoholics Anonymous and other twelve-step programs) in the treatment of addiction.

The basic operation includes three programs: a short-term (five- to eleven-day) detoxification, which includes evaluation, referral, and development of a specific recovery plan for the individual; a long-term (ninety-one-day) residential program that mingles AA-type activities and Christian-oriented counseling; and a transitional program for recovering substance abusers, who go through job and life skills training rather than merely returning to the streets on completion of their rehabilitation.

Substance abuse can't be ignored in fighting poverty in today's society, Bryant says, if only because some abusers resort to drug dealing, robbery, prostitution, and other crimes to maintain their habits, and many of them have lost the support of their friends and families long before they seek treatment. "We get people coming out from under bridges, literally," he said. "Not all of them are from poor backgrounds, either. But they've hit bottom by the time they get here."

Bryant argues that the cost of providing free treatment for indigent abusers actually saves the community money. Studies have shown that completion of long-term treatment (sixty days or more) is closely correlated with a decrease in future arrests and an increase in gainful employment. Even more striking is the high societal cost of "crack babies." Harris County public health officials estimate that it takes $30,000 to $50,000 a month to provide medical care for a single infant born addicted; in one case, the old Southeast Memorial Hospital, a private hospital, ultimately wrote off a bill for more than $100,000 for a teenage, addicted mother whose infant required three months of intensive care.

---

As we see again and again, similar mathematics applies in most of the effective local initiatives against poverty, not only in substance abuse. Investing early in solving community and individual problems, even when that investment involves a thorough, holistic approach, is almost invariably more efficient in terms of dollars and effort than waiting until the problem is out of control. By forming partnerships with government to help finance effective prevention and self-reliance efforts, nonprofit organizations can save taxpayers money in the long run.

# 6

# People Need Political Power

We might like to think we're past the head-banging days of the Pinkertons and the Molly Maguires, when private detectives beat up and sometimes killed activists who dared try to organize eastern coal miners; but one eternal verity remains: Those who enjoy power are rarely eager to share it with those who don't.

Since people in poverty rarely have power, this lesson is not without application at the grass roots. Some of the most effective organizations I've seen came about as a result of confrontational efforts by angry people who didn't care who they pissed off. The most effective of them, however, added a simple element that went beyond mere anger: once the particular battle was won, they built on success to do more. It worked that way in Holmes County, Mississippi, a predominantly black rural community where the delta land is so poor that even the soil along the roadside is an unhealthy looking ocher that turns into a coffee-with-cream gumbo after a rain. Although textbooks suggest that the civil rights struggle was over by the late 1970s, the news hadn't reached the dirt-poor courthouse town of Lexington, where blacks and whites still entered the doctor's and dentist's office through separate doors, and the all-white police force had a bad habit of beating up blacks. In 1978, amid charges that four white cops had beaten and raped a black woman, the community's blacks organized, calling their group the Rural Organizing and Cultural Center (ROCC), and mounted an economic boycott of the town's merchants.

The boycott lasted nine months. It attracted the attention of CBS's *60 Minutes*, which came to town and did a probing piece that embarrassed Mississippi's white establishment right up to the statehouse in Jackson. And it ended in total capitulation by the town's establishment. The four police officers were fired. The signs enforcing segregation came down. And local merchants agreed, in writing, to begin hiring blacks in responsible positions, such as cashiers and tellers, that had been systematically denied them before. Excited by their victory, ROCC's leaders set a policy that would ensure the organization's long-term success. Rather than deciding arbitrarily what should be next on the agenda, they asked the community to name its own priorities, and took seriously the answers that came back.

Perhaps surprisingly, according to Leroy Johnson, one of ROCC's early organizers and now its executive director, such niceties as social services or even efforts to address the community's lack of food, housing, and welfare programs ranked a distant third. In surveys covering more than a thousand Holmes County families, two more important priorities ranked as key goals. First, root racial prejudice out of the police and criminal justice system. Second, develop a system of quality public education. "Even though people didn't have enough to eat or a decent place to live, their first concern was dignity and respect," Johnson said. "Their second goal was to get the kids out of this life. Only after that came help with food and shelter."

Operating out of a cluster of small frame buildings on the outskirts of tiny Lexington, ROCC has grown to add food and shelter programs too. Its community gardening program offers residents a significant source of supplementary food, emphasizing organic gardening techniques without pesticides or chemical fertilizers. Its welfare advocacy programs teach recipients to demand their rights from social workers. ROCC's work in education has integrated the county school board and won a guarantee that one of the public school system's two top posts will be held by a black. At the same time, ROCC is active within the schools, riding herd on the curriculum to ensure that all students, regardless of race, receive relevant, useful courses and come out of school qualified for good employment. Toward that end, it sponsors summer education programs and a mediation process to work out problems between students and teachers.

But amid all these efforts, ROCC has never lost sight of its primary goal. Through jawboning and political pressure, it persuaded county jailers to spell out written rules and regulations, ending a century of arbitrary and capricious discipline. It integrated local police departments, and forced several of the county's worst small-town municipal forces to disband by showing that they could not meet even the state's lax standards for local law enforcement. "These changes have not been through the graciousness or the goodness of folks," Johnson said. "Every change has happened because there was a fight."

---

What worked for blacks in little Lexington worked as well for Hispanic Americans in San Antonio, the nation's tenth largest city and one of its poorest. According to a 1986 interim census survey, fully one-fourth of its population lives below the poverty line, and its 1988 per capita income ($13,436) was 19 percent below the national average, ranking the metropolitan area 244th among the nation's 319. More than 110,000 of the city's children—half of the student population—received free or subsidized school lunches in 1988–89, and only 59 percent of residents twenty-five and over have finished high school; an estimated one-fourth of the population is illiterate. Americans of Hispanic heritage form a slight majority, and blacks make up a tiny portion, less than 5 percent.

But there's something unusual about San Antonio: despite its problems, there's a sense of community pride that extends beyond the Alamo, the famous Riverwalk, and the bustling downtown. It is clean, its houses sport fresh paint, and there's no definable ghetto. In a political situation that may be unique in the United States, every citizen of this large city has a voice—and knows it. Communities Organized for Public Service (COPS), with a nineteen-year track record of community organizing, can take a large share of the credit for that.

Things were starting to change in San Antonio during the early 1970s. A small, rich, and conservative Anglo minority had ruled the city for most of the twentieth century, setting the public agenda through the Good Government League, a Chamber of Commerce–like organization. For decades, league leaders had consciously discouraged development and growth rather than risk the emergence of organized labor and the potential "difficulties" that an empowered Hispanic minority might cause. But the old guard was dying out, and those who were left were challenged for political power by well-to-do developers from outside who saw the city as a market ripe for the plucking.

San Antonio's ethnic divisions cut the city like a pie, along a diagonal line from northwest to southeast. Above it, the mostly Anglo North Side enjoyed the benefits of government and its services. Below it, the largely Hispanic West Side was more like a Latin American barrio than a modern American city. As former mayor Henry Cisneros noted in an article in *Commonweal* in 1988, San Antonio in the late 1960s was so poor that Peace Corps volunteers were trained in its barrios to simulate the conditions they would face in Latin America. "Thousands of Hispanics and black families lived in colonias, with common-wall, shotgun houses built around public sanitation facilities with outdoor toilets. The barrios had no sidewalks or paved streets, no drainage system or flood control. Every spring brought flooding; families were driven from their homes; children walked to school through mud sloughs. In the shadow of downtown San Antonio lurked a stateside third-world 'country.'"

A quarter of a century has seen this condition reversed, to the benefit of *all* the city's people, and the secret—the entire secret—was community organizing. It started with a seemingly unassuming man, San Antonio native Ernesto Cortes, who had been away learning community organizing from Saul Alinsky and his Industrial Areas Foundation. For many years, the IAF's primary interest had been in organizing industrial urban areas of the Midwest and Northeast, starting in Alinsky's own stockyard neighborhoods of South Side Chicago. Cortes came home in 1974 and applied the IAF's "institutional organizing" approach in a new setting. Rather than organizing individuals, he organized institutions, particularly the Catholic church, which had a long progressive tradition in south Texas.

"Ernie built around values that Hispanics hold dear," explains Pearl Caesar, now COPS's lead organizer. "COPS didn't totally change the system; rather, things were changing already—the new development mentality was breaking up the moneyed elite, which had been conscious of the Hispanic West Side but never integrated it. COPS came on the scene and changed the political climate. It started with a voter registration drive, but more important, it educated people on the issues and got them involved in power decisions."

City Hall casually slapped aside COPS's early efforts. The Anglo policymakers thought of the Hispanics as "Mexicans," illiterate and incapable foreigners, and assumed that their complaints would soon die down. But COPS continued electoral and economic pressure, registering Hispanic voters by the thousands and flooding City Hall with their voices. On the economic front, they slyly choked downtown department stores with Latino "shoppers" who examined merchandise, tried on expensive clothing, broke no laws—and bought nothing. Finally, municipal authorities started paying attention. A quick, sweet victory came when COPS successfully blocked a major development that would have polluted the city's aquifer, an underground stream that provides water so pure that it didn't need to be treated before being pumped into houses.

By 1977, in a COPS-supported referendum that saw 96 percent of the city's Hispanics vote as a bloc in favor, the city council switched from at-large to district representation, a measure that virtually guaranteed a Hispanic majority. When San Antonio elected a liberal woman mayor, then a Hispanic (Cisneros), the benefits of municipal government, including street paving, water and sewer service, and police protection, started flowing to all neighborhoods, not those on the North Side alone. "I can say unequivocally, COPS has fundamentally altered the moral tone and the political and physical face of San Antonio," Cisneros wrote in 1988.

With never a scandal or hint of corruption, despite intense scrutiny, COPS became a model organizing affiliate, leading to the establishment of a dozen other IAF groups in a broad swath of Texas, from the Rio Grande Valley north to Dallas. Its accomplishments are myriad. Caesar says the group's records indicate that, over the last two decades, COPS has been directly responsible for the expenditure of $750 million in development money in the city's Hispanic communities.

Here's the difference the money made: there are no more colonias in San Antonio—no neighborhoods with dirt roads, no houses without running water or toilets. "The city actually looks good. We have to tell visitors, reporters, 'We can't show you how it was, because it isn't like that anymore. You have to image how it might have been.'" The real secret, Caesar said, is this: "We teach ordinary people how to be public figures. We teach them how to work with the media, how to work with public officials, how to negotiate, how to compromise." And, when necessary, how to fight.

"San Antonio looks good on the outside because of COPS's work. But we need to get *inside* the houses and make sure that the kids who live there will be well educated, have good health care, and will have good job prospects in the future."

---

Similar concerns are at the foundation of El Centro de la Raza in Seattle. A seemingly sedate organization, the moral and cultural center for the Hispanic community of King County, El Centro fills multiple needs ranging from emergency services to excellent, affordable day care and job training. But like many other groups that stand up for the rights of their communities, El Centro got off to a raucous start. About twenty years ago, when agricultural mechanization began eliminating the jobs of unskilled farmworkers in the rich Yakima Valley, thousands of people, many of them Latino, moved from the no longer hospitable farming country to the cities of Puget Sound. Seattle's Hispanic population grew rapidly but almost invisibly because its members, constrained by the need to find low-cost housing wherever they could, were scattered widely throughout the metropolitan area rather than in a barrio or ghetto.

Along with other community leaders, Roberto Maestas, the wiry and intense founder of El Centro de la Raza, quickly realized that language was the major barrier keeping the former farmworkers from moving into the economic mainstream. But when Hispanics sought permission to use the abandoned Beacon Hill elementary school to house classes in English as a second language, school board officials responded with bureaucratic fervor: they didn't say yes, they didn't say no, and they threw the request before a committee that met periodically but took no action for months.

Angered by the frustration of seeing a much-needed building kept boarded up and empty by whim and caprice, Maestas and his group took bold action in October 1972. Getting permission to visit the vacant three-story building for an "inspection," once inside, several dozen activists refused to leave, saying they would stay in the building until a lease was signed. While the media watched with delight, the school board and city council soon agreed to negotiate seriously. "Thus, they established a classic confrontation situation," *Seattle Times* reporter Bruce Johansen wrote in an article during the protest. "What the confrontation did—what it was designed to do—was to shift the balance of power. As long as the Chicanos worked silently, the paper-shufflers—those who hold the people's resources in trust—held all the cards. The confrontation gave the Chicanos some leverage—and the city and schools a sense of urgency." Within weeks, El Centro had its permission. English classes started while the building was still being renovated, and a parade of services began to be offered soon after.

The organization has a mainstream reputation now. Maestas

says it hasn't been necessary to get into any confrontations for quite a while. But El Centro's readiness to fight for what is right remains institutionalized as one of its guiding principles: "To struggle for the creation of programs and services which a society must provide for the development of our community and its people."

## *Demanding Change*

The ultimate solution to poverty must rely, at least in part, on political organizing and advocacy by poor people themselves. If we argue that self-reliance is better than dependency and that social change is a more effective solution than charity, we have to acknowledge the lesson that the experiences of COPS and ROCC and El Centro de la Raza teach us: Change is unlikely to occur unless people insist on it.

Subtle differences divide various schools of organizing. In contrast with the IAF's mode of organizing community institutions, for instance, some organizations—most notably ACORN, the nationwide Association of Community Organizations for Reform Now—argue just as strongly that organizing efforts should aim to involve individuals, not institutions. But whether their focus is on crime, the environment, welfare programs, low-cost housing, small-farm policies, unions, safety and the workplace, or any of the scores of other issues that prompt people to get up and speak out, such efforts share one underlying assumption: You can't organize without getting out and knocking on doors, and you can't make people get involved in a hard fight over an issue that they don't consider important enough to fight for. This means that a good organizer has to be a good listener, capable of hearing what people want and flexible enough to abandon a bad plan without a backward glance when a better idea comes along.

That was certainly true in Portland, Oregon, according to Kathy Turner, who helped organize a blue-collar neighborhood that was rapidly sliding downhill as it became racially mixed and poor. The group that founded the Portland Organizing Project (POP) in a former Catholic rectory in 1985 was quite sure that the neighbors would want to do something about the fact that banks were redlining the community—that is, refusing to make loans for mortgages and home repairs. But they were wrong. The real local issue turned out to be quite different. Before even considering such matters as mortgage rates and appraisals, people wanted to rid their neighborhood of the crack cocaine houses that were proliferating. Police claimed that there were more than a thousand such establishments in this not-so-scary-looking neighborhood of single-family frame houses across the Willamette River from downtown Portland, and reports of violent confrontations with automatic weapons were spreading.

Because most of the crack houses were owned by absentee landlords—including the city's own housing authority—POP decided to push for a local law that would attack the landlords rather than their tenants. This stringent measure would allow the city to board up houses used for illegal activity and levy heavy fines against the property owners. Passage of the ordinance wasn't easy because the landlord lobby was powerful and the mayor not particularly supportive. But POP mobilized hundreds of residents, using church-based organizations and "phone trees" that yielded three hundred to four hundred calls a day to City Hall from members of fourteen churches, keeping public pressure and publicity hot until the council passed the law.

*Then* the neighbors, excited with their victory, were ready to take on the banks and savings and loans. Following an extensive door-to-door survey to poll members of the community about what issues concerned them the most, POP mounted a similar campaign against redlining. Victory came again, and three local banks eventually agreed to invest $33 million in low-interest housing loans in north and northeast Portland neighborhoods over two to three years.

Pick an attainable goal, and fight till you reach it. Then go on to another. That's the simple secret of successful organizing that POP knows well. Its next organizing effort persuaded the city to pass a jobs ordinance during the late 1980s establishing quotas under which 50 percent of jobs created by public investment through loans, grants, and waivers must go by first right of refusal to Portland residents, with 30 percent reserved for the city's low-income neighborhoods and 18 percent for blacks. None of these victories came easily, Turner said. Each required at least a year's hard work by hundreds of citizens. But the key elements of organizing people around issues that were truly important to them, and pursuing those issues relentlessly and consistently, eventually paid off.

## *Clients Helping Clients*

None of the single mothers who formed Clients Helping Clients in the Maryland suburbs of Washington, D.C., would tell you that the welfare system works well or that most people would prefer it to dignified work. Peggy Adams, the single mother of nine who founded the organization, says she was inspired to organize her fellow AFDC recipients when she saw a new applicant come reeling out of the welfare office with tears streaming down her face, crying with anger and frustration over the way she was treated. With organizational help from the Maryland Food Committee, a statewide advocacy group, she and Kathy Mindte, another welfare mother who bore similar scars, signed on as guides to help newer travelers along the same road.

Volunteers adopt new welfare recipients and walk them through the system, helping them learn the procedures and, when necessary, going to bat for them with welfare supervisors. The volunteers are able to intervene effectively because they know the system, and the system is coming to know them. WIC, AFDC, and food stamp workers who were defensive and paranoid at first are gaining confidence in Clients Helping Clients now because they've learned that this group doesn't speak up until all the information is in hand. They don't waste the system's time but deal efficiently with overburdened social workers, and the workers respond favorably. After the first few months, the Maryland public assistance offices began allowing the group to post fliers and even started referring troubled participants to its hotline, a remarkable testament when you consider that the group's basic goal is to do battle with an unresponsive system. "A lot of times, we can save them problems too" by screening clients and helping them understand what individuals need, Adams said.

The organization grows every month by enlisting women who've been helped to pass their knowledge to other frustrated and angry recipients. They also learn to lobby and advocate effectively for poor people, giving local and federal legislative bodies and reporters, which normally hear only from policy wonks and social workers, a direct look into the everyday lives of welfare recipients. Adams has testified before the Senate Budget Committee, and been quoted in the *Washington Post* and *Baltimore Sun* and appeared on local television news. "Clients need to learn that they don't have to be just pushed around but that they can make a difference," Adams said. "We register to vote, and we write letters to our senator and let him know that we want to see some action."

## *Organizing Farmworkers*

A chile pepper picker's life isn't pretty. Throughout the harvest season, which runs from July through the following February, a picker's day begins at midnight in El Paso, when he must show up at a labor recruitment site on a vacant lot on the gritty South Side, where labor contractors assemble teams of workers for the coming day. Even if they work for the same contractor all season long, it's a new deal every night, when workers must turn out to apply and be hired—or, if unlucky, rejected. Around two in the morning, the workers who make the cut board aging school buses for the two-hour drive to the fields around Las Cruces in New Mexico, where they arrive early and wait for dawn to begin work. With just one break at midday, they'll toil until late afternoon, returning home around six for a brief break to see their families and doze until midnight rolls around again.

The work is toilsome. Oils from the fiery peppers irritate the skin and can cause painful burns if a worker carelessly touches his eyes. And at the standard fieldwork rate of fifty cents a bucket for long green chilies or forty-five cents for dried New Mexico reds, a worker rarely claims more than $20 a day. Despite their critical role in bringing in one of New Mexico's major cash crops, pepper pickers, like most U.S. farmworkers, are ineligible for workers' compensation benefits—even though many of them become ill and occasionally permanently disabled by exposure to pesticides in the fields. (Studies reveal a cancer rate above ten times the national average among migrant farm laborers.)

The national craze for salsa and other ethnic foods has boosted the pepper industry, leading growers and producers to pour money into capital expenses and land. But they keep a tight grip on the cost of labor. It's this kind of exploitation—and similar abuses afflicting workers in the region's onion and lettuce farms—that Carlos Marentes and his wife, Alicia, have been fighting for years. They're starting to make some inroads, but they have a long row to hoe.

The Marenteses, who are originally from Juarez, Mexico, and were longtime activists with the old Texas Farmworkers Union, came to El Paso in 1980 to organize pepper pickers, the five thousand laborers who make up the single largest segment of the region's estimated fourteen thousand farmworkers. When the TFU failed under financial problems in 1983, the Marenteses and their fellows chose a new name—Sin Fronteras (Without Borders), reflecting the group's binational thrust—and kept right on working.

Sin Fronteras organizes workers to negotiate wages and working conditions with labor contractors, growers, and food producers.

But like many farmworkers' groups, Sin Fronteras is more than just a union. It is also a multipurpose agency prepared to do whatever needs to be done, from feeding farmworkers and finding them a place to sleep during the growing season to advocating for their rights and offering tax advice and assistance on immigration problems. Working out of a crowded El Paso storefront and using the donated gymnasium of Sacred Heart Catholic Church for meetings and a night shelter, Sin Fronteras is trying to raise $900,000 from city and private sources to build its new Centro de Trabajadores Agricolas, a modern, eight-thousand-square-foot building containing shelter facilities, office space, and room for a one-stop social services center.

The movement comes first, though, for Carlos Marentes, who has been agitating for development of a national farmworkers' coalition for a decade. "There are 4.2 million farm workers in the United States," he said. "If we could only organize them all, we'd have real power. For us, it is like a puzzle—and we are beginning to put together the pieces."

---

Agricultural field labor doesn't immediately spring to mind as a problem in Toledo, Ohio, an industrial city badly hit by the economic downturn that has ravaged the Rust Belt for more than two decades. But one of the region's strongest remaining contributors to the local economy is not smokestack industry but agribusiness. A good portion of the nation's tomatoes and pickling cucumbers grow in level fields of northwestern Ohio and southern Michigan. The huge farms here attract large numbers of migrant workers, mostly from Florida but with a smaller contingent from Texas. With an annual income of only about $7,200 for a family of six, these workers are often the poorest of the poor.

The Farm Labor Organizing Committee (FLOC), which follows the flow of migrants from Florida all the way up to Michigan, is doing its best to organize these workers and change their lives. Organizers Bonnie Bazala and Chuck Barret, a husband-and-wife team who share a single $12,000 salary, are trying to make that happen. He's in charge of development, building a donor base to supplement FLOC's income, which comes mostly from grants. A journalism graduate, she is working to get FLOC media coverage. Fernando Cuevas, the group's main organizer, a former farmworker from Florida who used to be a farm camp crew chief, and who is a self-described "bad guy," had his life turned around by a labor organizer and now is committed to spreading the word to other migrants who haven't yet figured out that they're exploited.

FLOC, like Sin Fronteras, is a labor union and more, representing about 6,000 of the 150,000 farmworkers hired by the cucumber and tomato farms—not a majority, Bazala says, but at least a start. The group was founded in 1968 by Baldemar Velasquez, a Brownsville, Texas, native and farmworker who followed the crops in the Midwest for years before settling down in the Toledo area. His organizing efforts saw him through an ugly strike in 1978 and a lengthy boycott, but they are finally starting to show some signs of progress.

Labor organizing here has traditionally been complicated by the three tiers of the food processing industry. Farmers hire migrant pickers directly, and in turn contract to sell their produce to the major processors, three of whom control almost the entire industry: Campbell's (through its pickle subsidiary, Vlasic), Heinz, and Dean's Foods, a Chicago firm whose most prominent subsidiaries are Aunt Jane's and Green Bay Foods.

Velasquez tried first to negotiate directly between workers and farmers, going from one migrant camp to another to sign on individual workers. When he met with only limited success, he came up with a new idea, one that both the AFL-CIO and labor experts recommended against: he decided to pressure the major processors to stipulate labor conditions in their contracts with farmers. This approach is based on the fact that of every food dollar consumers spend, 91.5 cents goes to the processing corporations, 6.5 cents goes to farmers, and 2 cents goes to farmworkers. Velasquez saw where the money was, and he followed it.

The processors initially argued that working conditions weren't their business. But seven years later, after a nationwide boycott and intense lobbying pressure, arranged by FLOC, from the leaders of many U.S. churches, Campbell's came to the bargaining table, yielding a precedent-setting contract in 1986. Heinz followed a year later, and Dean's finally succumed to negotiations, lobbying, and a national media campaign to end "sharecropping" in the pickle industry in 1993. Though the new contracts brought only nominal pay increases at first, some of their other provisions were far-reaching: Stoop labor was eliminated in the tomato fields, replacing payment for piecework with a minimum-wage hourly rate. Child labor was barred from contract farms, a grievance system was established, and workers with seniority were assured first crack at job openings. Also, while wages remained low (averaging $1,000 for the 1992 season), incentive pay boosts that wage significantly for workers who remain through the season.

---

While FLOC is busy organizing farmworkers, its neighbor Advocates for Basic Legal Equality (ABLE) sues those who exploit them. With oak-paneled walls lined with law books in neat rows on walnut shelves, ABLE's offices in the old redbrick Spitzer Building in Toledo look like those of a conservative law firm. But there's nothing conservative about the organization's approach, which resembles a radical revision of a Legal Aid Society.

The group goes back to the 1960s, when Gerry Lackey, a civil rights lawyer, and Tom Willging, a law professor at the University of Toledo, met at an antiwar meeting. It was a heady time for young, liberal lawyers. There was plenty of money around for legal aid to poor people. The War on Poverty was building up steam. The books were filling up with scores of new civil rights laws. And maybe best of all, the nation—or a lot of its young, bright members—was in an unprecedented mood to question authority. It didn't take long for the two young idealists to gather a crowd of like-minded people and form a public interest law group to work for the legal rights of Toledo's poor people and minorities.

Leaving the everyday legal needs of poor people to the established Legal Aid Society, ABLE took a different tack, choosing high-profile cases to set precedents on key social issues. In quick succession, ABLE won suits overturning city policies that had kept public housing developments out of the traditionally white, blue-collar Point Place neighborhood; barring increases in utility rates and service disconnections for poor people; and challenging racial discrimination in local police and fire department hiring and union apprenticeship programs.

Funded by the Legal Services Corporation, the state, and a variety of individual and institutional donors, ABLE's $1.8 million annual budget pays nineteen lawyers (none of whom takes a salary over $45,000), three paralegals, and seventeen support staff members. Though ABLE still pursues its high-impact approach, it also now offers routine assistance to poor people and migrant farmworkers who live outside the jurisdiction of Toledo's Legal Aid. In a fourteen-county farm region as large as Rhode Island and Connecticut together, an estimated 150,000 low-income residents and another 40,000 migrant farmworkers are eligible for its services.

ABLE's outreach workers have come up with delightfully creative ways to deal with the not-so-simple challenge of locating and educating a population that is anonymous, difficult to find, generally poorly educated, and usually not fluent in English. One successful approach mingles learning and entertainment. ABLE organizers have sometimes turned up at farmworker labor camps singing and playing guitars—unusual behavior for lawyers indeed. They have performed *teatros* (live skits, a popular Latino entertainment) at migrant camps. They produce radio shows on the Spanish-speaking radio station in Fremont, Ohio; and when I visited in 1990 they were looking for money to hire a *cuentista,* a traditional Latino bard who would go from camp to camp telling stories and singing songs. Once they rented a local movie theater in the town of Woodville, Ohio, near many migrant camps, where *La Bamba* drew crowds so large and enthusiastic that they had to repeat the program twice to accommodate everyone. "Along with the entertainment, we also take a few minutes of their time to talk about benefits, the minimum wage, eligibility for food stamps—a whole host of things," Joe Tafelski said. Added staffer Sandy Krawetz, "The beauty of it is to be able to go into a camp, first find a couple of children, and then they'll tell their parents, and people will just wander out on a summer evening. And we won't just tell them stories but also about their benefits and rights. And we'll tell them about their heritage, too; they may be doing menial labor, but we'll tell them about the Hispanic heritage and make them proud."

## Progress and Organizing in Idaho

One of the most attractive cities I saw along the road is Boise, Idaho, a clean, green oasis where arid sagebrush and potato-farming country meets the craggy Sawtooth Mountains. Among the fastest-growing cities in the Northwest, the town that French trappers named the Woods is filling up with refugees from California, but it seems to be handling its growth well, remaining surprisingly free of pollution, traffic problems, and crime. Its diverse economy has escaped the battering effect of the declines in the logging and mining industries that whacked northern Idaho and western Montana. With a rapidly growing high-tech and medical industry, the region's unemployment rate is virtually zero, and the rate of growth in average personal income is high.

But figures can be misleading, and it's no surprise that there's poverty here too. As in the other fast-growing towns in the Rockies, well-heeled newcomers have prompted a dramatic increase in housing prices that puts the squeeze on working poor people and elderly residents. What's more, advocates like to point out that Idaho looks good mostly because it started so low. As one of the nation's five poorest states in 1980, it had nowhere to go but up. Even so, the poverty rate increased from 12.6 to 13.3 percent during the 1980s, and more than a third of the state's poor people are children under eighteen. Idaho ranks only forty-second of the fifty states in per capita income, and it is by far the poorest of the four Pacific Northwest states. Furthermore, Idaho is a stronghold of the conservative, ask-no-aid culture of the Intermountain West. Its public assistance programs meet only the minimum federal requirements, with zero state or local funding. The maximum AFDC grant is as low as 27 percent of the poverty level, and despite extensive outreach, less than half of eligible children receive any assistance other than school lunches. Says local activist Leanna Lasuen of the Idaho Hunger Action Council, "Even though most low-income people in Idaho who are not elderly, disabled, or underage are working poor, local and state politicians are openly hostile to low-income people, regarding them as freeloaders, winos, or drug addicts. Prejudice is a major problem."

In Idaho as elsewhere, you can take the problems of poverty and double them for the migrant farmworkers who stream every harvest season into the potato and sugar beet country along the Snake River and the rich orchards of the Treasure Valley west of Boise. Farmworker organizing has made a real difference in some of the worst labor camps and exploitative situations that farm laborers once encountered here, but the region's Hispanic community—migrant and permanent residents alike—remains poorly paid, poorly housed, and poorly educated by a public school system that seems incapable or unwilling to alter a high school dropout rate in excess of 50 percent.

For well over twenty years now, under the charismatic leadership of Humberto Fuentes, the Idaho Migrant Council has been trying to do something about that. Fuentes, himself the child of a migrant farmworker family, started working his way up the migrant stream from south Texas to Idaho with his family as far back as 1952. After military service, he went to Treasure Valley Community College in Ontario, Oregon (adjacent to the orchards of southwestern Idaho), and then became a minority recruiter for the school. Inspired by Cesar Chavez, he and three other Hispanic organizers were fired because of their militant organizing efforts. They responded, with the help of the San Francisco–based Mexican-American Legal Defense Fund, by suing the college, charging that officials had flouted the federal requirement that recipients of Office of Economic Opportunity grants have some say about how the money can be used for migrant education and training programs. The group won the battle, Fuentes says, but lost the war: It achieved victory in court only to see the college abolish the programs. But then the group went on to win OEO funding of an independent, client-controlled group, which became the Idaho Migrant Council in 1971.

Since that time it has grown into a powerful organization operating dozens of programs, with a year-round staff of seventy that swells to three hundred while its summer Head Start program is under way in Idaho, western Montana, and western Wyoming. The group has an annual operating budget of $6 million. Despite political and financial reverses—most notably the harsh cuts of the Reagan years, in which five public health clinics were abolished because of lack of funds—the organization has continued to receive federal support from the old OEO, later replaced by the Office of Community Services and now the Job Training Partnership Act.

The council goes far beyond labor organizing. For example, it administers housing programs that have added hundreds of low-cost housing units for Hispanic farmworkers throughout the state. One project that members jokingly call El Milagro (the Miracle) converted a virtually uninhabitable labor camp of dilapidated buildings and old military barracks near Twin Falls into a modern apartment complex, using $3.5 million in federal Farm Labor Housing funds from the Farmers Home Administration. A manicured suburban subdivision just north of downtown Caldwell is the result of a sweat equity program in 1978 in which residents built their own houses. And on a highway east of Caldwell the council built an office and commercial development, El Mercado, which is now Canyon County's largest retail building. Built to raise both money and Hispanic pride (the designers consciously chose a red-tile and stucco Spanish decor), it has been such a success that the council, which had planned to use the upper floor for its offices, moved to a cheaper building so it could lease out its own quarters.

The Idaho Migrant Council also offers courses in English as a second language as well as extensive job-training programs. Federal funds targeted to aid migrant laborers help farmworkers learning new job skills with housing and transportation costs. Along similar lines, the group works to keep at-risk children of farmworkers in school. The support network for kids includes one-on-one counseling and referral programs and an annual conference at Sun Valley for 350 high school and junior high students who come together for a weekend of role modeling, competition, and talks.

"We decided at the beginning that the problem with farmworkers is not a single issue but a need for multiple approaches," says Fuentes. "It doesn't make any sense to assist a family with health care and then send them right back to a labor camp with no sanitation, where they'll get sick all over again. So we decided all along to look at housing, at education, at child care—a comprehensive approach to the problem."

## *Organizing Small Farmers and Ranchers*

I love the American prairie, particularly the part that stretches like a blanket across southern Minnesota, eastern Nebraska and South Dakota, and western Iowa. Far from being pool-table flat, the land undulates in lovely gentle hills, with lines of cottonwood and aspen trees separating green fields and dotted here and there with grain elevators and churches that seem too big for the little towns they're in, all spreading to the horizon under a brilliant wide bowl of sky. But there's something eerie about it too, eerie and lonely, because there are hardly any people left out here. Farm after farm stands empty, its houses and outbuildings decaying—or even worse, bulldozed to eliminate even the smallest obstacle to the miles of furrows plowed by agribusiness giants. Every village's Main Street looks half deserted, its empty or boarded-up storefronts alternating with those of businesses still struggling to survive.

Bipartisan national farm policy since the Eisenhower administration has concluded that the nation has more farmers ("excess human resources") than it needs, and federal efforts have quite consciously encouraged small farmers to leave the land and discouraged their children from going into farming. The much publicized, credit-driven farm crisis of the 1980s merely accelerated a flight from the land that had been well under way for a quarter of a century. In place of the small farms, corporate farms bring industrialized methods to the cultivation of huge expanses of land. And, small-farm advocates say, for every five farms that fail, one more Main Street business goes down, and a few more families pack up and move to Minneapolis or Denver or Dallas, where they find low-paying jobs if they're lucky.

Of course, much of the remembered agricultural bounty of small-town America is romance. Anyone who's done it will tell you that farming always has been hard work that pays little. The notion that all of Iowa, for instance, is such good farm country that corn sprouts practically without having to be planted is exaggerated. The fields where lush corn stands tall under the Iowa sun largely lie within the U-shaped crescent that drops down from the state's northern border to the neighborhood of Des Moines. Below that, particularly across the state's southern two tiers of counties bordering Missouri, rural poverty is endemic. Even in the rich glacial land of the northern sections there are plenty of the falling-down barns, abandoned farmsteads, and silent Main Streets that afflict the rest of the Great Plains. Iowa hasn't escaped the farm crisis, nor the racism and poverty-related problems associated with the flight of immigrants from the farms—and the Deep South, and Mexico—to America's large and middle-size cities.

During the first seven years of the 1980s, fully 7 percent of Iowa's residents left the state, ranking it after only West Virginia in population loss. Since the Des Moines area actually grew, the effect on farm communities was even more severe than statewide statistics suggest. Eliminating the state's ten urban or university counties, the other eighty-nine rural counties lost 11 percent of their population during the decade. And when recovery came in 1987, it was fueled by high-tech and white-collar industry lured almost entirely to Des Moines by strong corporate incentives and an exceptionally well-educated workforce.

Two excellent groups in Iowa illustrate a point I learned as a reporter: Community organizing isn't sexy. It requires long, hard, dogged work that often doesn't seem to yield any apparent change.

But it does make a difference, even if it's an evolutionary, incremental difference.

---

Founded by a coalition of church groups in Waterloo, Iowa, in 1975, Iowa Citizens for Community Improvement (CCI) cut its teeth on urban issues, not farm concerns, in the poorest sections of one of Iowa's poorest cities and the one with the state's largest black minority. After achieving a quick, relatively easy victory, when it prevailed on the city to force the owner of an old, abandoned motel building to tear it down, CCI went statewide, setting up urban chapters in Des Moines and Council Bluffs as well as a group for family farmers.

In one of its most controversial proposals, Full Court Press, CCI lobbied the Des Moines city council to pass legislation requiring that absentee landlords be rated on their record of maintaining their property and resolving tenant complaints. Landlords who fail to win a passing score are subject to more stringent codes and frequent inspections than well-behaved property owners. Their progress toward correcting deficiencies is closely monitored by the city housing department, and CCI takes advantage of explicit open records provisions to publicize the results.

CCI organizes communities to lobby the state legislature and local councils on farm issues, too. Its legislative agenda since 1981 has focused on easing the credit squeeze on farmers caught between low income and the high cost of borrowing for land and farming equipment and supplies. This is not a Mom, flag, and apple pie issue, even in Corn Belt Iowa. CCI generally turns up in the opposite camp from conservative Republican Governor Terry Branstad and Iowa State University, which is strongly in the agribusiness camp. And CCI probably loses more battles than it wins. In the process, however, it has earned a reputation as the state's preeminent small-farm advocacy group, and has signed on farmers all over Iowa. It has also developed an extremely simple but effective organizing technique. It identified the home towns and counties of all members of the state House and Senate agriculture committees, and then organized farmers in those counties early and well. When committee members get well-informed calls and letters on farm issues from local citizens who vote, it's hard for them to ignore CCI positions.

Outside the legislature, CCI has brought a federal banking law to bear on small-town banks with an effect that has other farm organizations throughout the country watching closely. The Community Reinvestment Act (CRA), a measure that requires commercial banks to "meet the credit needs of the local community" by extending services to poor people, has been primarily a tool of urban organizers, who use the act's public comment provisions to stall the expansion plans of banks that can't demonstrate a good record of lending and real estate investment in the inner city. Successfully redefining the terms of the law to cover small-town banks and their lending practices in farming communities, CCI persuaded Iowa's three largest bank holding companies (Norwest, Firstar, and Brenton) to start paying attention to low- to moderate-income farmers. Norwest alone set aside more than $13 million for low-interest loans to new borrowers who own small farms, and CCI director Joe Fagan estimates that the group's CRA actions overall have made $47 million available in new loans to Iowa family farmers. Under the standard CRA agreement, rural banks agree to make loans with interest rates and down payments as low as possible and to use government farm credit programs to help farmers get better terms on loans. What's more, Fagan says, before Norwest signed the CRA agreement, only 40 percent of its farm loans went to people with a net worth of $150,000 or less. Now 60 percent do.

CCI also promotes sustainable agriculture, the small-scale, environmentally conscious alternative agriculture that a lot of groups are beginning to scrutinize as a possible route out of the farm crisis. Because of heavy pesticide and fertilizer use, groundwater pollution is a significant issue in Iowa. A CCI–Iowa State survey of two thousand farm wells found that fully 25 percent were too polluted for pregnant women or children to drink from. Through individual organizing, educational efforts by Future Farmers of America chapters, and vocational classes in high schools, CCI is using that evidence to persuade farmers to switch to low-chemical fertilizers and pesticides less hazardous to groundwater. The group also sponsors "farmer-to-farmer workshops" on principles of sustainable agriculture. The evangelistic technique worked so well that the group added another twist. Finding that conservative country banks were reluctant to lend money for sustainable farming methods that the bankers considered newfangled and untried, CCI took a series of "farmer-to-banker" programs on the road, with successful farmers showing bankers what they had done and how they did it.

---

Iowa's other nationally respected small-farm organization, PrairieFire Rural Action, is more of a think tank for sustainable agriculture than a traditional community organizing group. Unlike CCI, it is not an umbrella group with individual members, but it nevertheless fosters state and national coalitions of farm, rural, religious, labor, urban, and community groups around farm issues.

In 1982, for instance, PrairieFire initiated the nation's first Farm Crisis Hotline, a telephone number that farmers could call for technical assistance, legal referral, and support. Throughout the decade, PrairieFire was involved with grassroots organizing, farmer protests in the Midwest and nationally, and developing and backing farm policy efforts such as the Iowa farmer-creditor mediation law, homestead rights for farmers forced off their land, state restrictions on land takeovers by nonfarm interests, and curbs on corporate centralization of food production. It also took a strong public stance against the agitation of white supremacist groups like Posse Comitatus and Aryan Nation.

With those battles largely behind the group in the 1990s, though, executive director David Ostendorf sometimes fears that small-farm groups are losing ground in the larger struggle. "The gut issue, which we haven't taken on, is the issue of income in agriculture. In many ways, we took on the crisis but didn't take on the gut systemic issue that we knew was underneath: control of the food system. Both then and now, farmers don't make a decent income." During the summer of 1992, corn prices in Iowa fell below $2 a bushel, which meant that it cost a farmer more to grow corn than he could recover in the marketplace.

There's an ugly dilemma here. When family farmers fight for crop prices sufficient to make a decent wage for themselves, they draw fire from advocates for urban poor people, who complain that higher food costs hurt their constituencies and diminish the role of WIC and other assistance programs. But Ostendorf and other family farm organizers argue that the nation's antipoverty campaigners need to work together on behalf of all the poor—farmers, poor urban mothers and their children, and the rest—rather than allowing the system to divide and conquer advocacy groups.

Meanwhile, as the farm credit crisis has eased and relatively few farmers are being forced off their land by foreclosure and bankruptcy, the media spotlight has moved on. Farm advocacy is no longer a priority for funders, and many of the well-known advocacy groups of the 1980s have closed their doors. PrairieFire has responded by moving in a new direction, shifting toward the creation of community-based economic development projects in rural America.

Farming is becoming increasingly centralized worldwide in large agribusiness enterprises. Only five corporations, for instance, control world grain production; two of those, along with one or two others, control livestock production. Farmers have thus largely lost the benefits of a competitive marketplace in their efforts to get good prices for agricultural commodities.

It's not only farmers who feel the economic pinch on the prairie. Packing industry workers may have it even worse. Throughout Iowa, Kansas, and Nebraska, the meatpacking industry, having broken the United Food and Commercial Workers during the Hormel strike in the late 1980s, has cut wages to near minimum (typically $6.50 an hour). Moreover, the industry now heavily recruits in the region's inner cities and in the Rio Grande Valley and Mexico for unskilled laborers willing to work for lower wages than the skilled union meatpackers are willing to take. "As in most industries, the recruitment issue is to take advantage of the most down-and-out," Ostendorf said. "The problem is that six-fifty an hour is better than sixty-five cents a day (which is the standard wage for many Mexican workers), so a lot of folks are coming up." With these low-paying jobs comes the standard litany of exploitation, including broken promises of decent housing and actual physical abuse of workers. The unexpected influx of Hispanic workers with little English into once lily-white, Protestant rural Iowa also raises thorny issues. Aside from plain ethnic bias and misunderstanding, small-town policymakers and politicians must now address literacy and social service needs that were never before much of a consideration.

PrairieFire has come up with a laundry list of initiatives to meet these new needs. Its Church Land Project, in partnership with the Catholic Rural Life Conference, mounted a comprehensive investigation of courthouse records to learn what Iowa's churches are doing with the nontaxed land they own. Uncovering a surprisingly large amount of such land—fifty thousand to seventy-five thousand acres—PrairieFire organizers hope that a moral argument will sway churches to demonstrate what Ostendorf calls "appropriate stewardship" of their land, putting sustainable agriculture and nonexploitative labor into practice as a model for the community.

Another PrairieFire effort, the Rural Cooperative Development Project, encourages groups of family farmers to band together in cooperatives in order to achieve economies of scale, allowing them both to save money and to compete with agribusiness. Its first such group, a poultry cooperative, involves about a dozen women from farms in southwestern Iowa. Each raises chickens on her own farm, but the women function cooperatively to buy chicks and feed, transport them to commercial processors, and sell them through markets, restaurants, and grocery wholesalers as high-profit organic free-range chickens.

The co-op's goals are modest: Each member pays just $50 to join and takes a few hundred chicks for $1 each. Spending another $1 apiece for feed and supplies, she can sell them for $3 each, yielding a likely annual income of $1,500 to $2,000 from several flocks during a successful year. Raising chickens isn't intended to be a full-time occupation, but it offers a way for farm women to supplement the family income without having to take a job in town.

---

All over the United States, wherever family farmers and ranchers struggle to earn a living, similar organizing groups have grown up to work with them, whether they're fighting in the state legislatures or marching on Washington or simply organizing farmers and ranchers to try creative new ideas that might help them make a few bucks.

In the northern Plains, seven state organizations developed at various times in the 1980s under the umbrella of the Western Organizations of Resource Councils (WORC) in Billings, Montana. They are forming grassroots organizations of individual farmers, ranchers, church and small-business people united to oppose federal and state policies that they argue have driven tens of thousands of small farmers and ranchers off their land.

I rode through the rolling Whetstone Valley and Big Stone Lake countryside of eastern South Dakota for hours one locust-buzzing

Sunday afternoon and early evening in the summer of 1992 with seventy-seven-year-old Barney Van Stralen and his wife, Gladys. They gave me a deep sense of this land in which their roots go back four generations and where their grandchildren still work the old family farm, an original 320-acre section from homesteading times. The Van Stralens demonstrate that hard, dogged individual organizing is a key to the fight against poverty. Organizing around issues raised by farmer members, Dakota Rural Action, one of the WORC groups, has achieved a number of successes in South Dakota. It spearheaded a state investigation into corporate domination of the livestock feeding and meat-packing industry, and won legislation enacting strict antitrust limitations. It pushed for state laws mandating a reduction in farm foreclosures and reforms in Farmers Home Administration lending practices. It helped establish a comprehensive recycling law, with regulations governing the disposal of hazardous waste and local landfills, and it launched community programs for waste reduction and recycling.

Travel to the rest of the northern Plains states, and you'll find more organizing going on under WORC's umbrella, conducted by local members working autonomously. Becky Ihli, organizer of the Boise-based Idaho Rural Council, knows what the farm crisis means as well as anyone: She saw her parents lose their family farm and home in Idaho's Treasure Valley in 1987. (She and her brothers still farm land in the orchard land of the valley.) The experience, though, drove her to a new full-time job: She sought out the Idaho Rural Council as a volunteer, then became an intern, then an organizer and finally its director, all because she saw there was something wrong and figured that *someone* needed to do something about it.

Founded in 1986, the Idaho Rural Council began as a one-on-one counseling and referral organization. Idaho farmers and ranchers called its volunteer-operated telephone hotline for information and emotional support. Recently, like many other farm-organizing groups, it expanded both its agenda and its scope. With more than three hundred dues-paying members all over the state and formal chapters in Boise and the Magic Valley agricultural region around Twin Falls, it now aims to bring not only farmers and ranchers but other members of rural communities as well as churches and civic groups together to make their voices heard on issues ranging from the farm debt crisis to hazardous waste disposal, concentration of agribusiness in the beef industry, use of bovine growth hormone in dairy operations, sustainable agriculture, and even the North American Free Trade Agreement. "A lot of people don't understand about farmers," Ihli said. "They think, 'Oh, farmers have got money because they've got land and all that stuff.' But it's not true. We get calls from people who are destitute—they have no money for food. People think farmers are rich, that they've got all these resources, but that's just not the case."

## *Large-Scale Agricultural Organizing*

Working out of a two-story brick building that was once the only hotel in Walthill, a tiny northeastern Nebraska farming town of 450, the Center for Rural Affairs is making ripples across the country. Marty Strange and Don Ralston, then VISTA volunteers, founded the center more than twenty years ago as an outgrowth of the local Community Action organization, a grassroots initiative of Great Society days where they worked. They thought it would be fruitful to study model farm policies and then urge farmers to lobby for the implementation of those that seemed most effective. It worked well enough to gain them a small national reputation as rural policy gurus, and they have dealt with issues as diverse as independent world banking, the structure of the hog industry, rural electric and water/sewage utilities, and the water-wasting disadvantages of center-pivot irrigation, the relatively new practice that creates those round fields that look so strange from an airplane flying six miles above the Plains. Among the group's significant victories was Initiative 300, an amendment to the Nebraska constitution that has survived challenges all the way to the U.S. Supreme Court. The amendment limits agribusiness operations in the state to corporations owned by families that actually work Nebraska land. "It's the best in the nation," Ralston says with pride.

---

Moving from the Grain Belt to the South, we find one of the oldest and most respected of all agricultural organizing groups working out of a crowded, cluttered office building in downtown Atlanta. The Federation of Southern Cooperatives is a legitimate icon of the civil rights struggle, and its leader, Ralph Paige, has been there since the beginning. The federation, which celebrated its thirty-fifth anniversary in 1993, got started in the aftermath of Dr. Martin Luther King's victories, Paige recalled. With the march to Selma in the history books and the Voting Rights Act and the Civil Rights Act in place, he said, "People started asking each other, 'Where do we go from here?'" For this advocate of the dirt-poor farmers and sharecroppers of the Southeast, the answer was to ensure "our God-given right to stay on the land and to have a decent way of life, through economic development, land retention projects, advocacy, and outreach."

Here and there across the South in the postwar period, poor black farmers independently formed cooperatives to gain economic power. Often organized by workers from the Student Nonviolent Coordinating Committee, the Southern Christian Leadership Conference, the Congress of Racial Equality, or the NAACP, they frequently began as alternatives to the white-dominated local economy, which many of them opposed through boycotts. "Finding themselves in the wilderness," as Paige says, a number of these groups joined in a coalition. Federal Office of Economic Opportunity money allowed the federation to hire organizers to go out and encourage the formation of more cooperatives, which got involved in projects ranging from low-cost housing and economic development to marketing agricultural produce. At one point as many as 130 co-ops were active in the federation, although that number has slipped in recent years because black farmers in the South, like their white counterparts on the Plains, are leaving the farm in large numbers. Only twenty-three thousand black farmers are thought to remain on three million acres of farmland, a fraction of their number two decades ago. Still, the federation continues, in a fashion very similar to the northern Plains resource councils, to train local leaders who then organize independent, self-governing local cooperatives.

Notes organizer Jerry Pennick, "Our co-ops operate on the one-man, one-vote principle, more in the way of sharing resources than profits. In credit co-ops, for instance, people pool their resources and lend them to their neighbors."

The Federation of Southern Cooperatives combines a firm conviction that organizing can change people's lives for the better with a hardheaded, frankly cynical perspective that black farmers have to help themselves. "Our people have been facing these problems for fifty years," Paige said. "I'm sorry for the farmers of the Midwest, but we've had a farm crisis for generations before those folks even knew they had a problem."

## *Industrial Organizing in the Border Country*

Until just three years ago, a boss who failed to pay his workers the wages they had earned was guilty of a mere misdemeanor in Texas, and even then it was hard to get a conviction. But that was before the women of El Paso's La Mujer Obrera (The Woman Worker) chained themselves to their sewing machines and later went on to mount a hunger strike. These widely publicized actions during the summer of 1990 got some of the womem sent to jail, but they also broke a legislative logjam that lawsuits and formal complaints had not been able to dislodge, getting this form of theft redefined as the felony it should have been all along.

La Mujer Obrera's community organizing is centered on the workplace rather than on neighborhoods. The original Centro de Obrero Fronterizo (Center for Border Workers) was formed in 1981, after a textile workers' strike against the Farah clothing company's El Paso plant. Organizer Cecilia Rodriguez concluded that women garment workers in particular were exploited and, without representation, were for all practical purposes invisible. "There was no place for women workers to meet and talk as women," said Maria Carmen Dominguez, now the group's lead organizer. "There was no representation of women's values and needs. There was a lack of respect for women as workers."

Conditions got worse as most of the major textile manufacturers closed and left the Texas side of the border for Mexico, turning over the industry to anonymous sweatshops that operated almost invisibly, often opening and then going out of business too rapidly to attract the attention of regulatory agencies, which in the border country have a justified reputation for weak regulation and lax enforcement.

La Mujer Obrera—still numbering only an estimated two hundred families—spreads out among the city's Spanish-speaking women workers with fliers, educational materials, and personal exhortation, emphasizing all their community's basic needs, from jobs to housing, health care, education, food, and *paz* (peace), by which they seem to mean "the pursuit of happiness."

In addition to its down-to-earth organizing in the sweatshops,

La Mujer Obrera reaches for those goals through such projects as La Escuela Popular (The People's School), which provides training in English, citizenship, women's and workers' issues; and two Spanish-language newspapers. The organization also produces an English language newspaper with translations of articles about Mexican politics from the Mexican news media. And in a major project for which they're still raising funds toward a goal of $850,000, they're planning a community-based economic development program that will help create jobs and train Spanish-speaking women to qualify for them.

Dominguez has no illusions of being able to solve all the problems of El Paso's women workers quickly, but she has strong and attainable dreams for the next five years. "I want to have more projects dedicated to addressing the needs of our community," she said. "Many more workers aware of their rights and involved in organizing. And continue to grow and strengthen our voice in the community."

## *Organizing to Fight Hunger*

Pittsburgh's great renaissance that replaced its smoky industrial buildings with the glittering Golden Triangle of skyscrapers and parks never reached up the Monongahela River to Homestead, a decaying steel town within the metropolitan area where rusting, vacant mills stand in silence on the river's steep slopes. The despair of poverty runs deep here, but it's countered by the sturdy spirits of Joni Rabinowitz and Ken Regal in the cluttered one-room office of Just Harvest, on the second floor of the former Bishop Boyle High School. It's a simple, lean, single-focus organization that is devoted to organizing their community around hunger issues.

"The thing that I think is unique about us," Rabinowitz said, "is that we are . . . successful in raising both city and county funds for other antihunger programs, but we still maintain our independence. We don't get funds. We build a constituency of service providers who get the money, but we're the ones on the firing line, not them. They don't have to worry about not rocking the boat because they get city money. *We* rock the boat."

For four long years after it became an independent organization in 1986, Just Harvest fought to get state money for school breakfast programs and to persuade Pittsburgh and Allegheny County governments to come up with funding to stock area food pantries. Both efforts were eventually successful. Just Harvest's current battle seeks to reverse the flight of major grocery chains from poor areas. Fully one-third of the large grocery stores in urban Pittsburgh closed during the late 1980s and early 1990s, leaving overpriced Mom and Pop stores—or no stores at all—in many low-income neighborhoods. Leaning on the private sector is a tough challenge, one that Just Harvest hopes to overcome by pushing the city council to establish a food policy commission with authority to review all the city's procedures and programs that touch on poverty and poor people, from zoning to transportation to tax policy. The proposed Pittsburgh Committee on Hunger and Access to Food would move beyond palliatives to address the root causes of hunger in the community. "The purpose of the commission would be to make the city government recognize its responsibility to take action to deal with these problems," Regal said.

## *Organizing Disabled People*

Access Alaska started, as most independent living centers for physically disabled people do, out of desperation. Eight disabled people, most of them under thirty, had no choice but to live among geriatric patients in Anchorage's Our Lady of Compassion nursing home, because there were no alternatives available for young, healthy people in wheelchairs. Working with an Anchorage schoolteacher who was assigned to go to the nursing home and tutor them, the group organized in 1983 as Independent Options Now. The group lobbied for state Medicaid money to allow them to hire personal attendants, making it possible for them to live on their own outside the nursing home. At about the same time, Alaska's vocational rehabilitation agency, using federal money, formed the Independent Quality of Living Center, which provided information and advice to severely disabled people. Within a year the groups recognized that they were duplicating each other's services and merged, then quickly grew from a one-person office to today's organization, with a staff of fourteen in Anchorage and eleven in Fairbanks, and a $1.2 million annual budget.

Modeled on the pioneer Center for Independent Living in Berkeley, California, and also drawing inspiration from Denver's ADAPT, Access Alaska fosters change for people with disabilities by working with individuals to make sure they get all the services for which they're eligible. It also identifies gaps in the system and works to fill them. Access Alaska pushed the state ahead of much of the country by obtaining an exemption from federal Medicaid regulations that normally force disabled people into nursing homes. Moreover, it persuaded the legislature to add additional state money to help pay for attendant services for those whose income is too high to qualify for Medicaid.

Access Alaska not only joined the national lobbying effort for the Americans with Disabilities Act but got a broader, more far-reaching state law ensuring civil rights for disabled people. It informs disabled people, service providers, and counselors of ADA requirements, and makes sure that employers and public facilities abide by the new federal law. It networks with low-cost housing organizations in the region to insist that all housing projects meet at least the legal minimum accessibility and preferably more. When necessary, Access Alaska raises hell, as it did when wheelchair riders mobilized with picket signs and bullhorns to protest inaccessible design at the $72 million Alaska Center for the Performing Arts in Anchorage. "We do that kind of thing when it's needed," said executive director Duane French, who uses a motorized wheelchair to get around. "We want to have a high profile in the community and encourage people with disabilities to get involved, run for office, and get involved not just in disability programs but in the community."

---

Disability rights is a key issue too for a group in Idaho, but it's hardly the only one. Whether it's getting a street light installed in rural Burley or a single-payer health plan implemented statewide, if community action is needed in Idaho, the Idaho Citizens' Network (ICN) will almost certainly be there to organize it. Based in a cozy old house with a shady veranda just a few blocks away from the state capitol, ICN mobilizes twenty-five thousand members in four chapters around the state, in Boise, Idaho Falls, Coeur d'Alene, and Kellogg, a small town in the depressed silver-mining country near the Montana border.

ICN credits its diversity and its statewide reach to its origins. It descends from three separate groups formed during the early 1980s: the Idaho Neighbors Network, focused on disability rights, women's welfare issues, and neighborhood problems in Burley; Idaho Fair Share, a statewide organization that addressed utility service for poor people; and the Idaho Disabilities Coalition, another organization based in Burley that united disabled people in the fight for accessibility. The three groups coalesced in 1987 to work jointly on health care issues, and not long afterward formally merged into ICN.

With a staff of eight, plus a larger group of fund-raising and organizing canvassers, ICN operates with a $200,000 annual budget. It pursues activities as diverse as Superfund cleanup initiatives in lead-contaminated Kellogg and a sit-in by wheelchair riders to protest the inaccessibility of Burley's City Hall, ultimately leading to construction of a new city building. ICN fought legislative cuts in Medicaid, and got an unprecedented $12 million allocated to finance personal care attendants for in-home services for disabled people. The organization is also setting up a worker-owned cooperative of in-home personal attendants to help disabled people with daily needs. "A lot of our stuff is traditional community organizing, just get down and do it," says Sherman. "We have some fun, and sometimes it's tough sledding."

## *Training Organizers*

There comes a moment when people stop thinking about what has happened to them and start thinking about what they can make happen. This principle of community organizing underlies the sixty-year-old Highlander Center, a school for grassroots community organizers in the Appalachian and southern states. Founded in 1932 by the long-time community organizer Myles Horton and a group of supporters as the Highlander Folk School, a "school for adults" where people of like spirit could meet, share experiences, and learn from each other, the center has continued with little change in its basic purposes.

Such famous organizers as Martin Luther King, Jr., have come here, earning the school notoriety among local segregationists, who considered the institution communistic. Contrary to the myth that her leadership of the Montgomery, Alabama, bus strike was merely the act of a tired woman who would not be moved, Rosa Parks was also trained here before the strike. And more recently, many well-known Appalachian organizers, like Becky Simpson of the Cranks Creek Survival Center, have won fellowships at the Highlander.

Horton organized the school, then in the town of Monteagle, Tennessee, to train southern union organizers. In the 1950s its primary focus moved to desegregation, and the resulting controversy caused state officials to yank its charter in 1960. Undeterred, Horton moved the institution to inner-city Knoxville, and then, about a decade ago, to its current setting about twenty miles east in New Market, Tennessee, on 110 acres of hilltop meadow with a view of the Great Smoky Mountains. While Highlander continues to be deeply involved in issues of race and poverty, its programs now reach into every area in which people are discriminated against—race, religion, gender, class, disability, sexual preference, and age—as it brings people together to learn from each other.

About once a year, a call for fellowship applications goes out to a broad network of organizations. Highlander makes as many grants as possible (fourteen of them in 1993, out of fifty-eight applications) to active, working organizers in the region. Fellows receive transportation assistance and a $200 monthly stipend to attend six weekend sessions at Highlander over the nine-month fellowship period, during which they stay in dormitories on the grounds, with child care provided. The sessions feature guest speakers, and fellows use Highlander's extensive library. "Mostly, however, we sit around this big room in rocking chairs and talk," said staffer Joyce Dukes. "It's laid back—blue jeans, very, very casual. No pressure, but there's a lot going on. It's a very participatory project. We've recognized that people learn a lot just by living and dealing with problems, and so a lot of peer learning goes on."

Highlander has earned a glowing reputation over its sixty years. When Myles Horton died in 1990, *New York Times* reporter Peter Applebome quoted staffer Candie Carawan in a story about Horton and the center: "From its start, this has been one of the few places that takes seriously the notion that grass-roots people, dispossessed people, who do not have money or power or much formal education can solve their own problems."

---

In inner-city Chicago there is another organization that, like the Highlander Center in rural Tennessee, teaches activists how to organize for change. Now called the National Training and Information Center (NTIC), it started a quarter of a century ago as a strictly local initiative devoted to public school issues in the Austin neighborhood on Chicago's West Side. In some respects, that's what it remains today, but the group that fought Mayor Richard J. Daley to win middle schools, a busing program, and less crowded classrooms has also become a national federation of more than three hundred community groups, a respected training center for community organizers, and a think tank on housing policy. It was NTIC that crafted the model legislation that became the Community Reinvestment Act; and that suggested to Jack Kemp, secretary of Housing and Urban Development in the Bush administration, the idea that was the basis of his HOME program. The center played a key national role in keeping Community Development block grants alive through the Reagan and Bush years, while at the same time it worked locally to oppose redlining by banks and insurance companies and residential abandonment by the FHA on the West Side of Chicago.

It didn't seem all that complicated back at the start, says executive director Gale Cincotta. The school issue was so hot that the Organization for a Better Austin mustered 129,000 members at its peak. Then it merged with a neighborhood group across the Chicago River to become the influential West Side Coalition, Chicago's first community organizing effort with ethnic whites, blacks, and Hispanics all working together for the common good.

Shel Trapp, one of the early neighborhood leaders who is now NTIC's training director, travels almost constantly to conduct workshops for community groups around the nation. NTIC also offers seminars and workshops for grassroots groups on a batch of issues: low-cost housing, crime and drug abuse, utility rates, health care, problems of rural areas, disability rights. It conducts research on poverty-related issues and provides technical assistance to help community groups get started and develop their own resources.

There's no secret to NTIC's success, Cincotta says, other than this: "Be steady. Be tenacious. Grab on like a bulldog and don't let go. Stretch the system." A recent success, for instance, was getting a major lending firm to stop redlining (in Chicago neighborhoods). The group conducted research (including congressional action to force HUD to release records) that proved redlining was occurring, then released the study to the public and went to the home of the institution's president to demand action. NTIC's aim was to show bank officials how the institution could live up to its commitments to serve the community and make money at the same time.

"We won't take no for an answer," Cincotta said. "We're not asking for something that we can't get. We ask insurance companies to sell insurance. We ask banks to loan money. That's what they do. Whether they like it or not, when you confront them with it, it's bad for them to say they don't want to put dollars in a neighborhood because it's black or it's poor. They've promised to be fair, to build housing. We just make them stick to what they say they'll do. You've really got to just be tenacious and stick with it."

This attitude informs just about every successful community organizing effort, and it illustrates more of the underlying principles that we find consistently in effective programs. Tenacity translates to management by objectives: Set your sights on practical, attainable goals, then march in a straight line toward accomplishing them. Leadership also makes a difference. The most effective grassroots leaders are charismatic, competent, flexible, unafraid to innovate, and unworried about breaking rules. They get past turf issues to join forces with other individuals and groups pursuing similar goals, and they get the community involved in their hopes and dreams.

# 7

# People Need Job Skills

If there's one sure cure for poverty, it's a good job and the skills to do it. Hunger and poverty disappear as problems for people who have fulfilling jobs that pay a living wage. To make this happen, job-training programs that work may be *the* single most effective grassroots tool in the struggle against poverty. Unfortunately, this is not an easy tool to build or use. It's particularly difficult to invent effective ways to move chronically unemployed, unskilled individuals into the labor market. Still, the best of the grassroots innovations show real promise, even if their victories are measured in small numbers and local impact.

---

The name St. Philip's College might sound like a high-tone prep school, but it's really one of San Antonio's three community colleges—no traditional redbrick campus but an all-business institution holding classes in a neat row of adobe-colored airplane hangars on what used to be Kelly Air Force Base. When I visited one hot spring afternoon in 1994, eleven serious students wearing trim blue uniform shirts listened alertly as Nelson Allday filled them in on the arcana of wave-form comparison, a complex matter involving poster-size graphs and charts with titles like "Pattern for Four Cylinders, Showing High Firing Line in No. 3 Cylinder." Allday, a rangy man with a Texas twang, leaned on his table and spoke of wiring harnesses and instrument clusters as the class followed along in their workbooks turned to the page on "Cab, Chassis, and Trailer Wiring Systems."

Allday's a good teacher. He keeps the class involved, and the students respond, jumping to answer as he fires out questions, breaking from the book to get them thinking about their own cars and how they work, and how this relates to the charts on the classroom wall.

"If I breeze down to U-Haul," he asks, pointing to a rough sketch of a trailer on the blackboard, "can I just breeze up to that thing and back up, hook on, and pull it away?"

"Naw! You'll get a ticket," a young woman blurts back. "You'll have no brake lights, no turn signals."

Before long, Allday has a wiring harness out on the table, yards of wires in a webby tangle, and the students are up, clustered around, pointing at it with pencils and telling him what goes where.

It's a typical day in a typical class at Project Quest, the San Antonio-based program that may just be the nation's most creative and hopeful effort to train a lot of people for a lot of good, high-paying jobs and do it fast.

Started as a project of San Antonio's outstanding COPS program, the community group described in the last chapter, Project Quest was designed to move jobs by the hundreds into the city's heavily unemployed Hispanic community and to jawbone local employers into earmarking good, skilled jobs for local people. The concept was based on an audacious set of principles, and as the first jobs come on line and find trained, willing workers to take them, it seems to be working.

Planning began in 1991 with a COPS task force of thirty-five volunteers headed by Father Al Jost, a Catholic priest and community activist. Analyzing the city's economy, the task force found that San Antonio had lost fourteen thousand skilled jobs in manufacturing, transportation, and communication during the 1980s. During the same period, it gained fifty thousand service sector jobs. While more than half of the new jobs were low-paying, often part-time, and high-turnover positions, twenty thousand of them—far more than the number lost—were high-wage, high-skill jobs.

So COPS set a simple goal: Identify specific jobs within that high-end category, and work with employers to devise competent classroom and on-the-job training that would turn out fully qualified graduates. Enlist unemployed residents of the mostly Hispanic West Side in the training courses; give them both moral and financial support to keep them on track through the training; and at the end of the course, place them in good, well-paying jobs that are there waiting for them.

Task force members sat down with the chief executives of the region's high-tech businesses, including aviation companies, hospitals, banks, and computer firms, and eventually won pledges from more than twenty firms to hire trainees for over five hundred jobs.

Project Quest was loosely modeled on the GI Bill, with a fund available to provide applicants financial assistance based on need to cover tuition, training fees, books, supplies, even transportation and day care, up to a maximum of $500 a month. Trainees must be drug- and alcohol-free; besides straightforward job training, they may receive additional help such as remedial work in language, math, and other basic skills as well as counseling and social service support.

This kind of individualized support doesn't come cheap. Project Quest's annual budget is $3.7 million—a sizable amount of money, but one that the state, the city, and the quasi-governmental Private Industry Council were more than willing to cough up on the basis of the program's promise and the competence of its staff. Now an independent nonprofit organization, Project Quest is directed by Jack Salvadore, a retired air force general who came to the program from a post as commander of the USAF Recruiting Service.

New in the summer of 1994, Project Quest quickly grew close to its expected dimensions, with 550 students in training, culled from more than 4,000 individuals who responded to its initial announcement. Most of the project's training programs require two years, so it's too early to measure its effectiveness in placing trainees in jobs. However, its first graduate, Cynthia Scott, moved directly from class to a $9-an-hour full-time job with benefits as a licensed vocational nurse at Baptist Memorial Hospital in San Antonio. A single mother of three children, she was a welfare recipient before she came to Project Quest, receiving $271 a month in AFDC.

"It's hard to get off the welfare system," she said. "They've made it difficult. You're not allowed to do this, you're not allowed to do that. When I graduated and started working, I went in and talked to my social worker, and he said, 'You know you won't be getting any more checks, don't you?' I said, 'Ha! I'll be getting checks, but not from you!' "

The program expects to graduate five hundred more workers with attitudes like that in the next year or two.

---

On Milwaukee's Hispanic South Side, Esperanza Unida (United Hope) was founded twenty years ago as a nonprofit community organization that supported labor rights, making sure that those who were eligible received workers' compensation and unemployment benefits. The group's founder and director, Richard Oulahan, a forty-six-year-old Irishman from Brooklyn, had learned Spanish in Mexico City, where he lived as a child with his family—his father was *Time* magazine's bureau chief there. He came to Milwaukee to attend Marquette University, then started Esperanza Unida as a community organizer. He decided to shift the organization's focus in 1985, when he realized that unemployment was rising and that existing programs were failing to make what seemed to him to be the obvious link between job training and economic development.

Adapting an idea from his friend and neighbor Terrance Brulc, who let neighborhood youngsters work on cars (and, rumor has it, deal a little dope and drink beer) in the back of an old service station he owned, Oulahan came up with a new approach: Use government job-training money not for make-work projects but to pay people to work in real jobs while they learned. "People don't realize this: It's legal for a nonprofit to run a business, so long as the money you generate is related to the purpose of the organization." So, for example, there's nothing to prevent an auto repair shop from operating as a nonprofit and charging market rates for competitive services, provided of course that the income goes back into the organization's budget and proper accounts are kept. In fact, Esperanza Unida's repair shop earned $700,000 in 1990, covering fully 70 percent of its $1 million annual budget, while it taught dozens of young folks from the neighborhood a marketable trade.

The group purchased an abandoned auto dealership in a fifty-eight-thousand-square-foot building in Milwaukee's Hispanic South Side in 1988, did basic renovations, and reopened as a working auto repair shop. Under the supervision of qualified mechanics who learned their trade in the auto industry, employees work at paying jobs in the garage, earning a decent wage while they learn to work on cars. During the program's ten-year life, the project has placed more than two hundred auto mechanics into permanent, quality jobs. The idea worked so well that the group soon expanded into half a dozen other trades, many of them aimed at giving people the experience they need to start their own businesses, while the incubator setting of the agency protects them from business failure (which knocks off 90 percent of small businesses in their first year of operation) as they learn.

For example, Esperanza Unida rehabilitates houses in Milwaukee's inner city, using trainees to help its qualified carpenter with the construction work. For $1, they purchase abandoned houses that the city would otherwise condemn, rebuild them for $30,000—less than half the cost of commercial rehabilitation—and sell them for no additional profit, making sound housing available to working poor people who could never afford the $60,000 market rate. "In vocational school, they build a wall and then tear it down," Oulahan says. "That doesn't make any sense. We build houses."

And, after discovering that some of the houses they repaired contained asbestos, a $5,000 removal job for a commercial firm, they trained one of their own people to do licensed asbestos removal. Once he was confident in his skills and business acumen, he was turned loose as an independent contractor.

Similar operations are under way with an auto body shop, which not only does commercial body work but rebuilds and sells old cars that people donate for the tax writeoff, and a parts shop, in which workers rebuild auto parts cannibalized from unsalvageable cars and sell them to the auto repair shop and over the counter.

Discovering that there was a market for trained welders, and for large metal waste bins, the organization got a contract to make waste bins, offering another opportunity to train people in a high-paying skill well suited for individual entrepreneurship. This particular effort, in fact, has proved even more successful than the auto repair shop, because welding skills, although technical and high-paying, are simple enough to turn out significant numbers of employable workers in a fairly short time.

Finally, concerned that many men but very few women were taking advantage of Esperanza Unida's jobs programs in traditionally male enterprises, Oulahan added a day care training program. In the old auto showroom, now converted into a colorful schoolroom, the organization trains dozens of neighborhood women to become licensed home day care practitioners, creating new small businesses in a neighborhood that heretofore had no home day care facilities, despite a great need.

This cluster of projects has trained more than 600 mostly minority individuals over seven years, has placed at least 425 of them into skilled, paying jobs in the community, and hired 35 more to staff the organization itself. It's a simple idea, but simple ideas aren't always easily implemented, Oulahan says, admitting that the whole thing is sometimes a struggle. Area businesses were nervous about hiring the trainees at first, and prejudice remains against both Hispanics and the blacks who come from the North Side and make up 20 percent of Esperanza Unida's job trainees. Old guard labor leaders still resist the idea of minorities moving into the skilled trades, but Oulahan says he is gradually winning over the "young Turks," and the old guard is dying off and retiring. "The Hispanic community here is still not as damaged as the black community—we still have the family structure—but there are serious problems," Oulahan said. "We've tried not to let things erode, and we still say that a decent job is the real answer to social problems."

## *High-Tech Skills in "Teaching Factories"*

America faces hard but simple choices in the world economy of the twenty-first century, says Dave Porreca, director of West Virginia's Robert C. Byrd Institute for Advanced Flexible Manufacturing Systems. Porreca cites the arguments of the best-selling economist Lester Thurow: "If our work force has only low skills, we will compete with all the other countries that have low skills to offer, and we can only win if we are the cheapest producers of low-skill products." The alternative? A trained work force that's trained and able to compete in a high-technology economy, using flexible manufacturing techniques that take advantage of computer and robotics technology to respond instantly to changing needs.

That's what the Byrd Institute, associated with Marshall University's Research and Economic Development Center, is all about. Financed by military grants—initially $2.9 million from the Air Force three years ago, and a $4 million current award from the Defense Department—the institute is on the leading edge of a development that's common in Japan and Germany but still rare in this country. The Byrd Institute, named in honor of the senator who helped establish it, fits nicely into a former bank building in downtown Huntington. Its centerpiece is a small but well-equipped "teaching factory" where small and mid-size West Virginia businesses can come to try out high-tech, computerized manufacturing equipment and have their employees trained to use it. This is critical for smaller companies, as most West Virginia firms are, because there's a direct link between a firm's ability to upgrade technology and its efficiency and productivity. The institute makes it practical for small companies to try technologies, like the $350,000 Cincinnati Milacron T-10 computerized milling machine, that only major corporations could otherwise afford.

It operates several programs, all of them intended to help the state's small and mid-size businesses remain competitive by mastering advanced technology. It currently deals primarily through businesses and trains their employees, although Porreca says he would like to establish an apprenticeship program for unemployed high school students and graduates. Mountaineer Archery, a local manufacturer of hunting bows, uses the Institute's equipment to "reverse engineer" its handmade bows, which will allow the firm to use robotic tools to make key parts rather than time-consuming hand techniques. This refutes the conventional wisdom that robotics causes unemployment by replacing line workers: By bringing its craft into the twenty-first century, the local firm may grow and hire more workers.

The Institute's telecommunications program will take advantage of modern communications linkages to assist the state's small business community, providing training videos and conferences downloaded via satellite and establishing electronic mail connections among home workers in isolated Appalachian communities. The Institute offers technical assistance to small businesses, and it provides training in computer-assisted design and computer-assisted manufacturing through Marshall's community college. One of its high-profile activities, the so-called computer integrated manufacturing cell, is a miniaturized working model of a robotics-style manufacturing line, on which students can operate actual computer control consoles to shape products from metal (or even wood or wax) to master these high-tech processes. "We've always been very good in the United States about inventing things," Porreca said. "But this is no longer as important. More important now is how you *make* things, and the Japanese and Germans have made this into a real science."

---

A similar teaching factory in Detroit accomplishes an equally hopeful result with a slightly different spin. Rather than seeking to build the economy by advising small business, Focus: HOPE takes jobless young people in the city's heavily poor and predominantly black neighborhoods and turns them into highly qualified high-tech workers for the new century.

After Father Bill Cunningham started a neighborhood group devoted to rebuilding human relations in the wake of Detroit's 1967 riots, he moved quickly into a commodities distribution program intended to build the health and strength of the community's poor mothers and their babies. Its "food prescription" program, passing out government surplus food in a setting very much like a supermarket, has become one of the largest of its kind in the nation, serving some forty-five thousand people every month.

But it was the crash of Detroit's auto industries during the late 1970s and 1980s, and specifically the closing of three large factories on the same block with Focus: HOPE's office, that inspired the group's most spectacular activities. Pulling together community support and creative financing, the organization bought the empty factory buildings and moved in, revitalizing them with actual, working industry that provides Detroit's people with advanced work training, good jobs, and as the name implies, hope. The project has grown to fill a three-block Industry Mall, in which one plant hires single mothers to rebuild General Motors auto transmissions, while another turned what was once a dead-end "work for welfare" program into a plant making diesel engine hoses and emission-control harnesses for automakers. In addition, Focus: HOPE's education program aims to convert Detroit's young people into a high-skill workforce, the 1990s equivalent of the once great labor force that made it the world's leader in the automobile industry but has now all but vanished.

In its twelve-year-old Machinist Training Institute, the modern equivalent of an apprenticeship program, former auto industry machinists share their craft with local young people. By 1992 the program had placed 684 graduates in precision machining and metalworking jobs at 125 Detroit plants.

Project Fast Track, acknowledging the unpleasant reality that many youngsters graduate from high school without a functional command of reading, writing, or mathematics, puts them back on track with a quick but intense computer-based remedial program that gets them ready to move into the Machinist Training Institute.

Finally, Focus: HOPE's new Center for Advanced Technologies, a larger counterpart to Huntington's Byrd Institute, has used a $40 million Defense Department grant to turn another huge old factory into a showplace training site. Graduates of the Machinist Training Institute will go on to a six-year course here, emerging as skilled technician-engineers competent to operate, maintain, repair, and modify the most modern automated manufacturing systems. No other institution in the country is now training workers at this level of expertise in the robotic manufacturing machinery that will be needed to revitalize U.S. industry in the competitive world economy of the coming decades.

## *A Man's Job?*

Women wearing jeans and hard hats, moving with calm confidence as they back roaring, lurching yellow bulldozers over an embankment and down into a highway construction cut? Hardly a traditional scene, but it's happening, and making a difference, in the isolated wooded valleys of northern West Virginia.

Women are coming off AFDC and elbowing their way back into the job market in Appalachia with the help of the Charleston-based nonprofit Center for Economic Options. The center's Nontraditional Jobs for Women Project gets attention because it breaks stereotypes by training women for highway construction jobs that Americans, particularly in conservative Appalachia, consider traditional for men. The twelve weeks of training cover not only basic engineering and math but actual experience driving earth-moving equipment. Meanwhile, the center doesn't just teach skills but sends out job development workers who aggressively negotiate with employers—some of them more than a little reluctant to hire women for "men's work"—to take on graduates and to establish pre-apprenticeship programs to move more women into the economic mainstream.

In addition to training women in nontraditional jobs and *getting* them jobs, this creative outfit does much more: It shows grassroots leaders in rural towns how to attract quality industry. It advises family farmers on moving into high-profit sustainable crops. And, in one particularly successful program, it has organized a knitwear cooperative, which is turning a traditional craft into a comfortable living for mountain women. Working at home, the co-op's thirty members created nine hundred sweaters in 1992 from wool provided by West Virginia sheep farmers, earning a total of more than $150,000. That's a significant chunk of change in West Virginia, which is statistically the nation's second most rural state, the only state that lies entirely in Appalachia, and consistently second to last of the fifty states in per capita income, employment, and many other elements of poverty. West Virginia has the lowest percentage of working-age women on the job of any state in the nation, with only 44 percent of its women between sixteen and sixty-five in the workforce in 1992, for example.

"Experts blamed the state's traditionally tight rural employment base for the apparent lack of opportunities for women," *Charleston Daily Mail* business editor Philip Nussel wrote then. The Center for Economic Options (which recently changed its name, and broadened its mission, from The Women and Employment Organization) has been doing something about that for more than a decade. Formed in 1980 in a public housing basement by women who were barred from construction jobs in the massive Charles Town Center mall, the grassroots organization filed a lawsuit against the city government. It quickly grew into an advocacy group offering information and referral and, before long, a smorgasbord of job training and economic development programs. Now located in a sprawling old painted brick house on the edge of downtown Charleston, the center operates on a lean $600,000 budget with a staff of ten full-time employees and nine part-time workers. A model of public/nonprofit partnership, it also mobilizes federal job training money, funding from the state Department of Health and Human Services, and foundation grants.

## *Getting People to Work*

For many of America's urban dwellers, getting back to work is as simple as getting a ride to work. That's the simple principle behind Chicago's Suburban Job-Link, which connects the residents of the poor inner-city neighborhoods with good employment opportunities in the suburbs. Unfortunately, this fundamental concept isn't always as simple as it seems. As the Chicago economist William Julius Wilson observed, the good, high-paying manufacturing jobs that lured a generation of African-American families from the South to northern cities in search of a better life have now largely fled to the suburbs, leaving behind a pool of poor, underemployed or unemployed people, largely blacks and Hispanics, who are willing to work but can't get to where the jobs are.

Suburban Job-Link seeks to change that—and has put together a track record over its two dozen years of operation—by helping residents of West Chicago's low-income neighborhoods find decent temporary jobs that may lead into full-time employment, and providing transportation to get them to work. In another of those remarkable up-by-the-bootstraps propositions that seems so simple but is all too rare, Suburban Job-Link makes enough money from its temporary employment program to finance almost all of its operations, including a fleet of nine express buses that whisk workers between the gritty North Lawndale neighborhood and their jobs around O'Hare International Airport around the clock.

Times have changed, founder and executive director John Plunkett says, since he and a group of friends emerged from the simmering political culture of the 1960s to start what they then called Just Jobs Inc. on the city's North Side in 1970. At the time, Chicago was known as "the city that works," and just about anyone willing to work could get a job, even if it meant long hours for low pay and being cheated out of overtime or worker's compensation benefits. Originally seeking to fight such abuses, Plunkett's group evolved as a nonprofit temporary job agency, operating in direct competition with profit-making job contractors who took advantage of their clients.

Over the years that followed, the economy changed and good jobs fled, creating a community of the 1990s in which Plunkett says many residents would be more than happy to have the kind of job that was considered exploitative two decades ago. So gradually, more by accident than by conscious plan, the temporary job agency added a van or two, then a school bus, and now runs nine sleek buses that shuttle some 450 riders a day from Lawndale to businesses around O'Hare and in the Morton Grove neighborhood north of the city at shift-change times: 7:00 A.M., 3:00 P.M., and 11:00 P.M., running even as late as 1:00 A.M. for the late shift at the Avon plant in Morton Grove, where a hardworking temporary can start at $5 an hour and soon move into a permanent job paying $10 or more. The ride costs $3.50 for a round trip that would require $12 or more for a complicated, lengthy series of bus and train rides, if it could be done at all. During its years of operation, Suburban Job-Link has found part-time work for more than twenty thousand Chicagoans, and it has converted those placements into full-time jobs for five thousand.

Industry went to the suburbs for many reasons, Plunkett says, and it isn't likely that it will ever come back to the inner city. "It isn't possible for us to go back to the fifties. We can't turn back the clock." But, he says, "We accept it as commonplace for suburbanites to commute in to the city for work. Why should we be surprised at the notion of city residents commuting the other way?"

## *Getting Back on the Ladder: Jobs for the Hard-Core Homeless*

Check out the stylish green awnings and then step down into the bright, modern coffee shop on the busy corner of Third and E in Washington's Judiciary Square district, just a few blocks from the

Capitol. Lawyers and lobbyists bustle past, and many of them slip in for an oversize cup of steaming coffee and a fresh muffin on their way to work. Green and white tile, shiny green tables, brass chairs, attractive framed art, and baskets of flowers make clear that this is no mere diner but a classy deli and coffee shop, where attentive workers in sharp green uniforms smile as they work in a shipshape kitchen behind glass windows in full view of the dining public.

The first restaurant in the neighborhood and still one of its most popular, Third & Eats is a standard, competitive restaurant in every way but one. Owned and operated by a nonprofit organization, Community Family Life Services, it exists primarily to provide real-world training for homeless people, offering them salable job skills in the food-service industry and a firm, respectable employment reference on their résumés.

"We pride ourselves on doing the weird and the unusual," executive director Tom Knoll once said, only half joking. Third & Eats is certainly evidence of that. Like Milwaukee's Esperanza Unida, it is one of the nation's few creative nonprofit organizations that operate real businesses in competitive situations as a way to move unemployed and homeless people into the labor market.

It's hardly a moneymaker, Knoll acknowledges. By traditional business standards, the restaurant expected to "lose" some $80,000 in 1994. Unable to persuade traditional banks to underwrite such a risky venture, the organization turned to the Lutheran Church–Missouri Synod's Church Extension Fund, normally reserved for church sanctuaries and schools, to provide its $400,000 startup costs. But restaurant revenues of $240,000 in sales do offset three-fourths of its $320,000 in expenses, and the "loss" actually means that more individuals were trained in its sixteen-week program and moved on into good jobs in the food-service industry. During the restaurant's first two and a half years, it placed 95 percent of its thirty-five graduates in jobs. "We take extreme risks here," Knoll says. "We're a faith-based organization, and our faith leads us to take greater risks than we might otherwise."

---

Chrysalis, an exceptional program on Skid Row in Los Angeles, succeeds at a challenge where many have failed: It finds jobs for long-unemployed men at risk of homelessness, primarily occupants of single-room occupancy hotels.

To be eligible for the program, men must be free of drugs and alcohol—a process that Chrysalis will assist through counseling and referral—and established in permanent housing. Participants begin with a short Job Search Prep Class in job hunting and self-improvement. When they've finished that, they get support and one-on-one help from Chrysalis as they set about the almost forgotten routine of hunting for a job.

Things that most of us might take for granted aren't so easy for men who've been down and out. Workers stand by to help them re-evaluate their skills and construct résumés that put the best face on a checkered curriculum and maximize the significance of scattered jobs and past experiences. Staff members assist with job seeking, using such obvious strategies as want ads and bulletin-board postings, along with cold calls to businesses listed in the Yellow Pages. They also contact regional employers regularly to ask about job openings and to make sure that Chrysalis participants get a fair chance at them.

Typewriters, computers, stamps and stationery, a telephone number, and mailing address: These everyday necessities of job hunting that loom large only when they're unavailable are all provided. Chrysalis also supplies clean clothes, bus fare, even a bag lunch on that all-important day of the job interview.

The support system works. In 1992, Chrysalis listed more than fourteen hundred men who used its support system to move into jobs. And Chrysalis stays in touch, tracking the progress of its clients for up to a year after they go on the job, ready to help with just about any problem that comes up.

In addition to its permanent employment program, Chrysalis also operates the Labor Exchange, a temporary employment agency offering homeless people the chance to earn money and gain work experience at short-term jobs. Designed for people who may not be ready for full-time jobs, the Labor Exchange offers some income while giving them a nonthreatening way to ease back into the world of work. This program generated an estimated thirteen thousand hours of paid work for Skid Row residents last year.

---

Along with its feeding and family services described in Chapter 5, Dallas's Trinity Ministry to the Poor brings an unusual approach to boost formerly homeless people back into the workplace. Its Client

Worker Training Program resembles a sheltered workshop for mentally retarded workers, but it serves a different purpose for these out-of-work adults. The program arranges contracts with local businesses that need simple, repetitive jobs done, such as assembling products and simple packaging. Individuals who report for job counseling are asked to work for two weeks in the hand assembly area, a large room where they sit around a long table working at such chores as putting Christmas trinkets into packages for a charitable mailing or organizing American Airlines tickets, itineraries, and paperwork into the appropriate order and stapling them into packets. Counselors observe how well individuals fit into a work setting, read and follow instructions, deal with authority, dress appropriately for work, and so forth.

"We've had a lot of people who are highly motivated but can't keep jobs," said volunteer coordinator Margie Smith. "We've had clients who were in as many as thirty jobs in a year. The hand assembly area allows us to find out in a real-world setting what their problem is. Do they get drunk? Authority problems? Do they lack self-esteem or discipline? The issue is not just to give them a résumé and send them to an interview but to help them keep a job. We find out what's sabotaging them, and then we deal with it."

As with Chrysalis, once a participant is ready to go out for job interviews, counselors work with him closely on interview skills, provide a decent set of clothes, and make sure the applicant gets to the interview on time and ready, willing, and able to make a good impression. Again, even after the program graduate has moved on to a full-time job, a case worker follows through for six months to deal with any unexpected problems.

## *Training Inmates and Ex-Offenders*

With her youthful smile, her trim blond hair in a neat ponytail, and the sweater thrown casually over her shoulder, Alice could almost pass for a Junior Leaguer—except for the delicate gold ring in her left nostril. But Alice got her education in a tougher school than one of the Seven Sisters. Just out of the San Francisco County Jail after serving a seven-month stretch for robbery, she has a minimum-wage job and is trying to go straight.

She and her co-worker Anthony, a slight young man with a twinkling smile who's done prison time for strong-arm robberies and a bank job, say they'll do almost anything to keep from going back to prison again.

"Nobody wants to go back to jail," Anthony says. "I'm off parole now, and this time I want to do good." Alice admits she stole to impress her boyfriend, a career criminal. "I was crazy. It just didn't make any sense."

They think they've found the answer in San Francisco's innovative Garden Project. The project, a half-acre garden on a long, narrow patch between a grocery store and a commercial bakery in a gritty neighborhood on the city's South Side, works like this: About twenty ex-offenders get a chance to reenter the world of work—earn a few bucks, get lunch, and make some friends—in a supportive setting that makes it easy for them to put their lives back together.

It's five hours a day of basic gardening, hands in the good earth and back warmed in the fresh sunlight, but it's not mere make-work: The produce is sold to some of the Bay Area's fanciest culinary outfits, including the Tassajara Bakery and the well-known restaurant Chez Panisse. A similar project, for prisoners in the county's San Mateo Jail, provides fresh produce for four large San Francisco soup kitchens and food pantries.

All that's required is a commitment to show up on time, get the work done, and make an effort to work on personal problems, says project director Cathrine Sneed, a former social worker who got the idea for the program while hospitalized with a life-threatening disease. As she told Anthony on his first day at work: "If you make a commitment to us, we'll make a commitment to you."

"Students" work four five-hour days a week, Alice said, earning only minimum wage; but through a negotiated agreement with the General Assistance Office, that income only nominally reduces their welfare grant. More important, she said, it restores a sense of the worth of work, and quite frankly, "It gives me something better to put on my résumé than twelve years as a stripper and seven months in jail."

The program grew out of a dream and a nightmare, said Sneed. In the early 1980s, when she was a counselor at the county jail, she was frustrated to see so many people returning on new charges only months after getting out. Given a copy of Steinbeck's *The Grapes of Wrath* while she was very ill, she was inspired by its characters' hope for a new life on the land. She later asked County Sheriff Mike Hennessey to let her and several prisoners restore the jail's long-abandoned farm as a work project. He agreed, and before long the prisoners were not only improving their attitudes through productive labor but also generating enough produce to supply several soup kitchens. That program, which continues under the direction of Arlene Hamilton, now provides 120 tons of produce a year, enough to fully stock four area soup kitchens.

But Sneed still wasn't satisfied: When prisoners got out of jail, they had to leave the garden behind. So, in 1990, in a remarkable partnership among the sheriff's office, the management of the Just Desserts bakery, and the somewhat grudging agreement of Southern Pacific, which actually owned the garden-to-be, Sneed and a group of volunteers cleared the weeds and garbage that had fouled the vacant lot and turned it into the Carroll Street Garden, lush with flowers, vegetables, and herbs.

In contrast with the charitable benificiaries of the horticulture program at the jail, the Carroll Street Garden has potential to become a self-supporting business. It already earns about $100 a week from sales of fruits and herbs to Just Desserts, San Francisco's largest bakery, and Chez Panisse. Better still, a number of program graduates have gone on to higher-paying jobs, mostly at the bakery and in the Tree Project, still another spinoff, in which men and women from the Garden Project are hired by the city at $8 an hour to plant trees in public places.

"This is miracle work," Sneed said, watching Anthony quietly watering plants. "They've done incredibly hurtful things to others, and themselves. This gives them a chance to do good things—and they do respond."

---

She didn't realize it at the time, but an odd incident more than a decade ago would lead Barbara Gifford into her life's work and inspire her to create Prison Ministries with Women, an unusual and effective program based in Atlanta that gives women ex-convicts the tools they need to stay straight.

Working as a resident volunteer at the Open Door Community Shelter, a nonprofit organization that offered a prison ministry, Gifford was asked to take charge of a monthly caravan that provided transportation and support to families visiting relatives who were inmates at the Hardwick Women's Prison near Milledgeville, Georgia. At about the same time, a woman named Emma, who'd been sentenced to life in prison at age sixteen for a murder she didn't commit, wrote a lawyer in South Carolina, asking for help getting out of prison. The lawyer passed the letter on to an Atlanta lawyer, who in turn routed it to the shelter, where officials asked Gifford if she'd like to correspond with the woman.

On Gifford's first trip to Hardwick, she met Emma—a confrontation that she now admits made her incredibly nervous. "I didn't know what we'd talk about," she recalled. "I was unnerved that I might have to stay in the meeting room for two hours with someone I didn't know and wouldn't know what to say to."

But the women hit it off instantly. Gifford quickly learned her new friend's story—how as a fifteen-year-old she had witnessed the man she called her common-law husband kill another man, then helped dispose of the body in a wood and fled with him to Florida. Later she was advised to skip a jury trial and plead guilty, with the understanding that she would be given probation. Instead, she was tried as an adult and sentenced to life imprisonment.

"We talked and talked," Gifford recalled. "I was so surprised when they told me it was time to go. We were two people becoming friends. It was extraordinary—mind-boggling. I don't remember to this day how I got from the prison gate to the van, it was just a religious experience. I *knew* God had called me to work with women in prison. That was it, and I never lost it."

Gifford started looking for ways to carry out this new commitment. She started a support group for women at Hardwick, billing it as a "prayer meeting" to satisfy suspicious prison authorities, making a four-hour round trip every Friday night for a year and a half in borrowed cars to talk with up to twenty women about everything from the Bible to their hopes and dreams.

Working with lawyers, legislators and a lot of supporters, they finally got Emma out of jail. During that period, Gifford became painfully aware how many women, once released, quickly returned under new sentences, having failed to make the transition back to life on the outside. "Why? They couldn't get jobs, they couldn't pay the rent, so they went back on the street and started all over again," she said. "It was a vicious circle. There was absolutely no support for women who got out of prison."

First, she started looking for money to open a house for women just out of prison, and got it, a couple of years later, from the

Presbyterian Women of the Church, who provided a $95,000 grant, sufficient to buy and renovate a five-bedroom house in southwest Atlanta. The center opened in 1989 as the Elizabeth Fry House, named for the nineteenth-century English Quaker woman who was one of the first prison reformers. Incorporating as a nonprofit, Prison Ministries with Women added other support services, ranging from a clothes closet and source of basic household goods and furniture to counseling, information, and referral for women just out of prison. In 1991 the group opened a second house, a duplex in southeast Atlanta, purchased from a bank for $500 and renamed the Sojourner Truth House. Residents in both houses, primarily recruited from the state's transitional work-release programs for women inmates, pay modest rent ($175 a month) and share the costs of utilities, making the houses financially self-supporting.

In addition to providing a safe, affordable living environment and essential support services for newly released female ex-offenders, Prison Ministries soon realized something more was needed: A training program leading toward good, skilled jobs. Staff efforts to work with the Private Industry Council, a national public-private partnership, and similar groups proved frustrating, because the council, restricted by tough government performance quotas, was reluctant to place ex-convicts or women with limited skills. So, pulling together volunteers and donations, the group rounded up eight computers, printers, and software for just $3,600 and started teaching computer skills. The course quickly evolved into a series of three-month modules involving three-hour classes three days a week. Women start by learning basic typing and computer literacy, then go on to advanced training in computer software like WordPerfect and Lotus 1-2-3 that are in considerable demand by area employers. A new job readiness course works to build job-seeking and interview skills and self-esteem, all elements that seem to be as critical as the computer training itself in getting women into full-time jobs.

In 1993, they set off on a course even more bold. Project Venture Forth, a new profit-making corporation, incorporates ten women who've been through the computer training course as equal shareholders in an independent computer services company. They'll market computer services such as accounting, bookkeeping, and word-processing, seeking an unfilled niche by providing those services evenings and weekends when most competitors are closed. The company leased computers and office space from Prison Ministries at first, but by plowing all profits back into the corporation, they hoped to grow quickly and provide many more jobs for more women.

---

Sheriff Joe Price of Harrison County, Mississippi, is a progressive example of the New South lawman, who recognizes that the stereotype of the dumb, bigoted southern cop was too close to reality for comfort, and who wants to replace the old ways with intelligent professionalism. In a series of farsighted programs that he and his predecessor, Larkin Smith, started years ago when he was Smith's assistant, Price is fighting crime and poverty from the criminal justice side by bringing quality vocational training and education to inmates in the county jail. "Inmates who spend their term in jail lying around learn to lie around," Price says. "Inmates who spend their time working at something useful learn to work at something useful." More important, if that work provides employable skills, they may just be able to turn them to honest use when they get out of jail.

It all started in 1984, when Smith ran for office on a pragmatic platform: He would cut the costs of running the jail by opening a prison farm, where inmate volunteers would work the fields and raise part of the produce needed to feed them. The farm paid off, and the inmates who worked there considered it a privilege and behaved well in order not to lose it. The idea was so good that it soon spawned similar projects. The local city and county governments now have all their vehicle repairs done at the jail's Training Center, a minimum-security residential area and multi-purpose workshop for seventy to eighty prisoners in training programs, mirroring Esperanza Unida in the way that inmates work alongside skilled mechanics to learn the fine art of auto repair. Similar programs are now available to teach inmates carpentry, building trades, welding, auto body work, and auto parts repair. A food preparation program gives inmates experience in catering as inmates prepare banquets for local churches, schools, and nonprofit groups. In a partnership with the local Gulf Coast Community College, the sheriff and the college pay the salaries of instructors who provide General Equivalency Diploma training to inmates. They use a forty-foot recreational van—seized in a drug arrest—as a mobile classroom to take GED classes to jails throughout the region.

No bleeding-heart liberal, Price has no illusions about prisoners, and he doesn't believe education programs can turn all their lives around. But he takes considerable pride in one statistic: Although 75 percent of inmates in regional jails eventually return on new charges, not a single one of his GED graduates has done so. Price, whose gray hair and lined face belie a youthful spirit, thinks there's a lesson in that: "The good ones, the ones who are willing to work—if we can just do the things to build their self-confidence and their self-esteem, we can make a difference."

This simple philosophy expresses one of the most basic premises of effective grassroots activism: You can't change people's lives on an assembly line. It's harder work to deal with individuals one-on-one, but identifying each individual's strengths and building on them is the only sure way to give people the tools they need to get themselves back into the mainstream.

# 8

# PEOPLE NEED WORK

GETTING PEOPLE READY FOR WORK, GIVING them the training they need, getting them jobs. All these tactics chip away at the wall of poverty. But it's hard to fight the frustration that comes when the jobs simply aren't there. Mills in New England closed and moved to North Carolina in the 1960s and '70s, and twenty years later those mills are closing and moving to Mexico. Entire industries shut down or through automation change beyond all recognition, and low-paying service jobs replace skilled trades, dispensing rough injustice to working people who assumed that some kind of "deal" would protect them and their lifestyle into retirement. The vagaries of a shifting economy sometimes seem far beyond the power of mere individuals and grassroots organizations to change. But the secret here, too, lies in the combination of creative thinking and hard work, tied with the reality that individual steps may be very small, but that enough small steps can add up to a substantial trip.

One powerful key to economic development on the small-scale, community level lies in nurturing the natural spirit of entrepreneurship in those who have it. Some of the most exciting initiatives in this area, ranging from community development banks to peer lending programs and entrepreneurial training, are paying off in new small businesses that are making a living for their operators and even creating new jobs when small new businesses thrive and grow big enough to start hiring employees of their own.

New businesses like, for instance, the one Cliff Williams runs. He loves country music, and he loves opera, and he used to think he might go to Nashville to find a career as a singer. But real life took a different turn, and Williams stayed home on the dry plains of Sweetwater, Texas, where it looked for a while as if he'd be stuck in a minimum-wage job bagging groceries at the Piggly-Wiggly store. But with an ambitious spirit that works twenty-four hours a day, and a boost from the folks at the West Texas Innovation Center, this round-faced, energetic Texan owns his own business and is well on his way to becoming a hot-sauce magnate.

Williams Food Manufacturing Company and its sole product, Mustang Picante Sauce, got started almost on a whim. Williams, like many of his neighbors, loves hot sauce on almost everything he eats. During his grocery-bagging days, money was so tight that he started making his own sauce from an old family recipe, staying up late and boiling down tomatoes, onions, and peppers just to save a few bucks. His family and friends liked Cliff's salsa so much that he started selling it on the side. He and his wife, Doris, rounded up a case of recycled mayonnaise jars, filled eighty of them with his finest, and sold them all in a few hours at a flea market.

"We turned fourteen dollars into six hundred dollars in a day," he recalled with a big smile. "You can't beat that." But converting a weekend gig at a flea market into a full-time business was a major challenge even for a hardworking young man like Williams. He works from eleven at night until five in the morning daily making his sauce, then catches a bare three hours' sleep before rising to hit the road to sell the product to supermarkets and restaurants throughout the region. He placed his product in forty-eight outlets during his first year of business in 1992, including one as far away as Las Vegas, and he says he's making a living.

What helped Williams turn a bright idea into a going concern was the West Texas Innovation Center, a nonprofit small-business "incubator" run by a small staff on a small grant in the shell of an old bowling alley on Sweetwater's dusty south side. There, director Gary Spaulding, a business education teacher with a background in international development, and training director Javier Franco, who brings his own experience in his family's store to bear, pass along their knowledge and technical support to dozens of would-be entrepreneurs in a community left devastated by the collapse of the oil economy during the 1980s.

The incubator, a spinoff of Sweetwater's People for Progress Inc., itself a model multipurpose organization providing a range of poverty-related programs, was started in 1988 with grants from the Texas Department of Agriculture as an effort to help rural agriculture diversify and expand. It supports emerging businesses like Williams Food Manufacturing with office space, technical assistance, and counseling, and a wealth of support services that would otherwise chip away at the tiny profits of a very new, very small business: reception and secretarial help, typewriters and computers, desktop publishing, even video editing and production and advertising time on the center's own cable television channel. Fees are nominal, based on a sliding scale depending on the business operator's financial ability, and the service may range from simple advice over the telephone to the full-scale incubator treatment, complete with office space. Williams, for example, is billed $75 a month for his spick-and-span kitchen and canning "factory" located in a small, windowless room in the former bowling alley.

It isn't easy to start up and spin off a profitable small business, and the numbers are still small. But the face of west Texas is beginning to change, at least a little, with businesses that the Sweetwater incubator has set sail: a small-game farm; an ostrich ranch; a fish farm; a business for an artist who makes wooden toys; and Williams's salsa factory. "It's hard work," he admitted. "But I have my own business, with my name on every jar. I can't believe I'm doing this—and I love it."

## *Community Development Banking*

The West Texas Innovation Center makes it possible for small entrepreneurs to get a start with little cash or credit, but in a market economy, money talks. Another approach to beating poverty by building business involves finding new ways to help people with little or nothing put together a stake.

Two events in 1985 fell into place to create a rare opportunity for that to happen in rural Arkansas, says George Sturgeon, president of the Southern Development BankCorporation, an unusual bank in Arkadelphia, a small town nestled in the pine groves where southern Arkansas's delta region rises into the Ozark foothills. First, Tom McRae, then president of the Little Rock–based Winthrop Rockefeller Foundation, who was worried about the inability of the state's lending institutions to finance small and medium-size businesses, read a report about Chicago's South Shore Bank, a community bank with the mission of rebuilding neighborhoods through creative financing for housing construction and mortgage loans. Then, a college friend of Hillary Rodham Clinton, who wasn't yet a household name and whose husband, Bill, was still the governor of Arkansas, came back from a trip to Bangladesh raving about an unusual concept called the Grameen Bank, in which groups of women band together to share small amounts of loan money and peer support to start their own businesses.

With lucky timing, a bright new dream reached critical mass. With the backing of the governor's office and support from WinRock and other regional foundations, the Southern Development BankCorporation was born. A full-scale bank holding company, its mission is rural economic development. It exists solely to finance and nurture businesses that may create jobs in the poorest parts of a very poor state. While it is expected to be self-supporting, its reason for being is not to pile up profits for stockholders but to keep money in motion to help individuals start businesses to boost the economy and create jobs.

In 1988 the organization purchased outright the Elk Horn Bank and Trust Company of Arkadelphia, a commercial bank that, like its new parent, operates legally as a full-service bank under federal regulations but applies a management philosophy very different from that of private banks. Its primary purpose is to make "development loans," that is, commercial loans that contribute to the development of the local economy—loans that other financial institutions would be unlikely to grant on similar terms in the normal course of business. As of 1991, the Elk Horn Bank was processing more than $2 million such loans. It also aggressively reaches out to family farmers, originating another $2 million in agricultural loans in an average year, offering the region's only alternative to federal farm financing. Southern Development BankCorporation also owns a real estate development subsidiary, Opportunity Lands Corporation, a for-profit operation that has developed two commercial centers providing office space and support services for small businesses and financing low- and medium-income housing developments.

Among the bank's array of nonprofit organizations, the Arkansas Enterprise Group runs a variety of services to support Arkansas entrepreneurs. Its Southern Ventures Inc., for instance, is a venture capital fund writing small-business loans too small and risky to interest commercial banks, hoping to encourage the development of small technology firms that pay high wages. It currently has nearly $2 million invested in ten companies whose products and services include bioassay radiochemistry testing, ceramic coating, and wastewater treatment. The group also operates AEG Manufacturing Services, a small-business incubator much like the West

Texas Innovation Center that offers free technical assistance to new businesses in the areas of marketing, management, and financial operations.

## *Grameen Banks*

The Arkansas Enterprise Group also oversees the Good Faith Fund in Pine Bluff, Arkansas, one of the nation's most successful small-business loan operations based on the Grameen Bank model. It's a little startling to realize that, here and there across America, individuals are forming grassroots groups to help each other start small businesses using an economic development model pioneered by women in rural Bangladesh. But this model, named after the original version in Asia, is getting a lot of attention because it works, and it works on a principle that seems too simple to be true. As it plays out in Pine Bluff, a desperately poor delta town with a black majority and very little money, four to six unrelated individuals get together under the Good Faith Fund's tutelage to form teams (known in Grameen jargon as "circles"). Each circle works as a unit, first receiving training in small-business operation, management, and finance, developing individual plans for the small businesses that they'd like to start. Then, acting as an initial loan committee for each other's plans, they take turns using a small loan as seed money to start their businesses. Each individual may borrow no more than $1,200 for the first loan, and only one loan may be out at a time. (Successful businesses may later come back for larger loans up to an ultimate limit of $5,000.) Circle members must decide which member deserves the first loan, based on a hard-nosed analysis of each member's business plan and chances of success. That member must begin repaying the loan before any other member is eligible to get one, which places not only a strong moral commitment on repayment but heavy peer pressure as well. This principle inspires a strong sense of responsibility and tends to rule out frivolous loans and unrealistic business plans.

As of 1992, the Good Faith Fund had made sixty-four loans totaling more than $140,000, drawing from a $500,000 portfolio supplied initially by WinRock, the C. S. Mott Foundation, and others. Loan repayment schedules range from as little as $13 biweekly on a $300 loan for a year to a maximum of $140 biweekly on a $5,000 loan for eighteen months. At those rates, even a very tiny business has a prayer.

Almost four out of five of the fund's participants were minorities and two-thirds were women. About a fifth of recipients remained on public assistance, but that number was dropping fast as a significant proportion of the businesses, in the early going, appeared to be successful. The businesses, many of them home-based and not all yet large enough to support a family, include automotive services, beauty shops, business services, crafts and gifts, day care, food services, repairs, and retail and specialty businesses. One man satisfied his lifelong dream of opening a barbecue and chitlins restaurant. Maxine Williams, who turned a flair for baking into the Sweet Tooth snack shop in Pine Bluff, told fund organizers, "My customers are very happy about my business here, because my snacks and candy are cheaper than any EZ mart around here." Her business is thriving, and Williams isn't on AFDC any more.

---

Another version of the Grameen concept pops up in the arid rolling hills of South Dakota's Pine Ridge Reservation. Here in a little geodesic dome in the village of Kyle, the Lakota Fund is distributing small loans and considerable hope. Its brochure tells the story: "You spend hours working on a beautiful star quilt. There's bills to pay, food to buy, places where you have to go. It's difficult if not impossible for you to get to town, much less to find a buyer for your work. So you trade it, pawn it or give it away. All that work, all that skill, all for nothing. This is a familiar scenario for a great many reservation artists who too often can't sell a piece for a decent price to even allow them enough to buy basic supplies to produce more work. Gaining marketing skills is just one benefit of becoming a member of a Circle Banking Project. You'll learn how to set fair prices and discover new markets and how to better utilize existing markets."

This is the genius of the Lakota Fund, one of the most effective fully operational Grameen Bank set-ups I've found. It may be more than just coincidental that, when Lakota Fund officials Gerald Sherman and Faith Stone decided in 1989 to consider replicating a Grameen Bank, they didn't stop halfway. "They didn't go to a model," said Dani Not Help Him, the Fund's native Sioux loan officer. "They went to the real one . . . in Bangladesh."

The idea of fostering small-business development had been around the Pine Ridge Reservation for a while. With hundreds of

Lakota capable of producing high-quality arts and handicrafts, an effort to turn traditional skills into ways of making a living was a natural. With the help of the First Nations Development Institute of Falmouth, Virginia, a small-business loan fund was operating by 1987, financed by foundation grants. But it wasn't working well; rates of delinquency and business failure were extremely high. Something was missing, and the Grameen concept of peer support and training seemed like the solution. When Sherman and Stone returned home, they quickly persuaded the fund's board and community leaders that it would work. With enthusiastic efforts from all participants, they converted the traditional loan operation into a Grameen-style bank and got the first Circles recruited and operating quickly.

Unlike the all-women Bangladesh original, the Lakota Fund's circles may include men and women and are made up of four to six members, who live in the same community but are not close relatives. Circle members receive a five-week orientation course covering both small-business topics (budgeting, marketing, costs) and social development (goal setting, planning, and the dangers of drug use and alcoholism). After circle members are certified, they decide among themselves which member should receive the first loan. The selected member submits a business plan for approval and then may borrow up to $400 in the first year, $800 in the second, and $1,000 in the third. Each successive member may get a loan after the previous borrower has made three payments. Circle members are also required to put $5 every two weeks into personal savings to build a nest egg for emergencies, and each loan recipient also receives (and must repay) $20 more than the requested loan amount, which is contributed to an Inner Circle Fund for the circle's discretionary use.

While Lakota Fund staff must approve the loan decisions, it rarely second-guesses them. Loans are repaid over twelve months at 15 percent interest, amortized daily, which works out to a payment of $17.44 every two weeks for the initial $400 loan. As anticipated, many of the small-loan recipients are artisans and craftspeople, but loans have also gone to a pig farmer, a caterer, the owner of a tire repair shop, and a member of a band.

The Lakota Fund's original small-business loan fund remained in business, too. But with the circles now operational as an entry-level option, and with the addition of training for potential borrowers, the fund has dramatically reduced its delinquency rates. To qualify for a larger loan, an individual must now either provide detailed financial books demonstrating two years of business activity or complete a six-week training course covering small-business essentials such as financial management, cash flow, budgeting, tax and license information, marketing, and basic bookkeeping. Loans from this program may be as large as $25,000, with interest ranging from 15 percent for smaller loans (under $1,000) to 11 percent for larger ones, payable over up to five years but refinanceable. Recipients have opened hair salons, electrical and gravel-hauling contracting businesses, video rental shops, an arts and crafts retail store, a restaurant, and a buffalo farm.

Overall, nine circles were operating in 1993, involving about forty small businesses, and sixty more entrepreneurs had small-business loans, for a total of about $180,000 out in loans of all types. In a community with poverty and unemployment at the level of Pine Ridge, one hundred working entrepreneurs is no small number, and the delinquency rate, seasonally ranging from 4 to 16 percent, is under control.

---

We've already been introduced to the Center for Rural Affairs in Walthill, Nebraska, an exceptional organizing program that's rebuilding optimism for family farmers on the prairie. This creative outfit runs a Grameen-type bank, too, the Rural Enterprise Assistance Project, known as REAP. In contrast with similar efforts in communities like the Arkansas delta country or the Pine Ridge Reservation, REAP is growing in a region where private enterprise and self-employment are not new ideas. Its goal is frankly not so much to raise people up from poverty but simply to keep them from falling into poverty, perhaps a marginally less fearful challenge, says Gene Severens, director of the program.

No buzzword artists here, REAP's midwestern participants don't call their peer groups "circles" but "small-business associations." In a particular stroke of genius, REAP adds a Main Street twist to the Bangladesh model: Each association must raise part of its loan fund from within its own community. For every dollar that the borrowers can raise from local businesses, banks, and institutions, the Center for Rural Affairs will come up with $3 from an endowment funded by the Ford Foundation, the C. S. Mott Foundation, and the Small

Business Administration. This requirement binds the association to its community and gives the community a stake in its success.

Also in contrast with the strict Grameen tradition, which holds membership in a circle to a small core of committed members, REAP solicits a larger group—up to fifteen members—and encourages each association to consider taking in new members. It skips as well the procedure of limiting loans to one member at a time, allowing as many members to take loans as need them.

In 1991, its first year, REAP assembled seven small-business associations totaling seventy-five members in twenty communities in eastern Nebraska. It made nineteen loans, totaling $23,000, to businesses ranging from a crafts shop to a lawn mowing service.

## *Training Entrepreneurs*

Sometimes a budding entrepreneur doesn't need money as much as knowledge: the know-how that's needed to turn a bright dream into the reality of self-employment in one's own small business. In Reno, the Nevada Self-Employment Trust, originally intended as a training program and loan fund for women who wanted to start their own businesses, found such a demand for training that its staff never found the time to get a Grameen-type fund up and running.

But the training quickly yielded a dozen success stories and more than a hundred people, mostly but not entirely women, who have completed its sixteen-week course of three-hour weekly sessions. The program started very simply, when its director, Janice Barbour, came to Reno with her husband in 1992 and joined the Nevada Women's Fund as an intern while working on her master's thesis on micro-enterprise development. Putting her studies into practice, Barbour formed an advisory committee of local social service providers. She examined model programs around the country and set up a training program, using $15,000 in grants from the Nevada Women's Fund and the Conrad Hilton Foundation.

Advertised only by word of mouth, the program addressed an obvious need: More than fifty people showed up for an orientation session, filling one class to its thirty-member capacity with a group on the waiting list standing by impatiently until another class could be scheduled. The course, taught at the Reno YWCA in Saturday day sessions or Tuesday evening classes, covers both business and personal development, with each student required to prepare a serious business plan. Students pay a nominal fee based on their income.

As with all entrepreneurial programs, progress is measured in small doses. Seven businesses started from the first two courses, Barbour said, including an older woman who "inherited" her son's quick-print shop, a learning-disabled woman who's now operating her own catering business specializing in low-fat and low-salt dishes, and a former welfare mother who went back to college, finished her degree in wetlands biology, and has established a three-woman cooperative providing environmental impact statements for government contractors. "No one's making $100,000 yet," she said. "But they're getting out there."

---

Turn to the other side of the country, find a similar story. Too many job-training programs overlook a simple reality, says Julie Reeder, community organizer with the Women Entrepreneurs of Baltimore (WEB): It makes no sense to train people for jobs if no jobs are available. WEB shows Baltimore women how to create jobs by training them as entrepreneurs, then backing them up with loan money and a focused array of support programs. This innovative approach links separate but important approaches that spell success: a comprehensive business skills training class; access to a loan fund to finance new businesses; resource sharing, mentoring, and volunteer business consultating from local experts; and community organizing to promote and support WEB businesses. This young program, founded in 1993, is already establishing a remarkable track record. More than 70 percent of its early graduates are currently operating their own businesses, which range from a merchant-police group and a masseuse to a pedicab business that takes customers around Baltimore's booming Inner Harbor area.

---

Bonnie Wright and Martin Eakes, who founded Durham, North Carolina's Center for Community Self-Help in 1980, started working in the fight against poverty by offering advice out of the back of a Volkswagen to worker-owned businesses. During a period when

North Carolina's textile mills were closing and abandoning their communities, Wright and Eakes tried to save workers' jobs by organizing worker cooperatives to take over the assets of the mills and operate them. It was a rocky road, sad to say, and their effort lasted only a short time. They concluded that it was almost impossible to turn people into leaders overnight when the workers had never been given any training or the opportunity to lead. And, more practically, they didn't have any money.

So, backing up, Wright and Eakes decided that the best way to follow up on the civil rights gains of the 1960s in the South was to build people up from poverty. Their plan: create and strengthen community credit unions in poor areas. This would make credit available to people who couldn't get it from traditional banks, it would encourage people to save money for housing, and most important, it would give them a stake to start their own small businesses.

Local credit unions have traditionally provided access to credit in poor black rural communities. Some black communities, particularly in agricultural areas in the northeastern section of North Carolina, have had tiny, minority-owned credit unions for fifty to sixty years. In addition to opening its own substantial community credit union in Durham, the Center for Community Self-Help also supports these rural credit unions in a partnership arrangement under which the small credit unions locate and screen prospective borrowers, whose loans are then financed by the center in Durham.

In addition to the credit union, which now holds about $24 million in deposits with $9 million in outstanding loans, the center's Self-Help Venture Fund, with $3 million available for loans and another $4 million in reserves, makes small venture capital loans to low-income people starting businesses, in a setting less strictly regulated than in traditional credit unions.

The center's North Carolina HOME Ownership Program, financed by a $2 million state grant in 1990, seeks private money to match state funds to create a revolving loan fund for small businesses and mortgage loans to low-income families. In its first year the program made forty-five home and thirty-eight business loans to borrowers, who said the money would create 850 jobs. Success stories included a community-owned grocery store in the town of Piedmont, a cucumber-buying station in Halifax County, a small child care business in Asheville, and a fifteen-unit apartment complex for low-income people in Goldsboro.

## *Community Development Corporations*

Grameen banks and entrepreneurial training efforts work well in local settings, but like all community economic development initiatives, the impact of a single group is necessarily small, and their value is limited to the relatively few individuals equipped by personality and talent to run small businesses. Another, broader approach, the community development corporation, is a nonprofit organization with the mission of locating and acquiring economic development money from government and private sources and using it to encourage small-business development in poor communities.

The Community Enterprise Development Corporation of Alaska in Anchorage, one of the few surviving community development corporations with its roots in President Johnson's War on Poverty, remains essentially true to its original mission set in 1968: It maximizes the impact of federal economic development money by investing it to make more money and placing it where it will do the most good. A membership organization formed by the twelve regional corporations established in Alaska by the Native Land Claim Settlement of 1971 as well as smaller village corporations, cooperatives, and tribal councils, the corporation focuses on rural and primarily Native Alaska, using federal money to help the state's rural residents move from subsistence lifestyles dependent on hunting and fishing into a cash economy.

That's not always easy, program Director Ann Campbell says. The state's three hundred villages exist in an isolation that makes even the poorest American Indian reservations in the Lower Forty-eight seem relatively prosperous. The typical bush village has about three hundred residents and no road system connecting it with its neighbors—only light-aircraft flights. The village economy supports no more than a dozen salaried jobs, typically an airline agent, a postal worker, a teacher's aide, a health aide, perhaps a city employee, and one or two employees in the village store. Everyone else depends on hunting or fishing, primarily for the family's own subsistence, or on welfare.

The corporation seeks to boost business development in the bush country through two direct approaches: technical assistance and direct lending. The direct lending programs, which generally have a loan portfolio averaging $10 million a year, leverage government money at low interest rates for businesses ranging from tiny to moderately small. For the smallest, the Micro Loan Fund, using Small Business Administration money, lends an average of $7,500 or less from a revolving loan pool of $230,000 for urban and rural business startups that can't get traditional bank loans. The Rural Development Loan Fund, originally financed by Health and Human Services funds and now by the Farmers Home Administration, provides loans up to $150,000 to businesses that will create new jobs through startup or expansion. It has generated nearly $4 million in financing to businesses such as air-taxi operations, rural general stores, sports lodges, and travel agencies. Finally, the Economic Development Administration Revolving Fisheries Loan Fund targets native commercial fishing in western Alaska. It was inspired by the growth of the herring fishing industry, which was luring commerce from all over the northern Pacific, while local fishermen were shut out because rural banks wouldn't make loans for boats and motors. Since 1983, this fund has processed 231 loans totaling over $2.5 million.

The corporation's Small Business Administration Technical Assistance Program, offers basic "hand-holding" for new entrepreneurs who come to the organization for small loans with big dreams but less than comprehensive business plans. A separately funded program, the Minority Business Development Center, gives business assistance to startup and expanding businesses run by Native Alaskans and other minorities.

A major program, Alaska Native Tours, offers technical advice to bush villages that want to encourage tourism while controlling its impact. The project's staff works with major tour companies, including Princess and Holland America cruises (which are responsible for more than 60 percent of Alaska's annual tourist traffic), to help village leaders establish activities to attract tourists. In the village of Gambell on St. Lawrence Island, an isolated islet near the international date line and just forty miles from Siberia, residents provide daylong "slice of life" tours in which visitors observe daily activities in an Arctic whaling town, including drumming, singing, and whaleboat demonstrations. Tourists pay $400 for the tour, including airfare from Nome. Native Tours handles all reservations, billing, and paperwork, and the village gets the proceeds.

Finally, the Howard Rock Foundation sponsors a college

scholarship program for Native Alaskan youth and the Bush Development Fund, a small competitive grants program honoring the most innovative community development projects. The 1992 grants funded four projects for a total of $80,000: a grocery and tourist equipment store in Alganak River, a firewood harvesting project in Fort Yukon, a retreat complex in Spirit Lake, and a restaurant in St. George.

---

Similar principles guide three related community development efforts in tiny Brinkley, Arkansas, deep in the delta country. The Arkansas Land and Farm Development Corporation directly descended from the work of Booker T. Washington through one of his disciples, Floyd Brown, who started an agricultural school on this site in 1919. It represents the lifelong dream of Calvin King, a charismatic leader who is doing everything in his power to see delta blacks gain economic clout through their own efforts, led by their own people. Now housed in a onetime reform school for girls, the corporation and its offshoots, the Delta Community Development Corporation and the East Central Arkansas Economic Opportunity Corporation, are making long strides toward that goal.

Blacks in the delta country have been poor and downtrodden since just after the Civil War, when freed slaves were brought in to work for low wages on large, white-owned farms. Most of the region's shrinking agricultural economy is based on agribusiness farming. Blacks owned 18 percent of farmland in eighteen Arkansas delta counties in 1935, a figure that has shrunk to 3 percent today; the number of small farms in the region declined by 24 percent between 1969 and 1982, while the number of large farms, over one thousand acres, increased by 16 percent.

Here are some of the programs that King and his associates have invented to try to turn those numbers around: The Land Retention Fund seeks grants and loans and uses them to purchase land and keep it in the hands of poor black farmers. Since the fund started in 1987, it has saved more than a thousand acres of black-owned farmland. The Floyd Brown Agricultural School, Agricultural Entrepreneurship Project, and Youth Enterprise Agriculture programs all serve similar ends: to train poor people, often welfare recipients or recent high school graduates, to operate small family farms as efficient and profitable businesses. Students, many of them single mothers, go through a twelve-week course that focuses heavily on farming as a business as well as on basic agricultural techniques. They emerge with a specific management plan, including paperwork for a $2,000 to $4,000 loan that they can then present to the Delta Community Development Corporation as a completed loan application. By bringing training, money, coaching, and technical assistance to bear as elements of a coherent strategy, says Community Development Corporation director Michael R. Jackson, the program maximizes each farmer's chance at success and, not coincidentally, his ability to repay the loan.

Although encouraging poor people to learn farming during a period when pundits are forecasting the demise of the family farm seems a bit like encouraging rats to leap on to a sinking ship, the idea is not as naive as it might seem. Because the region's primary agribusiness crops are either nonfood crops like cotton and soybeans, or are primarily intended for export like rice, there is almost no cultivation of row crops and edible produce in the region, even though poverty and its associated hunger are endemic. By providing fresh, low-cost produce as an alternative crop, small delta farmers can help attack hunger while filling a vacant market niche. King also envisions cooperative farming efforts on a cottage industry scale, in which five to ten farmers will work adjacent lands together, sharing the costs of capital investment and equipment.

On a larger scale, the Delta Community Development Corporation intends to raise money and recruiting efforts to establish food processing plants, including a cannery and a rice processing plant. To broaden the region's economic base, it also finances nonagricultural industry, including a sixty-worker plant producing "panelized housing," modular residences made in the factory in standard parts that can be trucked to a building site for quick and easy construction. In addition to creating jobs in an economy where they are rare, Jackson said, this plant serves the double-barrelled purpose of creating housing that can sell, fully assembled on purchased lots, for a market rate of $35,000 to $45,000, considerably below the region's current median housing price of $65,000 opening affordable housing possibilities to more working poor people.

## *Rural and Ethnic Cooperatives*

Out on the far side of Rockcastle County, Kentucky, where Bluegrass farmland rises and folds into Appalachia, the land is beautiful and the living tough: a third of the county's residents live below the poverty line. The area's ten percent official unemployment rate is certainly underestimated, and it's been a long time since coal or tobacco farming provided many people here a decent living.

But a political fight a decade ago gave the people of the old railroad town of Livingston some new ideas that are starting to pay off. Back in 1983 Livingston Fiscal Court, the county legislative body, proposed establishing a landfill on a clifftop above the town. Fearing that unsanitary effluent might seep through the region's limestone caves and into their pure underground water supply, residents banded together, fought the initiative to the state capital, and won.

"We got organized from this," said Ina Taylor, executive director of Livingston Economic Alternatives for Progress, known as LEAP, "and then we thought, 'Well, we can't depend on government to do for us what we need to be doing for ourselves.' "

First they formed the Rockcastle River Community Land Trust, an experiment in community landownership. This sputtered for a year or two, and then, when its members realized that a land trust didn't suit the Appalachian dream of individual property ownership, they shifted its focus from land to jobs. The land trust became LEAP, seeking members throughout the steep, wooded hills and hollows around Livingston, and its members began to invent ways to pool their resources and their common sense.

Its first effort, the Sweet Sorghum Project, is an agricultural cooperative whose farmers grow the traditional sweetener (akin to sugarcane) individually and pool their produce in a cooperative processing venture, where the stalks are stripped and boiled down into molasses. The sorghum project provides a source of income for four farmers. More important, it provides the raw material for LEAP's second major venture, the Opportunities for Women Project. This group of four Rockcastle County women, also a cooperative, buys sorghum syrup from its brother project, and uses it to make a line of Kentucky specialty foods from dessert toppings to candies. With marketing assistance from Eastern Kentucky University in Richmond, these items are sold under the Golden Kentucky Products trade name in state parks, regional gift shops, by mail order, in the group's little roadside retail shop on State Highway 55 in Livingston, and through a Kentucky Department of Agriculture gift catalog available in motels and tourist welcome sites. The cooperative's members shared $20,000 in 1992.

A third activity, the Livestock Project, is funded by the Heifer Project International, which provided a $20,000 grant for LEAP to purchase more than one hundred head of livestock (goats, sheep, milk cows, and beef cattle) to be distributed to group members with the facilities to care for them. Each recipient is expected to donate the first female offspring of the gift animal back to LEAP to be given to another family. The recipients are then free to keep the original animal as breeding stock or for wool, milk, or food.

Among smaller projects aimed at helping the county's poor people build self-sufficiency, LEAP distributes garden seeds and apple trees, and hopes to start an apple butter co-op when its first group of apple trees starts bearing commercially. It also invites in scores of church volunteers every summer for a two-week work camp to sweep the county with eager workers ready to perform home repairs for any resident who needs them.

## *Navajo Trading Post*

The back room of the eighty-three-year-old New Mexico trading post building that houses the Gathering Place looks a lot like your grandmother's attic—or, to be more exact, what your grandmother's attic would look like if she happened to be Navajo and a very good artist indeed. Works of fine American Indian arts and crafts fill every nook and cranny of the large room: Navajo blankets, with their spare, muted geometrical designs; sleek wooden tables with colorful sand art inlaid under safety glass; dolls and pottery and rugs and shirts, and lovable patchwork teddy bears, with constellations of Ojibway dreamcatchers rustling overhead. It's all the work of more than thirty Navajo artists and crafts people, who earned an estimated $25,000 in 1993 by producing quality arts and crafts for sale through a cooperative venture.

Out in the high desert country of western New Mexico, where rugged red mesas jut out of an arid and strangely beautiful countryside that seems to have been painted by an artist whose pallette contained mostly blues and reds and browns, there's a lot of poverty and not much hope of employment other than through art and craftsmanship. These pursuits probably make up at least part of the income for more than half of the Navajo population, said Angela Bianco, coordinator of the Gathering Place in the town of Thoreau. The people are young (median age under twenty-six) and poor (up to a third are unemployed) and marginally literate (fifth-grade achievement, on average, with widespread illiteracy among older people). Alcoholism, teen pregnancy, and domestic abuse are common, and services in the sparsely populated area are thinly spread.

Into this setting in 1987 came the Gathering Place, a dream of Bianco, a Sister of Loretto who had worked in social services at a local mission, and a group of Navajo people, who saw the local poverty and realized that if anything was to be done about it, they had better do it themselves. The first priority was jobs, and that led directly to establishment of the co-op, which originally involved a group of quilters, then expanded quickly to add other needle crafts, carpentry, and eventually a cooperative marketing venture for a variety of arts and crafts people. The co-op is informal. It simply provides training when necessary, technical support and advice, and marketing and publicity for the participants, each of whom sells finished crafts to the co-op for resale at a markup to the tourists who flood past Thoreau on Interstate 40—twenty thousand of them a day during the May-to-December tourist season, state officials say.

The co-op has marked considerable success in terms of prizes for some of its artists and pride for all its members, Bianco says. Financially, it's been less of a prize, mainly because it's been unable to attract enough business to make a full-time living for anyone. In the future the group hopes to raise money to hire a full-time manager to try to change that through aggressive marketing and publicity.

---

Oomingmak, the sturdy, long-haired creature that Alaska's Native people call the One with the Long Beard and Europeans call musk ox (even though it doesn't produce musk and is more closely related to sheep or goats than to cattle), is the ideal Arctic animal. Short, squat, and stocky, these four hundred- to eight hundred-pound grass-eaters have no long extremities to get cold. Their short legs, short tails, and even tiny ears under their downward-curling horns give the bulls their unique appearance. Long guard hairs protect the oomingmak from the elements, and when winter's snows begin to blow, a soft and woolly underhair that the Native Alaskans call *qiviut* (KEE-vee-oot) grows beneath the guard hairs like a warming blanket. In springtime, when the oomingmak no longer needs the warmth, this wool is shed—and therein lies the story of the Oomingmak Musk Ox Cooperative.

The story began years ago, when the late John J. Teal, Jr., met the Icelandic Arctic explorer Williamur Steffanson and learned about the musk ox, an integral part of the Arctic native subsistence economy with its roots in the Ice Age. Once abundant in Alaska, the oomingmak was hunted to extinction during the last century, then reintroduced from Greenland and allowed to return to the wild. Teal became fascinated with the idea of domesticating the animal, whose wool could become an indigenous cash product within the traditional Native economy. After experimenting with a group of musk oxen on a farm in Vermont, he rounded up private money and a Kellogg Foundation grant to capture thirty-three animals and establish them as a domestic herd on the campus of the University of Alaska in Fairbanks. By 1968, researchers had collected enough qiviut wool to have it spun into yarn, a task that the Alaskans farmed out to, of all places, a cashmere mill in Rhode Island.

During the Christmas season that year, project worker Ann Schell went to Nunivak Island, off the west coast of Alaska, and taught twenty-five Native women how to knit. They became the core of the cooperative, and through a combination of word of mouth and outreach to a dozen other villages on Nunivak and in the nearby Yukon-Kuskokwim Delta, Alaska's poorest region, the group of knitters eventually grew to between 200 and 250 women. Every village creates clothing with its own signature pattern, and the items—caps, scarves, stoles, and the Eskimo smoke ring cap-scarf combination—are sold in the co-op's little retail shop in downtown Anchorage or by mail order. The ash-brown garments are eight times warmer than sheep's wool by weight, never shrink, and are softer than silk—all powerful advertising points that justify their breathtaking prices: $65 for a child's cap, $165 to $250 for a scarf or stole, $425 for a tunic. Even so, the cooperative sells everything it can make, and undoubtedly could sell much more, pumping needed cash into an area with few jobs.

A single knitter may earn as little as $9 to as much as, rarely, $5,000 for a year's work, executive director Sigrun Robertson said. The group's seventy musk oxen produce about three hundred pounds of wool a year, and Robertson scrapes up that much more from other sources, including the University of Alaska's experimental herd, zoo animals, and a small amount of qiviut gathered from the wild by Native collectors, enough to make a total of about thirty-five hundred garments a year. Sales cover the co-op's $450,000 annual budget and put between $75,000 and $100,000 annually into the village economy—between 10 and 20 percent of the village's total work income for the year.

That's half of Teal's dream. The other half, creating self-sustaining musk ox herds in the Native villages, has been harder to realize. An effort to start one such herd at Unalakleet, on the shore of Norton Sound, eventually had to be abandoned because of the difficulty of air-freighting hay for the animals and in getting Native caretakers for the herd, which requires constant attention during the spring and summer, the time when people are most occupied with hunting and fishing necessary for subsistence. Accordingly, the herd was moved back to Palmer, in an agricultural area about fifty miles northeast of Anchorage, where it is administered by the staff of the Musk Ox Farm, a subsidiary nonprofit.

The gossamer qiviut garments appeal to tourists, and constant crowds stream through the Anchorage store and visit the green, mountain-bordered Matanuska Valley that houses the farm. But all is not well. Even after twenty-five years, domesticating musk oxen is still an experimental project, and the herd is slowly dying, down now from one hundred animals to fewer than seventy. Several calves died during one week in the summer of 1993, succumbing to diarrhea, which workers fear may be linked to a mineral deficiency in their diet. Bolstering the herd with another large roundup may be the only way to keep it at a commercially feasible size, but that would require an investment of $150,000 to $250,000 that the group doesn't have. Robertson also has her eye on a supply of qiviut wool that she could claim for $50,000 — if she had $50,000—which co-op knitters could convert with their quick needles and their skills into ten times that amount.

"In trying to improve the economics of Native villages, one is walking a thin line," Robertson observes in an unpublished paper about the project. "Improve too much, and the culture may be destroyed. On the flip side, the Co-operative may be not helping enough: knitting is hardly something that will someday allow a young Native Alaskan to get a job working with computers. Is a purposefully labor-intensive cottage industry really the way to improve people's chances for a better future? Not for everyone. The Musk Ox Producers' Co-operative, however, provides a way for many villagers to continue living in the way that they prefer, and makes it a little easier to survive."

## *The Other Side of Palm Beach*

A rich businessman who acquired an ancient religious relic, purportedly a piece of the True Cross, offered to donate to the Catholic church a large piece of property he owned in the orange groves near Indiantown, Florida, for use as a shrine. Instead, the archbishop of Miami urged that he build a parish church for the local people, the only one within thirty miles.

Father Frank O'Laughlin, an Irish-American priest with a social conscience, was assigned to the new Holy Cross Church, and it didn't take him long to see two roads out of the horrible cycle of poverty that trapped the region's cane cutters and citrus pickers: better jobs, and a decent education for their children. O'Laughlin and his flock created a model school and low-cost housing initiatives that have changed the complexion of the town and the lives of its Guatemalan workers. In an effort to build self-reliance for parents as well as pupils, the parish created the cooperative InDios, a play on the Spanish words for "Indians" and "In God." Sister Teresa Auad, a Bolivian nun trained in Wisconsin who came to Indiantown in 1985, first spent a year working in the fields getting to know the women and winning their confidence. Determining that a sewing business best fitted their interests and abilities, she patched together a rickety combination of grants and gifts to acquire a dozen professional sewing machines and train a few dozen women to use them. The underlying principle here, like all of Holy Cross's efforts, is to benefit the children. By creating full-time, year-round work for at least a handful of mothers, the families can pull at least one parent in each family out of the migrant stream and establish them in year-round housing, allowing the children to stay in school and advance, rather than having to follow their families north with the crops before school's out.

Initially, InDios sewed exotic garments in the Guatemalan style and marketed them through Bloomingdale's and other high-fashion stores. This got InDios a lot of national publicity, which inspired people and organizations to give the group money. Ultimately, however, the colorful styles got more publicity than sales. With the pro bono assistance of a Boston firm, the InDios artisans moved into a more financially stable niche, making clerical shirts that have a market among not only Catholic clergy but priests and ministers of numerous other denominations as well.

Now twenty-six strong, the women of InDios turn out 250 shirts a week. They are trained in a six-month apprenticeship during which they work eight hours but are paid for seven; the extra hour's pay is banked to accumulate the co-op entry fee of $2,000. They pay themselves only minimum wage but earn bonuses for special projects and additional piecework, which works out to about $400 every two weeks—not great riches, but to a migrant farmworker family that's had almost nothing, it looks like a dream.

## *Saving Factory Jobs*

Sometimes it's simpler to save jobs than to try to create jobs. Here's a lesson from the Boston area. The three-story redbrick building that houses Market Forge in Everett, Massachusetts, looks pretty much like any other older factory in this industrial town. But a bold yellow sign on the wall just inside the front door makes it clear that this is no ordinary plant. OWNERS AT WORK it reads, and this is a statement of fact: All 140 employees of this bustling plant that makes commercial kitchen equipment for restaurants—the union workers, clerical staff, and administrators, from the janitor through the president of the company—own equal shares in 100 percent of its stock.

During the autumn of 1993, the plant's workers and management, with the technical advice of a Boston-based nonprofit organization called the ICA Group, bought their own company, a century-old Everett firm, in a complicated deal that made them all partners in an employee stock ownership plan (ESOP). This is no dreamy commune in which workers debate each morning and vote on what products they'll make that day, but a hardheaded business arrangement, a unionized plant with professional management—in fact, company president Hal Hamilton and his staff survived the ownership transfer and remain at their posts. The distinction between this and the more customary capitalist arrangement is simply that the stockholders are not distant and anonymous individuals and institutions but the people who work in the plant. This approach, known as the Mondragon model after a movement encouraging worker-owned businesses in the Basque region of Spain, is making inroads in America, primarily because of the efforts of the ICA

Group, an organization that "saves and creates jobs through the development of worker-owned and community-based businesses," as its executive director Jim Megson says.

Opened in 1898, Market Forge was originally a metal-working forge in Boston's Quincy Market area. It thrived through the world wars and moved into manufacturing commercial kitchen equipment in the late 1940s, Hamilton said. Beatrice Foods Corporation bought the company in 1968, and it continued as a major force in its rather specialized field until 1985, when it fell victim to a malady of the times. Market Forge and four other Beatrice subsidiaries were taken over in a leveraged buyout by Specialty Equipment, a consortium of banks that announced upfront that it intended to sell off or close the plant. The business was viable, but "it wasn't in Specialty Equipment's long-range plans," Hamilton said.

The plant's United Steelworkers' union local approached the ICA Group, presenting it with a situation ready-made for its mission: a going concern with a sizable workforce that had been marked for closing but with the potential of being saved through an ESOP buyout. "It would take years to create that many jobs," ICA's Megson said. "If you can save that many in situ, you've done something remarkable."

Specialty Equipment had given the union ninety days' notice of its plan to close the plant when union president Dave Slaney approached Megson and asked for help. They flew to Chicago the next morning and persuaded Specialty Equipment's president to give them four weeks to come up with a preliminary study proving that the buyout could work. That report (with ICA waiving half of its usual $20,000 consulting fee) led to a letter of intent, which began a negotiating process that lasted over two and a half years, involving such threatening shallows and shoals as pension-fund arrangements, disputes over responsibility for retirees' health benefits before the sale, and environmental permissions required for the plant.

On October 31, 1993, however, the deal was done; the sale went through for an undisclosed multimillion-dollar price financed by a combination of traditional bank loans and personal sacrifices by the workers, who agreed to take pay cuts to make the transaction work. Market Forge's employees took possession of their own plant. "We've done well," Hamilton said six months later, looking over the plant floor from his pleasant but decidedly unostentatious office. He declined to disclose specific figures but smiled when he said, "We've become profitable. We're well past the break-even point."

This kind of deal is getting to be routine for the ICA Group, a thoroughly professional consulting firm that thrives on the kind of plant closings that are commonplace with leveraged buyouts: sound plants with potential for profit-making success, being closed or sold because they don't fit the short-term profit plans of their new owners. Funded by a combination of earned income from its fees (which covers about half of its $500,000 annual budget) and grants from foundations and religious institutions, the group was organized in 1978 by activists angered by the closing of Youngstown Steel in Ohio, a move that devastated the factory's company town. ICA (originally the Industrial Cooperative Association) was initially an advocacy group with the mission of publicizing the Mondragon model in the United States to encourage the development of worker-owned companies as new industries and buyouts. During the 1980s it moved into nationwide technical assistance and consulting because its organizers found that publicity alone wasn't enough to make things happen.

Besides negotiating the Market Forge buyout, ICA has helped hundreds of workers save their jobs—six hundred during 1991 alone—through employee buyouts of companies as diverse as a high-tech maker of optical filters in Vermont, a plastic mold-maker in Massachusetts, and a jewelry maker in Oregon. It also helped establish a new worker-owned company, Valley Care Cooperative, a home health care service in Waterbury, Connecticut.

"The Mondragon model works," Megson says. "We can point to some of these things, show people what's available, and say, 'There! Copy this.' We're able to offer people a hopeful message: 'There *are* some solutions. Some things are working, and here they are, folks.' We want to create jobs for people who don't have them, and we want to save jobs for people on the verge of losing them. If we can save these jobs, these people won't be on welfare."

What could be simpler than that? It's a clear example of the "Mr. Goodwrench" principle. An investment—even a significant investment—in keeping a viable business afloat with its payroll intact will pay considerable dividends, in contrast to a depressed community populated by unemployed workers and an idle factory.

# Conclusion

# Lessons for All Americans

WHY HAVE SO MANY OF OUR WELL-INTENDED efforts to change the lives of poor people failed? With the examples of hundreds of programs that *do* work to guide us, the answer to this frustrating question begins to come clear: We have simply failed to ask the right questions, to treat the right symptoms, and to set the right goals. This failure of goal-setting follows a consistent pattern, and it reflects the difference between dispensing charity and nurturing change.

If the goal is merely to address a short-term symptom and not the underlying malaise, nothing changes. It isn't always easy to communicate this difference, because well-meaning people, believing that charity is decent and kind, sometimes don't understand that it can be both good and insufficient. Some see charity as a supplement to (or worse, a replacement for) our current welfare system, which admittedly doesn't work very well. But neither, frankly, does traditional charity, which offers a hand out but not a hand up—even in the cases where it comes with no particular strings attached.

So we face the frustration of having soup kitchens that feed hungry people but don't ask why the same people keep coming back hungry again. Shelters provide beds for homeless people, but make little effort to learn what in these people's lives is keeping them on the street. We build housing for homeless people, but we don't necessarily consider the needs of the people who will live there. We establish job-training programs but don't ask whether the graduates actually get jobs, or were trained for jobs that even exist. We try to treat the symptoms, but we don't always recognize the disease. In short, returning to the simple notion that opened this book, we give people fish—and often a scanty portion at that—but we all too rarely teach them to fish.

The most effective grassroots initiatives that do teach people to fish consistently return to several basic premises: Changing people's lives is labor-intensive work. You can't rush a thousand people through a program and expect them to walk out with jobs and lives that are whole. It's necessary to work one-on-one with people, respecting their intelligence and capabilities and at the same time being as tough as you need to be. It takes competent, creative, and honest people to run successful programs, once they've got the resources that they need to get the job done; and they have to be left pretty much alone in order to do it.

But the most important lesson we learn at America's grass roots is this: Even the most apparently intractable groups of people in poverty are composed mostly of decent folks who just want a chance to make a living and support themselves and their families. If you give them a reasonable chance to work their way out of poverty—a chance that they can recognize as honest and practical—just about everyone will grab for it.

The spread of visible homelessness, hunger, and poverty in our country since the early 1980s has left scars on individuals and on the political landscape. But it has also left a surprising legacy of hope as Americans of good spirit have stepped in to do a job that needed to be done. Based on the programs I've seen and the hundreds of creative poverty fighters I've met across the nation, I'm convinced that we can look to these small-scale, local efforts to find responses to the problems of poverty that are not only more effective but more humane than our current social service and welfare programs. These grassroots innovations are not based on the inventions of office-bound bureaucrats or policy gurus but on the commonsense ideas of everyday Americans who've seen a problem and pitched in to help fix it.

How can we turn the best grassroots programs into national models for fighting poverty through self-reliance and personal initiative? We need to take a completely new look at the way we deliver welfare and social services. We must build on the strengths of poor people rather than assume that their weaknesses will forever defeat them. We must foster individual self-reliance, recognize it in people and nurture it. And we must take fullest advantage of every opportunity to build partnerships between government and the nonprofit groups that have demonstrated creativity, competence, and skill at what they do.

---

Let's take a closer look at ten specific principles we've learned from America's most effective grassroots poverty fighters. Each of these principles holds clear lessons for nonprofit groups and the people who lead them. If we can pass these lessons along to every state, county, city, and town with the evidence of the programs that work best, and establish similar efforts with the guidance but not the heavy hand of government, we can put poverty on the run.

1. **Establish partnerships between federal, state, and local governments and nonprofit organizations, ensuring that every community has competent programs delivering a complete range of services that foster individual self-reliance.**

This is by no means a call for blanket funding for nonprofit organizations without regard to their capabilities or their mission. Neither taxpayers nor government will soon forget the scandals in some early Community Action agencies and Community Development grant programs, when naive supervisors dumped money into poor communities without sufficient oversight, only to be surprised when program workers showed up for work in new cars, sporting fancy jewelry.

But the local programs that have demonstrated competence and the ability to help people get themselves back into the community and back to work should stand as models for nationwide replication and taxpayer support. Government has a proven ability to write checks, but the record of welfare programs like Aid to Families with Dependent Children and the often unpleasant and error-ridden approach of welfare bureaucrats builds no confidence in the system. Just as authorities like David Osborne advise reinventing government by fashioning partnerships between it and the private sector, it's equally worth while to examine similarly inventive partnerships between government and the best nonprofit organizations. Nonprofits have demonstrated a consistent ability to understand local problems and overcome them with creative, flexible approaches. But they rarely have sufficient resources. When we bring together government money and local enterprise, with appropriate oversight and full access for citizens and the media, good things start to happen.

San Antonio's Project Quest, for instance, drew on $3.7 million in federal and state money, and needs a similar amount each year for its training program, which will place six hundred workers into high-paying, skilled jobs in two years. That breaks down to a little more than $6,000 a year for each worker's training and support. This is not a bad deal for people like Cynthia Scott, the program's first graduate, who went directly to a hospital job paying her $18,720 plus benefits. Before enrolling in Project Quest, Scott was receiving an AFDC dole that paid her $3,252 a year to support herself and her three children.

**2. Manage by objectives. Set smart goals and come up with simple, direct approaches that will take you straight to them.**

This fundamental principle of modern management theory is too often overlooked in the nonprofit sector. "Train one hundred workers" or "build one hundred houses" are lofty objectives, but "Get one hundred workers trained and placed in permanent jobs" and "get one hundred families established in decent houses that they can afford" are better, more specific goals. The best nonprofit managers understand management by objectives, and they plan their programs by setting the goals they really want to accomplish and then coming up with pragmatic ways to get the job done.

Milwaukee's Esperanza Unida followed a straight, focused path to a clearly defined goal: Look for economic niches in the community, available jobs that reward attainable skills with good pay and benefits—auto repair, welding, building trades, family day care. Then start small nonprofit businesses in which young people can learn those skills under experienced mentors, while the business earns money to help support the organization itself.

**3. Foster self-reliance by building on people's strengths.**

We must turn on its head the foolish notion that underlies Aid to Families with Dependent Children, which requires that mothers who accept its grant decline work—even part-time work—and avoid forming families for fear of losing the dole and health care benefits for themselves and their children. DC Central Kitchen, the organization in Washington, D.C., that collects usable food leftovers and turns them into healthy meals for hungry people, understands this concept and puts it into practice by hiring homeless men to do its work, learning employable skills in the process. It stands out from scores of other restaurant-gleaning programs across the nation that do a good job of feeding hungry people but mobilize affluent volunteers to do the work, missing the chance to employ and train the very people they are trying to help. All the grassroots Grameen banks, small-business incubators, and nonprofit venture loan organizations, in similar fashion, recognize that a pool of skills, talent, and ambition exists among even the groups most hammered by poverty. By giving people the tools they need and a quick loan to get started, these organizations foster the development of businesses that may eventually boost the economies of their own communities.

**4. Use the holistic approach, bringing a full array of tools to bear on each individual's problems.**

For many years, government social services programs and nonprofit charities alike have typically focused on doing a single job and, it is to be hoped, doing it well. On the government side, unemployment offices handled unemployment insurance, food stamp offices distributed food stamps, welfare offices handled AFDC, social security offices were responsible for payments to elderly and disabled people, and so it went. Officialdom neither thought about nor apparently cared about the time and convenience of recipients, who were expected to trudge from one office to another, waiting in line at each to fill out separate forms and await separate decisions from separate bureaucrats. The lessons we've learned from "one-stop shopping" welfare operations like those in Westminster, Maryland, which consolidated both the offices and the forms they use, are valuable because they not only reduce the human toll on the recipients but cut the cost of running the welfare bureaucracy for government as well.

For nonprofit poverty fighters, *holistic* has a different meaning. With few exceptions, the grassroots programs that have proved themselves most effective at turning people's lives around do so not by focusing on a single problem but by identifying every problem that stands between individuals and recovery, and finding ways to get the assistance that these individuals need. As Margie Smith of Trinity Ministry to the Poor in Dallas cogently observed, "The

Band-Aid approach or the 'quick fix' that addresses only the symptoms has got to stop."

Failure to comprehend this dooms the most well-intended programs. The best job-training program won't keep its graduates at work if it ignores the need for drug and alcohol counseling. A food pantry that gives away unfamiliar or difficult-to-prepare foodstuffs shouldn't be surprised if the recipients of its largesse seem ungrateful. A program that puts formerly homeless people into permanent housing can't expect them to stay there if they can't pay the rent. These conclusions may seem thoroughly reasonable, but a surprising number of bureaucrats and grassroots program leaders have been too easily satisfied to ignore them, preferring to do a single task and declare that the rest of the effort, alas, is "not our job."

**5. Deal with individuals, one-on-one. Poverty is not best fought on an assembly line.**

The Recovery Program in Atlanta's Cafe 458 is as good an example as I've found to illustrate this simple but sometimes frustrating principle. Working with only a dozen homeless drug addicts at a time, giving them food and conversation and emotional support and even that unruly thing named love, the Cafe's committed staff can only work with a handful of individuals at a time, saving six while they'd love to be salvaging a thousand. It's a slow, painstaking, and infinitely rewarding process, but it's not one that can be mechanized and used to churn out clean, working, mentally healthy people by the battalion.

Food stamps and AFDC and other necessary interventions handle people by the numbers. They make a difference, but they provide no warmth or humanity, nor, frankly, do they build self-reliance. That's a task requiring more personal effort. As Phil, one of Cafe 458's clients who came from the drug life to a fulfilling job as a counselor, told us: "Daily, long-term, that is what's needed. You can't do it in a short period of time. It takes building a foundation. The dedication of the people who work here is long-term."

And it works.

**6. The "Mr. Goodwrench" principle: Intervene early and anticipate problems before they occur.**

As television's "Mr. Goodwrench" warns, you can maintain your car before it falls apart, or you can wait until an emergency compels you to respond. The best grassroots programs presume a similar principle about the much more important business of maintaining people's lives before they fall apart.

Two of the most effective government welfare programs rest on this principle. The federal nutrition program for Women, Infants and Children, known as WIC, has been shown to save $3 in health care costs for every $1 it spends on food for pregnant and nursing mothers and children. Despite this record, in most states it receives funding sufficient to feed only about half of the eligible population. Head Start, one of the greatest surviving success stories of the Great Society of the 1960s, boasts significant achievement preparing youngsters for success in elementary and secondary school.

At the grassroots level, the Mr. Goodwrench principle informs all of the effective programs that understand the importance of nurturing, feeding, and educating children and ensuring their health and strength. Holy Cross School in Florida's sugarcane country, for instance, gets the children of Guatemalan refugees off to a strong start in life that may help them avoid the problems that have stymied their parents. Short-term intervention is a pragmatic initiative too, as in the Louisville school system's inventive notion of rounding up the younger sisters of pregnant teens and giving them good advice about avoiding the mess that Big Sis got herself into. Tacoma's Martin Luther King Center brings the Mr. Goodwrench principle to bear in locating families on the brink of becoming homeless and doing whatever it can—through advice, referrals, or emergency cash—to keep them in the housing they're in. We see it again in Cities in Schools in Charlotte, North Carolina, and other education programs that single out students whose grades and behavior suggests that they are at risk of dropping out, and giving them the help and support they need to regain their confidence and stay in school.

### 7. Leadership makes a difference: The best grassroots leaders are charismatic, competent, flexible, unafraid to innovate, and unafraid to break the rules (if not the law).

If any one thread runs through all the best grassroots organizations, it's the presence of a leader who's bold, creative, and willing to take risks. Richard Oulahan demonstrated that at Esperenza Unida when he defied conventional wisdom by setting up a commercial business—an auto repair shop—as a nonprofit job-training agency. People like Oulahan may stop and check the facts, but they don't simply back away when they hear the old worried song, "You can't *do* that!"

Kent Beittel, the street minister in Columbus, Ohio, who's coming up with new ways to reward homeless people for working their way off the street, is proud to be a maverick. So is Carolyn Lanier, who's made the food bank in Lubbock, Texas, a model for the southern Plains, over the now diminishing protests of the national food bank bureaucracy. Sylvia Cannon rewrote the rules to make her welfare office in Carroll County, Maryland, into a national model. In Seattle, Roberto Maestas and his crew literally took the law into their own hands to capture the building that the establishment wouldn't give them for El Centro de la Raza. Scratch any grassroots community organizer anywhere, like Carlos Marentes of the El Paso chile-pepper pickers, or Tirso Moreno in the Florida orange groves around Orlando, or Baldemar Velasquez in the Ohio tomato and cucumber country, and you'll find a hell-raiser who'd rather question authority than bow to it.

None of this suggests that grassroots leaders should be rebels without a cause. Without exception, the honor roll I've listed here represents people who know how to work within the system and do it very well. But the best leaders know when to lead, and they know when leadership means getting out in front of the establishment, the conventional wisdom, and even sometimes their own board of directors.

### 8. Join forces, fill the gaps, coalesce. Work together to meet the community's overall need.

Just as the holistic approach pays dividends in working with individuals, grassroots groups can profit when they recognize a common cause and join hands with other organizations fighting similar or related battles. The Montana-based Western Organization of Resource Councils provides an excellent example of a working umbrella organization: It creates a network of information and planning that statewide organizations of family farmers and ranchers in seven states can share. This spares the effort and expense of reinventing the wheel, while each state group, and community organizations within the state, retain autonomy. Statewide coalitions of organizations working on behalf of hungry and homeless people offer similar benefits, with particularly good models in Maryland, Idaho, Alabama, and Minnesota.

The social services arena and nonprofits in general have a bad reputation for turf battles, but in at least three communities—Anchorage, Alaska; Reno, Nevada; and Nashville, Tennessee—I found unusually effective, yet thoroughly informal, webs of grassroots organizations that are moving toward covering the gaps in services in their regions by recognizing that a team effort can often accomplish what an individual can't. These towns offer powerful examples of the battles that can be won when good people and good groups work together.

### 9. Involve the community in what you do. There's strength in support as well as in dollars.

Even if we build government partnerships to support and replicate the best grassroots initiatives against hunger and poverty, it's safe to predict that the nonprofit world will never be fat with cash and property. Many of the strongest organizations enlist individuals and businesses within their communities as willing partners, providing both work and contributions.

Phoenix's Homeward Bound and Bridge programs, for instance, mobilize churches and businesses to provide both financial support and volunteers to help get homeless families back into the mainstream, and they are building a remarkable record of success with as many as nine of every ten families they serve. Nashville's Room in the Inn houses hundreds of homeless people on winter nights entirely through joint efforts by dozens of the city's churches. Dr. Scott Morris of the Church Health Center in Memphis mobilized scores of physicians to deliver health care to uninsured working people. In Anchorage, Alaska, Bean's Cafe enlists its community with fund-raising and volunteer-motivating initiatives that range from bean soup cook-offs to the sale of a slick cookbook.

Most of the people in a community will recognize, when it's pointed out, that it's best for them and their town, too, when something's being done to fight local problems of hunger, poverty, and homelessness. Give them half a chance, and they'll get busy doing something about it.

### 10. One more time: Change is better than charity. "Teach a man to fish."

Putting it all together, one thing becomes clear: There is no silver bullet that will slay poverty, no single solution that will cure it and all its evils. But in my travels to hundreds of outstanding organizations in all fifty states, I've seen the shape of something better: a golden blanket, a gentle and supporting weave that can cover the needs of people who haven't been able to share the American dream. This blanket can be woven in any community that chooses to replicate the best grassroots programs, the innovative partnerships that, with the essential ingredient of government support, can put domestic hunger and poverty out of business.

Ending poverty will require more than just giving people free lunch and grocery baskets. It demands a network of services that don't just feed people but help them feed themselves. Food, housing, education, child care and family support, counseling and health care, job training and economic development, political organizing: They're all connected and can all be provided, as a matter of local and national policy, by people of goodwill working with their government, all of us doing what we do best.

# Appendix

# GETTING INVOLVED

FIGHTING POVERTY THROUGH GRASSROOTS action is not a job for bureaucrats, politicians, or policymakers but for ordinary people who get involved by rolling up their sleeves and getting busy.

Every community in the nation boasts outstanding programs that are changing people's lives by building self-sufficiency—teaching people to fish. Here's a sample of more than 180 grassroots initiatives in every state and the District of Columbia, including all the groups mentioned in this book. They thrive on volunteers and can always use willing hands.

**ALABAMA**

Alabama Coalition
Against Hunger
Gerald Sanders
P.O. Box 409
319 W. Glenn Ave.
Auburn, Ala. 36830
(205) 821-8336.

Upper Sand Mountain Parish,
United Methodist Church
The Rev. Dorsey Walker
P.O. Box 267
Sylvania, Ala. 35988
(205) 638-2126

**ALASKA**

Access Alaska
Duane French
3710 Woodland Dr., Suite 900
Anchorage, Alaska 99517
(907) 248-4777

Anchorage Neighborhood
Housing Services
Cynthia Parker
2700 Woodland Dr., Suite 500
Anchorage, Alaska 99517
(907) 243-1558

Bean's Cafe
Maggie Carey
1101 E. Third Ave.
P.O. Box 110940
Anchorage, Alaska 99510
(907) 274-9595

Community Economic
Development Corporation
of Alaska
Ann Campbell
1577 C St., Suite 304
Anchorage, Alaska 99501
(907) 274-5400

Crossover House
John Bajowski
1000 E. Fourth Ave.
Anchorage, Alaska 99501
(907) 258-4512

EARTH
Mike O'Callaghan
1540 Medfra
Anchorage, Alaska 99501
(907) 277-8889

Oomingmak Musk Ox
Cooperative
Sigrun Robertson
604 H St.
Anchorage, Alaska 99501
(907) 272-9225

## ARIZONA

Association of Arizona
Food Banks
Ginny Hildebrand
P.O. Box 36368
Phoenix, Ariz. 85067
(602) 252-9088

The Bridge
Suzanne Viehmann
3603 N. Seventh Ave.
Phoenix, Ariz. 85013
(602) 943-4871

Homeward Bound
Pamela A. Martin
29 W. Thomas Rd.
Phoenix, Ariz. 85013
(607) 263-7654

Native Seeds/SEARCH
Mahina Drees
2509 N. Campbell Ave., No. 325
Tucson, Ariz. 85719
(602) 327-9123

## ARKANSAS

Arkansas Land and Farm
Development Corporation
Calvin King
Route 2, Box 291
Brinkley, Ark. 72021
(501) 734-1140

Good Faith Fund
Julia Vindasius
400 Main St., Suite 118
Pine Bluff, Ark. 71601
(501) 535-6233

Southern Development
BankCorporation
George Sturgeon
605 Main St., Suite 203
Arkadelphia, Ark. 71923
(501) 246-3945

## CALIFORNIA

Asian Neighborhood Design
Maurice Lim Miller
80 Fresno St.
San Francisco, Calif. 94133
(415) 982-2959

Chrysalis
Mara Manus
516 S. Main St.
Los Angeles, Calif. 90013
(213) 895-7777

Downtown Women's Center
Adrienne Pingree
325 S. Los Angeles St.
Los Angeles, Calif. 90013
(213) 680-1600

Food for Children
Neil Thompson
815 W. Market St.
Salinas, Calif. 93901
(408) 758-1523

F.O.O.D. Crops
Christina Macias
11270 Merritt St., Suite A
Castroville, Calif. 95012
(408) 633-6001

Food from the 'Hood
5010 11th Ave.
Los Angeles, Calif. 90043
(213) 295-4842

The Garden Project
Cathrine Sneed
35 S. Park
San Francisco, Calif. 94107
(415) 243-8558

House of Ruth
Sr. Jennifer Gaeta
605 N. Cummings St.
Los Angeles, Calif. 90033
(213) 266-4139

LAMP (Los Angeles Men's Project)
Yvonne Williams
627 S. San Julian St.
Los Angeles, Calif. 90014
(213) 488-0031

Para Los Niños
Patricia Tomlin
845 E. Sixth St.
Los Angeles, Calif. 90021
(213) 623-8446

PATH Shelter (People Assisting the Homeless)
Michele Smollar
2346 Cotner Ave.
Los Angeles, Calif. 90064
(310) 996-0034

Step Up on Second
Susan Dempsay
1328 Second St.
Santa Monica, Calif. 90401
(310) 395-8886

Senior Health and Peer Counseling Center
Bernice Bratter
1527 Fourth St.
Santa Monica, Calif. 90401
(310) 829-4715

## COLORADO

Brothers Redevelopment Inc.
José Giron
1111 Osage St., Suite 210
Denver, Colo. 80204
(303) 892-8345

CHARG Resource Center
David D. Burgess
920 Emerson St.
Denver, Colo. 80218
(303) 830-8805

Colorado Women's Employment and Education (CWEE)
Laurie A. Harvey
1111 Osage St., Suite 230
Denver, Colo. 80204
(303) 892-8444

## CONNECTICUT

Hartford Food System
Kathy Cobb
509 Wethersfield Ave.
Hartford, Conn. 06114
(203) 296-9325

## DELAWARE

Delmarva Rural Ministries
Gina Miserendino
26 Wyoming Ave.
Dover, Del. 19901
(302) 678-2000

National Council on Agricultural Life and Labor
Joe Meyer
P.O. Box 1092
Dover, Del. 19903
(302) 678-9400

## DISTRICT OF COLUMBIA

DC Central Kitchen
Robert Egger
425 Second St. NW
Washington, D.C. 20001
(202) 234-0707

The Family Place
Dr. Ana Maria Neris
3309 16th St. NW
Washington, D.C. 20010
(202) 265-0149

Community Family Life Services (Third & Eats)
The Rev. Thomas Knoll
305 E. Third St. NW
Washington, D.C. 20001
(202) 347-0511

## FLORIDA

Office for Farmworker Ministry Farmworker Association of Florida
Tirso Moreno
815 S. Park Ave.
Apopka, Fla. 32703
(407) 886-5151

Florida Impact
Dr. Debra Susie
837 E. Park Ave.
Tallahassee, Fla. 32301
(904) 222-3470

New Hope Community/ Holy Cross School
InDios Worker Cooperative
Sr. Marie Celeste
15929 S.W. 150th St.
Indiantown, Fla. 34956
(407) 597-2203

## GEORGIA

Atlanta Community Food Bank
Bill Bolling
970 Jefferson St. NW
Atlanta, Ga. 30318
(404) 892-9822

Cafe 458
Jillian Grable
458 Edgewood Ave. NE
Atlanta, Ga. 30312
(404) 525-3276

Federation of Southern Cooperatives
Ralph Paige
100 Edgewood Ave., Suite 814
Atlanta, Ga. 30303
(404) 524-6882

Food Bank of Coastal Georgia
Pauline Knight
5 Carolan St.
Savannah, Ga. 31401
(912) 236-8779

Georgia Citizens Coalition on Hunger
Sandra Robertson
818 Washington St. SW, Rm. E-02
Atlanta, Ga. 30315
(404) 584-7141

Habitat for Humanity International, Inc.
Millard Fuller
121 Habitat St.
Americus, Ga. 31709
(912) 924-6935

Prison Ministries with Women
Barbara Gifford
P.O. Box 1911
Decatur, Ga. 30031
(404) 622-4314

Summerhill One-to-One
Sonya Tinsley
250 Georgia Ave. NE, Suite 308
Atlanta, Ga. 30312
(404) 521-1216

## HAWAII

Angel Network Charities
Ivy Olson
5339 Kalaniaole Hwy.
Honolulu, Hawaii 96821
(808) 377-5477

The Institute for Human Services
Debbie Morikawa
350 Sumner St.
Honolulu, Hawaii 96817
(808) 537-4944

Kokua Kalihi Valley
Comprehensive Family Services
Jory Watland
1846 Gulick Ave.
Honolulu, Hawaii 96819
(808) 848-0976

Self-Help Housing Corporation
of Hawaii
Claudia Shay
1427 Dillingham Blvd., Suite 305
Honolulu, Hawaii 96817
(808) 842-7111

## IDAHO

Backwoods Solar Electric Systems
Steve and Elizabeth Willey
8530 Rapid Lightning Creek Rd.
Sandpoint, Idaho 83864
(208) 263-4290

Idaho Citizens' Network
Roger Sherman
904 W. Fort St.
Boise, Idaho 83701
(208) 385-9146

Idaho Hunger Action Council
Leanna Lasuen
4649 Overland Rd., Suite 526
Boise, Idaho 83705
(208) 336-7010

Idaho Migrant Council
Humberto Fuentes
104 N. Kimball St.
Caldwell, Idaho 83606
(208) 454-1652

Idaho Rural Council
Becky Ihli
P.O. Box 236
Boise, Idaho 83701
(208) 344-6184

## ILLINOIS

Bethel New Life
Mary Nelson
367 N. Karlov St.
Chicago, Ill. 60624
(312) 826-5540

Lakefront SRO
Jean Butzen
4946 N. Sheridan Rd.
Chicago, Ill. 60640
(312) 561-0900

Lawndale Christian Development
Corporation
Wayne Gordon
3848 N. Ogden Ave.
Chicago, Ill. 60623
(312) 762-6389

Metro East Church-Based
Citizens' Organization
Sr. Cecilla Hellman
771 Vogel Pl.
East St. Louis, Ill. 62205
(618) 398-6284

National Training and
Information Center
Gale Cincotta
810 N. Milwaukee Ave.
Chicago, Ill. 60622
(312) 243-3035

Suburban Job-Link Corporation
John Plunkett
2343 S. Kedzie Ave.
Chicago, Ill. 60623
(312) 522-8700

## INDIANA

Eastside Community
Investments Inc.
Dennis J. West
3228 E. Tenth St.
Indianapolis, Ind. 46201
(317) 633-7303

## IOWA

Iowa Citizens for Community
Improvement
Joe Fagan
1607 E. Grand Ave.
Des Moines, Iowa 50316
(515) 266-5213

PrairieFire Rural Action
The Rev. David L. Ostendorf
550 11th St.
Des Moines, Iowa 50309
(515) 244-5671

## KANSAS

The Land Institute
Wes Jackson
Route 3, Water Well Road
Salina, Kans. 67401
(913) 823-5376

## KENTUCKY

Brighton Center
Robert Brewster
741 Central
Newport, Ky. 41071
(606) 431-5649

Community Farm Alliance
Hal Hamilton
200 Short St., No. 10
Berea, Ky. 40403
(606) 986-7400

Cranks Creek Survival Center
Rebecca (Becky) Simpson
Route 568, Box 32
Cranks, Harlan County, Ky. 40820
(606) 573-2812

Jefferson County Public Schools
Dr. Stephen Daeschner
P.O. Box 34020
Louisville, Ky. 40232
(502) 473-3251

Livingston Alternatives for
Progress (LEAP)
Ina Taylor
P.O. Box 246
Livingston, Ky. 40445
(606) 453-9800

Louisville Coalition for
the Homeless
Sue Speed
333 Guthrie St.
Louisville, Ky. 40202
(502) 589-0190

## LOUISIANA

Hope House
Sr. Lillian Flavin
916 St. Andrew St.
New Orleans, La. 70130
(504) 522-5881

Louisiana Welfare Rights Organization
Viola Francois
3111 Bruxelles St.
New Orleans, La. 70119
(504) 529-1113

Orleans Parish Community Correctional Center Literacy Training Program
Henry Helm
2800 Gravier St.
New Orleans, La. 70119
(504) 822-8000

## MAINE

HOME, Inc. (Homeworkers Organized for More Employment)
Lucy Poulin
P.O. Box 10
Orland, Maine 04472
(207) 469-7961

## MARYLAND

Clients Helping Clients
Peggy Adams
1711 Connecticut Ave. NW
Washington, D.C. 20009
(301) 963-6206

Emergency Services Center
Alex Jones
10 Distillery Drive
Westminster, Md. 21157
(301) 848-8880

Friends of the Family
Rosalie Streett
1001 Eastern Ave., 2nd Floor
Baltimore, Md. 21202
(410) 467-2556

Maryland Food Committee
Linda Eisenberg
204 E. 25th St.
Baltimore, Md. 21218
(410) 366-0600

Mid-Town Churches Community Association Inc.
Esther R. Reaves
435 E. 25th St.
Baltimore, Md. 21218
(410) 889-3291

Light Street Housing Corporation
M. Gregory Cantori
809 Light St.
Baltimore, Md. 21230
(410) 539-0134

Women Entrepreneurs of Baltimore (WEB)
Julie Reeder
28 E. Ostend St.
Baltimore, Md. 21230
(410) 727-4921

## MASSACHUSETTS

City Year
Michael Brown and Alan Khazel
11 Stillings St.
Boston, Mass. 02210
(617) 451-0699

The ICA Group Inc.
James D. Megson
20 Park Pl., Suite 1127
Boston, Mass. 02116
(617) 338-0010

Machine Action Project
Bob Forrant
1176 Main St.
Springfield, Mass. 01103
(413) 781-6900

Massachusetts Affordable
Housing Alliance
Lew Finfer
25 West St., 3rd Floor
Boston, Mass. 02111
(617) 536-1200

Project Bread
Annette Casas Rubin
11 Beacon St., Rm. 400
Boston, Mass. 02108
(617) 723-5000

## MICHIGAN

Ann Arbor Community
Development Corporation
Michelle Vasquez
2008 Hogback Rd., Suite 2A
Ann Arbor, Mich. 48105
(313) 677-1400

Community Farm of Ann Arbor
Paul Bantle
1525 S. Fletcher Rd.
Chelsea, Mich. 48118
(313) 994-9136

Focus: HOPE
Fr. Bill Cunningham
1355 Oakman Blvd.
Detroit, Mich. 48238
(313) 494-5500

Genessee Area Skills Center
Technology Center
Doug Weir
G-5081 Torrey Rd.
Flint, Mich. 48507
(810) 760-1444

Warren-Conner Development
Coalition
Maggie DeSantis
10100 Harper
Detroit, Mich. 48213
(313) 571-2800

## MINNESOTA

Land Stewardship Project
Ron Kroese
14758 Ostlund Trail North
Marine on St. Croix, Minn. 55047
(612) 433-2770

Sabathani Community
Center Inc.
James Cook
310 E. 38th St.
Minneapolis, Minn. 55409
(612) 827-5981

Sustainable Resources Center
May Morse
1916 Second Ave. South
Minneapolis, Minn. 55403
(612) 870-4255

## MISSISSIPPI

Harrison County Sheriff
Joe Price
P.O. Box 1480
Gulfport, Miss. 39502
(601) 865-7060

Rural Organizing and Cultural
Center (ROCC)
Arnett Lewis
103 Swinney Ln.
Lexington, Miss. 39095
(601) 834-3080

V'BURG Special Initiative Program
Linda Perry
P.O. Box 150
Vicksburg, Miss. 39180
(601) 634-4522

## MISSOURI

Ad Hoc Group Against Crime
Alvin Brooks
P.O. Box 15351
Kansas City, Mo. 64106
(816) 861-9100

Farm Alliance of Rural
Missouri (FARM)
William E. Dellinger
P.O. Box 1094
Jefferson City, Mo. 65102
(314) 636-6005

Grace Hill Neighborhood Services
Betty Marver
2600 Hadley St.
St. Louis, Mo. 63106
(314) 241-2200

Guadalupe Center
Chris Medina
1015 W. 23rd St.
Kansas City, Mo. 64108
(816) 472-4770

Hosea House
Amanda Pulliam
2635 Gravois
St. Louis, Mo. 63118
(314) 773-5438

## MONTANA

Alternative Energy Resources
Organization (AERO)
Al Kurki
25 S. Ewing, Suite 214
Helena, Mont. 59601
(406) 443-7272

Montana Hunger Coalition
Minkie Medora
P.O. Box 314
Missoula, Mont. 59624
(406) 728-4100

Montana People's Action
Jim Fleischmann
208 E. Main St.
Missoula, Mont. 59802
(406) 728-5297

Western Organization of
Resource Councils (WORC)
Pat Sweeney
2401 Montana Ave., No. 301
Billings, Mont. 59101
(406) 252-9672

## NEBRASKA

Center for Rural Affairs
Nancy L. Thompson
P.O. Box 406
Walthill, Nebr. 68067
(402) 846-5428

Nebraska Association of
Farm Workers
Virgil Armendariz
2900 "O" St., Suite 631
Omaha, Nebr. 68107
(402) 743-4100

## NEVADA

The Children's Cabinet
Sarah Longaker
1090 S. Rock Blvd.
Reno, Nev. 89502
(702) 785-4000

Nevada Self-Employment Trust
Janice Barbour
P.O. Box 50428
Reno, Nev. 89513
(702) 849-0852

## NEW HAMPSHIRE

Capitol Region Food Program
Maria Manus Painchaud
P.O. Box 709
Concord, N.H. 03302
(603) 225-0933

## NEW JERSEY

New Community Corporation
Msgr. William Linder
233 W. Market St.
Newark, N.J. 07103
(201) 623-2800

## NEW MEXICO

The Gathering Place
Angela Bianco
P.O. Box 838
Thoreau, N. Mex. 87323
(505) 862-8075

Intermountain Youth Centers
David Giles
P.O. Box 426
Santa Fe, N. Mex. 87504
(505) 986-8481

Zuni Sustainable Agriculture Project
Pueblo of Zuni
Donald Eriacho
P.O. Box 630
Zuni, N. Mex. 87327
(505) 782-5851

## NEW YORK

Binding Together Inc.
Philip Caldarella
75 Varick St., 6th Floor
New York, N.Y. 10013
(212) 334-9400

Community Food Resource Center
Kathy Goldman
90 Washington St.
New York, N.Y. 10006
(212) 349-8155

National Federation for Teaching Entrepreneurship (NFTE)
Steve Mariotti
64 Fulton St., No. 700
New York, N.Y. 10038
(212) 233-1777

Part of the Solution (POTS)
Martin Carney
2763 Webster Ave.
Bronx, N.Y. 10458
(718) 220-4892

World Hunger Year
Sue Leventhal
505 Eighth Ave., 21st Floor
New York, N.Y. 10018
(212) 629-8850

Wyandanch Homes & Property Development Corporation
Peter Barnett
1434 Straight Path
Wyandanch, N.Y. 11798
(516) 491-7285

## NORTH CAROLINA

APPLE
Union County Department of Social Services
Bill Sharpe
P.O. Box 489
Monroe, N.C. 28110
(704) 282-0200

Center for Community Self Help
Martin Eakes
413 E. Chapel Hill St.
Durham, N.C. 27701
(919) 683-9686

Cities in Schools of Charlotte/Mecklenberg County
Cynthia Marshall
525 N. Tryon St., Suite 200
Charlotte, N.C. 28202
(704) 335-0601

Community of Readers Coalition
Greensboro Public Library
Steve Sumerford
900 S. Benbow Rd.
Greensboro, N.C. 27406
(919) 373-2392

Literacy South
Hanna Fingeret
331 W. Main St., Suite 202
Durham, N.C. 27701
(919) 682-8108

## NORTH DAKOTA

Abused Adult Resource Center
Diane Zainhofsky
P.O. Box 167
Bismarck, N. Dak. 28202
(701) 222-8370

Standing Rock Sioux Reservation
Food Distribution Program
Charles (Red) Gates
P.O. Box D
Fort Yates, N. Dak. 58538
(701) 854-7238

## OHIO

Advocates for Basic Legal
Equality (ABLE)
Joseph R. Tafelski
740 Spitzer Bldg.
Toledo, Ohio 43604
(419) 255-0814

Cleveland Works
David C. Weiner
812 Huron Rd. SE, Suite 800
Cleveland, Ohio 44115
(216) 589-9675

Farm Labor Organizing
Council (FLOC)
Baldemar Velasquez
507 S. St. Clair St.
Toledo, Ohio 43602
(419) 243-3456

The Open Shelter
Kent Beittel
370 W. State St.
Columbus, Ohio 43215
(614) 461-0407

## OKLAHOMA

Education and Employment
Ministry Inc.
Theo (Doc) Benson
14 N.E. 13th St.
Oklahoma City, Okla. 73104
(405) 732-7662

SPARK (Special Program for Arts
and Reading for Kids)
Peggy Garrett
1008 N. McKinley
Oklahoma City, Okla. 73106
(405) 235-6855

## OREGON

Oregon Food Bank
Rachel Bristol Little
2540 N.E. Riverside Way
Portland, Ore. 97211
(503) 282-0555

Portland Organizing Project
Kathy Turner
4610 N. Maryland
Portland, Ore. 97217
(503) 282-0087

## PENNSYLVANIA

Just Harvest
Joni Rabinowitz
120 E. Ninth Ave.
Homestead, Pa. 15120
(412) 464-0739

Sixth Street Shelter
Michelle Lawson
219 N. Sixth St.
Allentown, Pa. 18102
(215) 435-1490

## RHODE ISLAND

New Visions of Newport County
Jean Hicks
19 Broadway
Newport, R.I. 02840
(401) 847-7821

## SOUTH CAROLINA

Eastside Revitalization Program
Patricia Crawford
90 Mary St.
Charleston, S.C. 29401
(803) 724-3766

## SOUTH DAKOTA

International Organic Gardening Training Program
Oglala Lakota Community College
Dr. Leland Bear Heels
Kyle, S. Dak. 57752
(605) 455-2321

The Lakota Fund
Elsie Meeks
P.O. Box 340
Kyle, S. Dak. 57752
(605) 455-2500

Slim Butte Community Farming Project
Tom Cook
P.O. Box 859
Chadron, Nebr. 69337
(308) 432-2290

## TENNESSEE

Church Health Center
Dr. Scott Morris
1210 Peabody Ave.
Memphis, Tenn. 38104
(901) 272-0003

Council on Community Services
Rusty Lawrence
2012 21st Ave. South
Nashville, Tenn. 37212
(615) 933-3443

Downtown Clinic for the Homeless
Dr. Lawrence Madlock
411 Seventh Ave. South
Nashville, Tenn. 37219
(615) 862-7900

Downtown Service Center
Dick Achuff
526 Eighth Ave. South
Nashville, Tenn. 37219
(615) 862-7935

Highlander Research and Education Center
Jim Sessions
1959 Highlander Way
New Market, Tenn. 37820
(615) 933-3443

Knoxville Transit Authority (K-Trans)
Shop & Ride
David White
1135 Magnolia Ave.
Knoxville, Tenn. 37917
(615) 546-3752

Mid-South Family Health
Care Center
Yvonne Madlock
409 Ayers
Memphis, Tenn. 38105
(901) 525-4395

Room in the Inn
Fr. Charles Strobel
606 Demonbreun St.
Nashville, Tenn. 37219
(615) 254-7666

## TEXAS

Austin Community Gardens
Barbara Nagel
4814 Sunshine Dr.
Austin, Tex. 78756
(512) 458-2009

CEDEN Family Resource Center
Emily Vargas Adams
1208 E. Seventh St.
Austin, Tex. 78702
(512) 477-1130

Center for Maximum Potential
Building Systems (Max Pot)
Pliny Fisk
8604 F.M. 969
Austin, Tex. 78724
(512) 928-4786

Communities Organized for
Public Service (COPS)
Consuelo Torar
P.O. Box 830355
San Antonio, Tex. 78283
(210) 222-2367

Interfaith Hunger Coalition
Judy Durand
3217 Montrose
Houston, Tex. 77006
(713) 520-4620

La Mujer Obrera
Maria Carmen
2120 Texas
El Paso, Tex. 79923
(915) 533-9710

Project QUEST
Jack Salvadore
310 S. Frio St., Suite 400
San Antonio, Tex. 78207
(210) 270-4690

Proyecta Azteca
Jesus Limon
P.O. Box 1014
San Juan, Tex. 78589
(210) 787-2233

The Shoulder
Nancy Branson
7655 Bellfort
Houston, Tex. 77061
(713) 649-7200

Sin Fronteras Border
Agricultural Workers Project
Carlos Marentes
514 S. Kansas
El Paso, Tex. 79901
(915) 532-0921

South Plains Food Bank
Carolyn Lanier
4612 Locust Ave.
Lubbock, Tex. 79404
(806) 763-3003

Trinity Ministry to the Poor
Pam Schaefer
134 Oak Lawn Ave.
Dallas, Tex. 75207
(214) 653-1711

West Texas Innovation Center
Gary Spaulding
1901 Lamar St.
Sweetwater, Tex. 79556
(915) 235-4806

## UTAH

Crossroads Urban Center
Glenn Bailey
347 S. 400 East
Salt Lake City, Utah 84111
(801) 364-7765

Disabled Rights Action
Committee (DRAC)
Barbara Toomer
255 W. 1300 South
Salt Lake City, Utah 84115
(801) 484-9314

Utah Issues
Bill Walsh
1385 W. Indiana Ave.
Salt Lake City, Utah 84104
(801) 521-2035

Utahns Against Hunger
Steve Johnson
845 W. 100 South
Salt Lake City, Utah 84104
(801) 328-2561

## VERMONT

Bennington-Rutland Opportunity
Council Inc.
Beth M. Flood
257 S. Main St.
Rutland, Vt. 05701
(802) 775-0878

Chittenden Community Action/
Vermont Tenants Inc.
Virginia Winn
191 North St.
Burlington, Vt. 05402
(802) 862-2771

## VIRGINIA

New River Community
Action Inc.
Terry Smusz
106-B S. Franklin St.
Christiansburg, Va. 24073
(703) 382-6186

## WASHINGTON

El Centro de la Raza
Roberto Maestas
2524 16th Ave. South
Seattle, Wash. 98144
(206) 329-9442

Martin Luther King
Ecumenical Center
David Boyd
1424 Tacoma Ave. South, Suite A
Tacoma, Wash. 98402
(206) 383-1585

Seattle Food Committee/Food
Resource Network
K. C. Spengler
509 10th Ave. East
Seattle, Wash. 98102
(206) 329-0492

Washington Food Policy
Action Center
Linda Stone
525 E. Mission
Spokane, Wash. 99202
(509) 484-6733

## WEST VIRGINIA

Robert C. Byrd Institute
for Advanced Flexible
Manufacturing Systems
David Porreca
1050 Fourth Ave.
Huntington, W. Va. 25755
(304) 696-6275

Center for Economic Options
Pam Curry
601 Delaware Ave.
Charleston, W. Va. 25302
(304) 345-1298

## WISCONSIN

Esperanza Unida
Richard Oulahan
1329 W. National Ave.
Milwaukee, Wis. 53204
(414) 671-0251

The Key New Readers Newspaper
Suzanne Zipperer
Milwaukee Area Technical
College
700 W. State St.
Milwaukee, Wis. 53233
(414) 278-6664

## WYOMING

Nutrition and Child
Development Center
Terry Barnett
4150 S. Poplar St.
Casper, Wyo. 82604
(307) 237-1496

Poverty Resistance Inc.
Mary Anne Budenske
440 S. Wolcott
Casper, Wyo. 82601
(307) 266-9928

# Acknowledgments

THE HUNDREDS OF CREATIVE AND CARING Americans who are fighting poverty in their own communities are the heroes of this book. My contribution has been to tell their stories and to assemble them into broader lessons; their contributions are, quite simply, changing the face of poverty. They have my greatest admiration and deepest thanks.

Without the vision of Bill Ayres, the executive director of World Hunger Year and Harry Chapin's partner in starting it all, the program Reinvesting in America, and thus this book, would never have come to be. I often think that Harry too, wherever he is, must have had a hand in making it happen. "Circle" and "Cat's in the Cradle" came on the car radio too many times during my years on the road for me to believe otherwise! The contribution of Dr. James Chapin, Harry's older brother and chairman of the board of World Hunger Year, was also monumental as we created Reinvesting in America and got it running, well before we had any idea whether we could make it work or even pay for it.

For making that financing possible, we owe particularly grateful thanks to good friends who were there when Reinvesting in America was still no more than an untested idea—friends who believed in the idea, and in us, and supported it with their dollars: Bruce Springsteen and Barbara Carr; Ken Kragen for USA for Africa; Sandy Chapin and the Chapin Foundation; Marge Benton; and Kraft General Foods. Hearty thanks go to World Hunger Year's supporters, particularly those with New York's K-Rock 92.3 FM, who have been responsible for the annual Hungerthon fund-raiser that has been the primary source of income for Reinvesting in America. The organization could not have survived these years without the help of Mel Karmazin, Tom Chiusano, Peggy Panosh, Mark Chernoff, and all the DJs and staff, especially Hungerthon host Pete Fornatale. Thanks go also to all the other donors who've given Reinvesting in America support, including Bill Shore and Share Our Strength; Jennifer Simons and the Simons Foundation; Lucie Arnaz and Larry Luckinbill; Steve Apkon; Chemical Bank; Mazon: A Jewish Response to Hunger; the Public Welfare Foundation; the

Newman Foundation; Spring Air Mattress; ASCAP; and more than ten thousand individual donors who believed in our idea.

World Hunger Year's staff, my colleagues, supported me with faith and friendship as I spent much of my life for four years traveling some two hundred thousand miles to find the nation's best grassroots programs. Special thanks go to them: Peter Mann, Sue Leventhal, Noreen Springstead, Amalia Guerra, Vivian Wong, Jonathan Greengrass, Jenifer Urff, Mary Painter, Bettina Damiani, Ana Cardenas, Joan Behan, Judith Broadhurst, Dick Donahue, and the other staff members and volunteers who made our offices in New York City not only a professional place where good work was done well but also something like a family. Thanks go also to all World Hunger Year's board members for their support, including (in addition to those already mentioned) Larry and Jane Levine; Tom Chapin and Steve Chapin; Jennifer Chapin; Deni Frand; Charlie Sanders; John Poelker; Robin Batteau; David Buskin; Al Handell; Paul Kurland; Ann Ruckert; Sam Weisman; Pat Beninati; Steve Beninati; Susan DeMarco; Bruce Llewellyn; Graham Nash; Senator Patrick Leahy of Vermont; Senator Byron Dorgan of North Dakota; Representative Ben Gilman of New York; former U.S. Representative Tom Downey of New York; former U.S. Representative Bob Carr of Michigan; and all the other WHY board members, past and present.

Among national leaders in the antihunger movement who've supported Reinvesting in America with faith and good advice, special thanks goes to Dr. Larry Brown; Rob Fersh; Representative Tony Hall of Ohio; Bob Greenstein; Christine Vladimiroff; David Maywhoor; David Beckman; Barbara Howell; Sam Harris; John Riggan; Ed Barron; and many more.

I owe a considerable debt to my agent, Jon Matson, who saw early on that my job could yield a major book and who helped me turn a mass of jumbled field notes into a marketable proposal and then this manuscript. The role of my editors at Addison-Wesley was equally significant, and I'm deeply indebted to Bill Patrick, who helped me find a strong and consistent voice, and Sharon Broll, who was a wizard at spotting my digressions away from the main theme and gently guiding me back on track.

Thanks also to personal friends who gave me moral support and practical advice, particularly Claire Shottenfeld and Martha Barnette, who were there when I needed them.

And most of all, thanks to my wife, Mary Woodford Johnson, who read the book first, gave me consistently sound advice, and always made me smile, even on the hard days.

# Index

## A


ABC-TV, 105
Abel, Leonard, 145
About Face, 115
Abused Adult Resource Center, 139–141
Access Alaska, 179–180
Access to food, 28–30, 80–81, 178
ACORN, 157
Adams, Emily Vargas, 138–139
Adams, Peggy, 159
ADAPT, 179
Advocates for Basic Legal Equality, 163–164
AEG Manufacturing Services, 208
AFDC. *See* Aid to Families with Dependent Children
AF L-CIO, 162
Afraid of Bear, Loretta, 26
Agribusiness, 161, 167–169, 172, 174, 175, 218–219
Agricultural Entrepreneurship Project, 218
Agricultural Leadership of America, 39
Aid to Families with Dependent Children, 126, 127, 128, 131, 159, 165, 193, 210, 231, 232, 234
Air Force, 190
Alabama, 8, 76, 89–91, 181
Alaska, 1–4, 20–22, 83–84, 145, 179, 216–218, 222–225
Alaska Center for the Performing Arts, 3, 180
Alaska Fish and Game Department, 22
Alaska Native Tours, 217
Alcoholics Anonymous, 12, 134, 137, 148
Alcoholism, 58, 69, 222
Alinsky, Saul, 154
Allday, Nelson, 185–186
Allentown, Pennsylvania, 61
American Indian nutrition programs, 23
American Institute of Architects, 97
American Public Transit Association, 30
Americans with Disabilities Act, 179, 180
Americus, Georgia, 77
Amoco, 130
Anchorage, Alaska, 1–4, 20–22, 83–84, 145, 179, 216
Anchorage Community Mental Health Services, 145
Anchorage Neighborhood Housing Services, 83–84
Applebome, Peter, 182
Apple computers, 111
Appropriate technology, 96–97
Arizona, 40–41, 43–47
Arkadelphia, Arkansas, 207–208
Arkansas, 207–209, 218–219
Arkansas Enterprise Group, 208–209
Arkansas Land and Farm Development Corporation, 218
Arrington, W.W., 142
Aryan Nation, 171
Arzola, Rose, 58
Association of Community Organizations for Reform Now, 157
Atlanta, Georgia, 11, 16, 200, 202
Atlanta Braves, 124
Auad, Teresa, 225
Aunt Jane's, 162
Austin, Texas, 97, 138
Austin Community Garden, 35
Avon, 195
Ayres, Bill, xi, xiii
Aztec Project. *See* Proyecto Azteca


## B


Bajowski, John, 145–146
*Baltimore Sun*, 159
Bangladesh, 207, 209
*See also* Grameen Bank model
Baptist Memorial Hospital, 187

Barbour, Janice, 213–214
Barnet, Ann, 134
Barret, Chuck, 161–162
Barthelemy, Sidney, 129
Battered women, 139–141
Baumgart, Martin, 27, 28
Bazala, Bonnie, 161–162
Beacon Hill Elementary School, 156
Bean's Cafe, 20–22, 145, 237
 and Bean-a-Fit drive, 22
Bear Eagle, Steve, 28
Bear Heels, Leland, 28
Beatrice Foods Corporation, 227
Begay, Clara, 115
Beittel, Kent, xiii, 63–66, 236
Bellew, Lynn, 20–21
Benjamin Franklin High School, 114
Bennett, Barbara, 21–22
Beth-Anne Campus, 82
Bethel Lutheran Church, 81
Bethel New Life, 81–83
Bianco, Angela, 221–222
Big Brothers/Big Sisters, 125
Billings, Montana, 173
Binion, Richard, 50
Bishop, Janet Spector, 50
Bjornsrud, Marlene, 44
Boarding houses. *See* Single-room-occupancy hotels
Boise, Idaho, 164–165
Bolling, Bill, 16
Bonn, Germany, 27–28
Book 'Em!, 72
Boss Crump organization, 141
Boston, Massachusetts, 226
Boys and Girls Clubs, 107
Branstad, Terry, 169
Brenton, 170
Bridge, The, 43–45, 46, 48, 119, 237
Brinkley, Arkansas, 218–219
Broglio national poll (1992), 38
Brown, Floyd, 218
Brulc, Terrance, 188
Bryant, James W., 148
Bryn Mawr Church of Philadelphia, 26
Burlington, Vermont, 91–94
Burlington Community Land Trust, 93
Burlington Housing Board of Review, 93
Bush, George, viii, 6, 7
Bush administration, 107, 182, 183
Bush Development Fund, 218
Business Development Loan Fund, 84
Byrd Institute, 190–191, 192

## C

Caesar, Pearl, 154–155
Cafe 458, viii, 11–15, 43, 234
California, 5, 15, 39–40, 57–61, 123, 144, 146–147, 196, 198–200
California Gray Bears, 40
Cambodian immigrants, 54
Campaign Against Childhood Hunger, 63
Campbell, Ann, 216
Campbell's, 162
Canneries, 90
Cannon, Sylvia, 127–129, 236
Capone, Al, 111
Cap-Rock Winery, 17
Carawan, Candie, 182
Carroll County, Maryland, 129
Carroll County Food Sunday, 128, 129
Carroll Street Garden, 200
Carr's grocery store, 3
Carter, Jimmy, viii, 77, 78
Carvalho, Barbara, 6
Casa Guadalupe, 60
Case management, 52, 56, 60, 62, 72–73, 94, 136
Casper, Wyoming, 121–122
Castillo, Gloria, 88
Castillo, Isaac, 88
Catch 'Em in the Cradle, 116
Catholic Archdiocese of Phoenix, 45
Catholic Diocese of Kansas City, 112
Catholic Rural Life Conference, 172
Cawein, Howard, 16
CBS-TV, 151
CCI, 169–171
CEDEN, 138–139
Center for Advanced Technologies, 192
Center for Budget and Policy Priorities, 75
Center for Community Self-Help, 214–216
Center for Economic Options, 193–194
Center for Hunger, Poverty and

Nutrition Policy at Tufts University, 38
Center for Independent Living, 179
Center for Maximum Potential Building Systems Inc., 96–97
Center for Rural Affairs, 175, 212
Center for the Study of Social Policy, 135
Centro de Obrero Fronterizo, 177
Centro de Recursos Familiares, 138–139
Centro de Trabajadores Agricolas, 161
Chaffee, Georgia, 103–104
Champlain College, 94
Chapin, Dr. James, xi
Chapin, Harry, xi, xiii
Charging Crow, Michelle, 26
Charity, 4, 157, 229, 237
*Charleston Daily Mail*, 194
Charles Town Center Mall, 194
Charlotte, North Carolina, 109–110
Chavez, Cesar, 166
Chehraz, Sara, 55
Chez Panisse, 199, 200
Chicago, Illinois, 15, 48–51, 81, 182, 194–195
Chicago Legal Aid, 49
Child care, 61, 108, 122–123
Child Care Food Program, 122
Child labor, 162–163
Children and families, services for, 120–126, 133–140
Children and Youth Project, 135
Children's Cabinet, 120–121
Chittenden Community Action Program, 92
Christian Development Corporation, 111
Christian Relief Services, 27
Christmas in April, 83
Christmas in May, 84
Chrysalis, 196–197, 198
Churches, 1, 6, 8, 44–45, 54, 68, 196
  community gardening, 32, 33
  homelessness, 70
  land ownership, 172–173
  political activism, 158, 169
Church Extension Fund, 196
Church Health Center, 142–143, 237
Church Land Project, 172
Church of the Savior, 134
Cincinnati Milacron T-10, 190
Cincotta, Gale, 183
Circle Banking Project, 210
Cisneros, Henry, 45, 47–48, 154, 155
Cities in Schools, 109–110, 235
Civil Rights Act, 176
Clavelle, Peter, 92
Cleveland, Texas, 87
Clients Helping Clients, 158–159
Client Worker Training Program, 197–198
Clinton, Bill, 6, 45, 108, 207
Clinton, Hillary Rodham, 207
Clinton administration, vii, ix, 5, 107
CNA Insurance, 82
Coalition for the Homeless, 72
Cole, Judy, 60
Colonias, 86–88, 154, 155
*Commonweal*, 154
Communities Organized for Public Service, 153–155, 157, 186
Community Action agencies, 231
Community Action Program, 94
Community centers, 82, 107
Community development corporations, 207–209, 216–219
  *See also* Grameen Bank model
Community Development grants, 31, 183, 231
Community Empowerment Zones, ix–x
Community Enterprise Development Corporation of Alaska, 216–218
Community Family Life Services, 196
Community gardening, 25–28, 30–35, 90
  and ancient food crops, 40–41
Community Health Agency, 144
Community of Hospitality, 12
Community of Readers, 115–116
Community Pantry of Hollister, 40
Community Reinvestment Act, 170, 183
Computers, 111, 202
  in education, 102, 114–115
  and manufacturing processes, 190–191
Condominium Conversion Ordinance, 93
Congress, vii, ix, 75
Congress of Racial Equality, 176
Conrad Hilton Foundation, 213

Cook, Tom, 26–27
Cooperatives, 8, 84, 90–91, 173, 175–176, 220–226
Cornell School of Hotel Management, 19
Cortes, Ernesto, 154
Council of Community Services, 71, 72
*Courier-Journal*, xi
Cox & Wright grocery stores, 29
Crack babies, 148–149
Cranks Creek Survival Center, 181
Cranston-Gonzales Act, 45
Creating jobs. *See* Entrepreneurs
Credit unions, 215
Criminal Justice program, 140
Crisis Intervention Center, 140
Crossover House, 145–146
Crossroads, 69
Cruz, Nancy, 83
Crystal City, Texas, 96
C.S. Mott Foundation, 209, 212
Cuevas, Fernando, 161–162
Cunningham, Bill, 191–192

# D

Daily Bread Food Bank, 16
Dakota Rural Action, 174
Daley, Richard J., 182
Dallas, Texas, 136
*Dallas Morning News*, 136
Dave Johnston Power Plant, 121
Davidson College, 109
Day centers, 22, 70, 82, 146–147
DC Central Kitchen, 18–20, 233
Dean's Foods, 162
Deinstitutionalization, 5, 75, 146
Delta Community Development Corporation, 218–219
Dempsay, Mark, 146
Dempsay, Susan, 146–147
Department of Agriculture, 8, 22, 23
  Child Care Food Program, 122
Department of Agriculture, Kentucky, 220
Department of Agriculture, Texas, 97, 206
Department of Commerce, 4, 80
Department of Defense, 8, 190, 192
Department of Health and Human Services, 8, 194, 217
Department of Housing and Urban Development (HUD), vii, 8, 31, 45, 51, 76, 81, 182, 183
Department of Labor, 8, 56, 108, 114
  Employment Training Act, 107
Department of Social Services, Carroll County, Maryland, 127
Department of the Interior, 8
Depression, the, 6
  and poverty, xiii
Dermody, Mike, 120
Desert Storm, 15
Detroit, Michigan, 191–192
Disabled people, 179–181
Dominguez, Maria Carmen, 177–178
Donner Fund of New York, 20
Dow, Bill, 90
Downtown Clinic for the Homeless, 69–70, 72, 144
Downtown Service Center, 69–70
Downtown Women's Center, 57–59
Drees, Mahina, 41
Driscoll, Tim, 39
Drug and alcohol abuse programs, 12–15, 69, 147–148, 197, 234
Duke Power, 109
Dukes, Joyce, 182
Durham, North Carolina, 113, 214–215
DuValle Education Center, 106–107

# E

Eakes, Martin, 214
EARTH, 3–4
Earth Summit, 97
East Central Arkansas Economic Opportunity Corporation, 218
Eastern Kentucky University, 220
Ebenezer Baptist Church, 11
Economic Development Administration Revolving Fisheries Loan Fund, 217
Economic Opportunity Council, ix
Education, 106–108, 110–112
  computers in, 111
  declining quality, 100–101
  high technology, 190–193
  and social services, 109
Education for Justice, 132
Egger, Robert, 18–20
Eisenhower administration, 167
El Centro de la Raza, 155–157, 236
Elderly, 144–145

Elizabeth Fry House, 202
Elk Horn Bank and Trust Company, 208
Ellwood, David, 5
El Milagro, 166
El Paso, Texas, 160, 161, 177–178
Emergency Services Center of the Carroll County Department of Social Services, 127–129
Employee stock ownership plan, 226–228
Employment and Training Center, 82
Employment Training Act, 107
Energy advocacy, 34, 90–91, 94–97
Entergy Corporation, 51, 114
Entrepreneurs, 205–214
  training, 213–214
Erlich, Elaine, 125–126
ESL classes, 60
ESOP. *See* Employee stock ownership plan
Esperanza Unida, viii, xiii, 8, 187–190, 196, 203, 232, 235
Eugene, Georgia, 102
Everard, Don, 131–132
Everett, Massachusetts, 226
Exemplary Local Government, 97

# F

Fagan, Joe, 170
Families Reading Together, 116
Families with a Future, 82
Family Place, 134–135, 136
Family Preservation, 121
Family Resource Center for Development, Education and Nutrition, 138–139
Family Stabilization Program, 137
Family Support Centers, 135–136
Family Training Center, 52
Farah clothing company, 177
Fargo Food Bank, 140
Farm Bureau, 40
Farm Crisis Hotline, 171
Farmers Home Administration (FHA), 166, 174, 183, 217
Farming
  credit crisis, 167–168, 172
  family, 36–40, 90, 170–171, 208
  hotlines, 171, 174
  technology, 97
Farm Labor Housing funds, 166
Farm Labor Organizing Committee, xiii, 161–163
Farmworkers, 86–88, 113–114, 165–167, 225–226
  political activism, 159–167
Farragut High School, 111
Farrow, Frank, 135
Federal Aviation Administration, 44
Federal Community Development Block Grant, 51
Federal Economic Development Authority, 80
Federal Food Distribution Program, 22
Federal General Accounting Office, 76
Federal General Assistance Office, 199
Federal Nutrition Program for Women, Infants and Children (WIC), 22, 103, 115, 127, 159, 235
Federal Office of Community Services, 166
Federal Office of Economic Opportunity, 166, 176
Federal Reserve
  and unemployment policy, 126
Federation of Southern Cooperatives, 175–176
FHA. *See* Farmers Home Administration
Fingeret, Hanna, 113
Firstar, 170
First Nations Development Institute, 211
Fisk, Pliny III, 96–97
Flavin, Lilianne, 131–132
Florida, 16, 40, 85, 225
Floyd Brown Agricultural School, 218
Focus: HOPE, 101, 191–193
Food banks, 7, 15–20, 39–40, 125–126, 128
Foodchain, 20
Food City, 29
Food Organizations Organizing and Distributing Crops (F.O.O.D. Crops), 39–40
Food pantries, 32, 33, 36–37
Food Research and Action Center, 38, 63
Food Stamp Act of 1973, 23

Ford Foundation, 212
Fort Yates, North Dakota, 23, 25, 140
Foti, Charles C., 115
Fourth Ward Garden, 33
Franco, Javier, 206
French, Duane, 180
Friends of the Family Inc., 135–136
Friskics-Warren, Bill, 71–72, 73
Fuentes, Humberto, 165–167
Full Court Press, 169
Fuller, Millard, 77–78
Fulton County Stadium, 124
Fund for Humanity, 78
Future Farmers of America, 170

# G

Gannett Corporation, xi
Garden Project, 199–200
Gardens of Plenty, 90
Gates, Charles (Red), 1, 22–25
Gathering Place, 115, 221–222
GED, 52, 104, 105, 106, 107, 112, 114, 132, 203, 204
General Electric, 102
General Equivalency Diploma. *See* GED
General Motors, 192
Georgia, 11, 16, 77, 102–104, 124–126, 200, 202
GI Bill, 187
Gifford, Barbara, 200–201
Gleaning Program, 133
Golden Kentucky Products, 220
Good Faith Fund, 209–210
Good Government League, 153
Gordon, Marlene, 108
Gordon, Wayne, 111
Government
  farm policy, 167–168
  homelessness, 75–76
  job training, 108
  social service programs, 5, 7–8
  unemployment policy, 126
Grameen Bank model, 208–213, 216, 233
*Grapes of Wrath, The* (Steinbeck), 199
Greater Chicago Food Depository, 16
Greater Kansas City Hispanic Scholarship Fund, 112
Great Society, 7, 175, 235
Green Bay Foods, 162
Green Builder Program, 97
Greensboro, North Carolina, 115–116
Greenspot plots, 35
G Street Shelter, 55
Guadalupe Center, 112
Guatemalan immigrants, 225–226
Guest House, 69
Gulf Coast Community College, 203
Gulf Oil, 130
Gunderson, Sue, 34

# H

Habitat for Humanity, viii, 77–79, 80, 86, 97
Halverson, Jill, 57–58
Hamilton, Arlene, 200
Hamilton, Hal, 226, 227
Hardwick Women's Prison, 200
Harris County, Texas
  Southeast Memorial Hospital, 148–149
Harrison County, Mississippi, 203–204
Harrison County Training Center, 203
Harry Chapin Food Self-Reliance Awards, xii, 133
  and Reinvesting in America program, xii–xiii
Harry Chapin Foundation, xii
Harvard, 5
Head Start, 107, 166, 235
Health care, 142–145
  elderly, 144–145
  farmworkers, 160
  homelessness, 72–73
  mentally ill, 69–70, 145–147
Hearn, Patti, 101
Heifer Project International, 221
Heinz, 162
Helm, Henry, 114
Henderson, Susan, 105
Hennessey, Mike, 199–200
Hidalgo County, Texas, 85–89
Highlander Center, 181–182
Highlander Folk School, 181
HIPPY, 104
Hispanic community, 32, 59, 96, 112–114, 123, 134–135, 160–161, 165–167

- housing, 86–88
- migrant farmworkers, 160–161
- political activism, 153–157, 177–178
- poverty line, 138
- unemployment, 186

Hmong immigrants, 34–35
Hodgkinson, Harold (Bud), 102
Holistic approach, 52–53, 119–121, 137–138, 233, 238
Holland America cruises, 217
Holmes County, Mississippi, 151–153
Holy Cross Church, 85, 225
Holy Cross School, 235
Holy Name Church, 67
Holy Trinity Catholic Church, 137
Homeless Coalition, 72
Homelessness, 43–73, 123
- causes, 5, 47, 75–76
- demographics, 47–48
- health care, 69–70, 72–73
- mental illness, 56–61, 145–147
- prevention of, 53–56

Homeless Veterans Reintegration Project, 56
HOME program, 182
Homeward Bound, 45–47, 48, 119, 237
Hope House, 131–132
Hormel, 172
Horton, Myles, 181–182
Hosea House, 36–38
House of Ruth, 59–61
Housing Act, 75
Housing costs, 75–76
Housing Exchange, 54–55
Housing Replacement Ordinance, 93
Housing Strategy Group, 93
Houston, Texas, 31–34
- Chamber of Commerce, 31
- Food Bank, 147

*Houston Chronicle*, 32
*Houston Post*, 32
Howard, Maureen, 54, 55
Howard Rock Foundation, 217–218
HUD, vii, 8, 31, 45, 51, 76, 81, 182, 183
Hunger statistics, 38
Hunter, Hilton, 19
Huntington, West Virginia, 190, 192

# I

Iacocca, Lee, 110
IBM, 92, 102, 109
ICA Group, 226–228
Idaho, 94, 95, 133, 164–167, 174–175, 180
Idaho Citizens' Network, 180–181
Idaho Disabilities Coalition, 181
Idaho Fair Share, 180
Idaho Foodbank Warehouse, 133
Idaho Hunger Action Council, 133, 165
Idaho Migrant Council, 165–167
Idaho Neighbors Network, 180
Idaho Power Company, 94
Idaho Rural Council, 174–175
Ihli, Becky, 174–175
Illinois, 15, 48–51, 81–84, 110–112, 182, 194–195
Immigrants, 34–35, 53–54, 58, 112–114, 123, 131
Incubators, small-business, 188, 206–207, 208, 233
Independent Options Now, 179
Independent Quality of Living Center, 179
Indiantown, Florida, 225
InDios, 225–226
Industrial Areas Foundation, 86–87, 154, 155, 157
Industrial Cooperative Association. *See* ICA Group
Industry Mall, 192
Ingwerson, Donald W., 99–102, 103, 106
Initiative 300, 175
Inner Circle Fund, 211
Inner cities, 29, 30, 142, 178
- riots, 30, 80, 81

Inspiration Cafe, 15
Interfaith Hunger Coalition, 31, 32–34
Intergenerational Gardening Project, 35
Iowa, 168–171, 172
Iowa Citizens for Community Improvement (CCI), 169–171
Iowa State University, 169

## J


Jackson, Michael R., 219
Jefferson Community College, 105
Jefferson County, Kentucky, 99–104
Jenkins, Major, 49
Jewish Council on Urban Affairs, 49
Job banks, 71
Job Search Prep Class, 197
Job training, 19–20, 62, 81, 107–108, 185–194, 196–204
  entrepreneurs, 213–214
  ex-offenders and incarcerated, 198–204
  goals, 185–186
  homeless, 60–61
  mentally ill, 147, 198
  minorities, 188–190
  nontraditional jobs, 193
Job Training Partnership Act, 108, 166
Johansen, Bruce, 156
Johns Hopkins Medical School, 135
Johnny Appleseed, 113
Johnson, Dave, 39
Johnson, Leroy, 152–153
Johnson, Lyndon B., 216
Johnson, Michelle, 56
Jones, Alex, 129
Jordan, Clarence, 77
Jost, Al, 186
Journey House, 117
J. Paul's restaurant, 19
Just Desserts bakery, 200
Just Harvest, 178–179
Just Jobs Inc., 195


## K


Kansas City, 112
Keepers of the Beautyway, 115
Kellogg Foundation, 223
Kelly Air Force Base, 185
Kemp, Jack, 183
Kenan Family Literacy Program, 104–106, 107
Kentucky, 99–104, 106, 107, 219–221
*Key, The*, 116–117
King, Calvin, 218
King, Martin Luther Jr., 11, 175–176, 181
King, Rodney, 123
Kingdome, 53
Knoll, Tom, 196
Knoxville, Tennessee, 29–30
Knoxville Food Policy Council, 30
Koinonia Farms, 77
Kozol, Jonathan, 100
Krawetz, Sandy, 164
Kroger grocery stores, 29–30
K-Trans, 29–30


## L


Labor Exchange, 197
Lackey, Gerry, 163
La Escuela Popular, 177
Lakefront SRO, 48–51, 84
Lakota Fund, 210–212
Lakota Produce Growers Organization, 28
Lakota Sioux, 1, 22–25, 210–212
  and gardening, 25–28
La Mirada Apartments, 44
La Mujer Obrera, 177–178
Land Retention Fund, 218
Lanier, Carolyn, 16–18, 236
Lassman-Eul, Mark, 77
Last Chance Shelter, 55
Lasuen, Leanna, 165
Lawndale, Illinois, 110–112
Lawndale College Opportunity Program, 111
Lawndale Community Church, 111–112
Lay Advisers, 143
Legal Services Corporation, 163
Lehigh Valley, Pennsylvania, 61
Lettuce Link, 35
Lewis, Mattie, 58–59
Lexington, Mississippi, 151–153
Linder, William, 80
LINK, 37–38
Literacy, 113–117, 132
  and single mothers, 104–106
Literacy South, 113
Little, Rachel Bristol, 16
Little Finger, Leonard, 28
Livestock Project, 221
Livingston Economic Alternatives for Progress, 220–221
Livingston Fiscal Court, 220
Loaves and Fishes, 67
Los Angeles, California, 59, 123, 146, 196

and homelessness, 57–61
Los Angeles County Mental Health Association, 146
Louisiana, 114, 129–132
Louisville, Kentucky, 99–102, 106, 107
*Louisville Times*, xi
Loussac-Sogn SRO, 84
*Love in the Mortar Joints* (Fuller), 78
Low-cost housing, 45–46, 51–53, 75–97
availability, 76–77
counseling programs, 83
and new technology, 94–97
principles to create, 84–85
*See also* Anchorage Neighborhood Housing Services; Bethel New Life; Habitat for Humanity; New Community Corporation; Proyecto Azteca; Single-room-occupancy hotels
Low-Income Family Training and Support, 133
Lubbock, Texas, 16
Lubbock Correctional Facility, 17
Lutheran Church–Missouri Synod Church Extension Fund, 196


## M


Mabus, Ray, 51
McAllen, Texas, 86
McDonnell-Douglas Corporation, 46
McGee, Charles, 120
Machinist Training Institute, 192
McKinney Act grants, 47, 145
McKnight, Ken, 71
McRae, Tom, 207
McWilliams, Hunter, 30
Madlock, Larry, 70, 144
Madlock, Yvonne, 144
Maestas, Roberto, 156–157, 236
Mallett, David, 31
Management by objectives, 12–15, 48, 65–66, 137, 183–184, 232
Mandela House, 55
Marentes, Alicia, 160
Marentes, Carlos, 160, 236
Marine Corps, 115
Marist Institute for Public Opinion, 6
Market Forge, 226–227, 228
Marquette University, 188
Marshall, Cynthia, 109
Marshall University, 190
Martin, Pamela, 46
Martin Luther King Center, 53–56, 235
Maryland, 129, 135–136, 158–159, 214
Maryland Food Committee, 159
Maryland General Assembly, 135
Maryland Social Services Administration, 135
Massachusetts, 226
Matthew 25, 68
Max Pot, 96–97
Mayfield Memorial Baptist Church, 110
Mbandaka, Zaire, 78
Means, Russell, 26
Meatpacking industry, 172, 174
Medicaid, 128, 131, 142, 179, 181
Medi-Cal, 58
Megson, Jim, 227, 228
Memphis, Tennessee, 141–142, 144
Memphis Plan, 143
Mercy Academy, 131
Metcalfe, Mississippi, 52
Methodist churches, 89
Mexican-American Legal Defense Fund, 166
Michigan, 191–192
Micro Loan Fund, 217
Mid-South Family Health Care Center, 144
Migrant workers. *See* Farmworkers
Miller, Greg, 19
Milliken, Bill, 109
Milwaukee, 8, 116, 117, 187
Milwaukee Area Technical College, 117
*Milwaukee Journal*, 117
Mindte, Kathy, 159
Minneapolis, Minnesota, 34–35
Minneapolis Community Development Agency, 34–35
Minnesota, 34–35
Minority Business Development Center, 217
Miskito Indians, 97
Mississippi, 51–52, 76, 151–153, 203–204
Mississippi Power & Light, 51
Missouri, 36–38

Missouri Association for Social Welfare, 38
Mitchell, Ellen, 31, 32
Mitch Snyder Shelter, 18–20
MIT-Harvard Joint Center for Housing Studies, 75
Mobile Outreach Team, 70
Mohawk Indians, 26
Molly Maguire, 151
Mom the Teacher, 115
Mondragon model, 226, 228
Montana, 173
Monterey County, California, 39–40
Monterey County Food Bank, 40
Montgomery, Alabama, 181
Moreno, Tirso, 236
Morris, Scott, 142–143, 237
Morris, Zel, 71
Mother Hen Day Care Center, 82
Motivation Education & Training Inc., 87
Mountaineer Archery, 191
"Mr. Goodwrench" principle, 53, 54, 228, 234, 235
Murone, Sherry, 125, 126
Musk Ox Farm, 224
Mutual Housing, 84

# N

NAACP, 176
Narcotics Anonymous, 12
Nashville, Tennessee, 67, 69, 70, 71–73
*Nashville Banner*, 67
Nashville Council on Aging, 72
Nashville Health Department, 70
Nashville Metropolitan Council, 72
Nashville Metropolitan Court System, 69
Nashville Metropolitan Health Department, 69
National Association of Food Distribution Programs on Indian Reservations, 23
National Atmospheric and Oceanic Administration, 4
National farm policy, 167–168
National Training and Information Center, 182–184
Native Alaskans, 216–218, 222–225
Native Land Claim Settlement, 216
Native Seeds/SEARCH, 40–41
Navajo Indians, 221–222
Nebraska, 114, 175, 212
Nebraska Association of Farm Workers, 113–114
Neighbors Making a Difference, 84
Neild, Joey, 55, 56
Nelson, Mary, 82–83
Nevada, 120–121, 213–214
Nevada Self-Employment Trust, 213–214
Nevada Women's Fund, 213
Newark, New Jersey, 30, 80
New Community Corporation, 30, 79–81, 82
New Hope Community, 85
New Jersey, 30, 80
New Jersey Housing and Mortgage Finance Agency, 80
New Mexico, 115, 221–222
New Orleans, Louisiana, 114, 129–132
New York City
poverty in, 6
*New York Times*, 182
Nigro, Laura, 15
Ninth Street Elementary School, 123
Nontraditional Jobs for Women Project, 193
Nordstrom's department store, 145
North American Free Trade Agreement, 175
North Carolina, 109–110, 113, 115–116, 214–216
North Carolina Center for Literacy Development, 113
North Carolina HOME Ownership Program, 215–216
North Dakota, 1, 22, 23, 25, 139, 140
Norwest, 170
Not Help Him, Dani, 210
Nussel, Philip, 194
Nutrition and Child Development Inc., 121–122

# O

O'Callaghan, Michael, 2–4
Ochoa, Ella, 114
Oglala Lakota College, 25–26, 27, 28
Ohio, 63, 161, 163, 164
O'Laughlin, Frank, 225

One-stop shopping, 127–129, 233
Ontario, Oregon, 166
On-the-Job Training, 114
O'odham Indian Reservation, 41
Oomingmak Musk Ox Cooperative, 223–225
Open Door Community Shelter, 200
Open Shelter, viii, xiii, 63–66
Opportunities for Women Project, 220
Opportunity Lands Corporation, 208
Oregon, 16, 157–158, 166
Organization for a Better Austin, 183
Orleans Parish Community Correctional Center, 114–115
Orrego, Maria Elena, 135
Osborne, David, 231
Ostendorf, David, 171–173
Oulahan, Richard, 188–190, 235
Our Lady of Compassion, 179
Outreach Project, 56

# P

PACE, 104
*Packer* magazine, 40
Paige, Ralph, 175–176
Paint the Town, 84
Para Los Niños, 123–124
Parent-Child Program, 138
Parks, Rosa, 181
Partnerships, government, private enterprise, schools and non-profit organizations, viii, xii, 4–5, 7, 82, 109, 149, 230–231
Pathmark Corporation, 30
Pathway Program, 115
Pathways shelter, 116
Peace Corps, 154
Pennick, Jerry, 176
Pennsylvania, 26, 61, 178–179
People for Progress Inc., 206
Perry, Linda, 51–53, 76
Pew Charitable Trust, 72
Phelps, Chris, 54–55
Phoenix, Arizona, 43–47
Phoenix Suns, 46
Piggly-Wiggly, 206
Pima Indians, 40–41
Pine Bluff, Arkansas, 209
Pine Ridge Reservation, 25, 210
 and gardening, 27–28
Pinkerton detectives, 151
Pittsburgh, Pennsylvania, 178–179
Pittsburgh Committee on Hunger and Access to Food, 179
Plenty Wounds, Jody, 28
Plunkett, John, 195
"Points of light," viii, 7
Political organizing, 151–167, 169–184
 disabled people, 179–181
 family farmers, 169–176
 farmworkers, 159–167
 Hispanic community, 153–157, 166–167
 industrial, 176–178
 training, 181–184
Pollution, 170, 180–181
Porreca, Dave, 190–191
Portland, Oregon, 16, 157–158
Portland Organizing Project, 157–158
Port of New Orleans, 130
Posse Comitatus, 171
Poverty, 38, 138, 148, 203
 causes of increase, 5
 economic realities, 205
 education, 101, 102–103, 113
 government policies, vii
 ten principles for fighting, 231–238
 solutions, vii–x, 18, 20, 43, 46–47, 119, 149, 185, 230
 symptoms, 229
Poverty line, 6, 25, 138, 153, 220
Poverty rate, 165
P-Patch community gardening, 35
PrairieFire Rural Action, 171–173
Prenatal Education Program, 138
Presbyterian Women of the Church, 202
Price, Joe, 203–204
Princess cruises, 217
"Priority:Home!," 47
Prison Ministries with Women, 200, 202–203
Private Industry Council, 187
Privatization, 5
Project Fast Track, 192
Project Quest, 186–187, 232
Project Self-Sufficiency, 94
Project Venture Forth, 202–203
Project Worth, 107–108

Proposition 13, 5
Proyecto Azteca, 87–89
Public schools, 99–106, 109–110
  computers in, 102
  and poverty, 101
Pulitzer Prize, xi
Pulliam, Amanda, 37
Pyramid, the, 142

## Q

Queen of the Angels Church, 80

## R

Rabinowitz, Joni, 178
Ralston, Don, 175
Randall, Bob, 33
Reach for the Academic Difference, 121
*Ready or Not, Here We Come* (Hodgkinson), 102
Reagan administration, 5, 20, 32, 48, 67, 166, 183
  cuts in service programs, 72
Recession of 1981, 6–7
Recovery Program, 12–13, 234
Recycling, 17, 174
Recycling Center and Material Recovery Facility, 82
Redlining, 157–158, 183
Reeder, Julie, 214
Refugees, 134
Regal, Ken, 178–179
Reno, Nevada, 120–121, 213
Rent to Own program, 88
Research and Economic Development Center, 190
Resolution Trust Corporation, 88
Reynolds, Earlie, 56
Riddle, Roy, 17
Rio Grande Valley, Texas, 77, 88–89
Robert C. Byrd Institute for Advanced Flexible Manufacturing Systems, 190–191, 192
Robertson, Sigrun, 223, 224
Robert Wood Johnson Foundation, 72
Rockcastle County, Kentucky, 219–221
Rockcastle River Community Land Trust, 220
Rodriguez, Cecilia, 177
Room in the Inn, 67–69, 70, 72, 237
Running Strong for American Indian Youth, 27
Rural Cooperative Development Project, 173
Rural Development Loan Fund, 217
Rural Enterprise Assistance Project, 212–213
Rural Organizing and Cultural Center, 151–153, 157
Rural-Urban Linkage Project, 37–38
Russian Commonwealth of Independent States, 97
Ryle, Ed, 45

## S

Sacred Heart Catholic Church, 161
Safe Shelter, 140
St. Anne's Hospital, 82
St. Francis Shelter, 145, 146
St. Joseph Center, 15
St. Joseph's Church, 80
St. Louis, Missouri, 36–38
St. Philip's College, 185
St. Regis Mohawk reservation, 26
St. Thomas projects, 131, 132
Salvadore, Jack, 187
Salvation Army, 43, 69
San Antonio, Texas, 153–155, 185–187
Sanchez, Gilbert, 8
Sanders, Bernie, 92
Sand Mountain, Alabama, 8, 76, 89–91
Sand Mountain Parishes, 8, 89–91
San Francisco, California, 199–200
San Francisco County Jail, 198
San Juan, Texas, 87
San Mateo Jail, 199
Santa Monica, California, 146–147
Saunders, Lou, 116
*Savage Inequalities* (Kozol), 100
Savannah, Georgia, 125
Schaaf, Laurie, 131–132
Schaefer, Pam, 136, 137–138
Schaffner Elementary School, 104, 105, 107
Schell, Ann, 223
Scott, Cynthia, 187, 232
Seattle, Washington, 155–156

Seattle Food Committee/Food Resource Network, 35
*Seattle Times*, 156
Second Harvest Food Bank of Coastal Georgia, 125–126
Second Harvest Food Bank of the Central Coast, 39–40
Second Harvest network, 15–16, 40
Section Eight, 84, 85
Self-Help Venture Fund, 215
Self-Reliance Center, 34–35
Self-Sufficiency Program, 82
Senate Budget Committee, 159
Senate Select Committee on Hunger, 133
Senior Health and Peer Counseling Center, 144–145
Seven Sisters, 198
Severens, Gene, 212
Shannon County, South Dakota, 25–27
Shell Oil Company, 130
Shelters, 57–58, 59–61, 63–66, 140
  *See also* Homelessness
Sherman, Gerald, 210, 211
Shober, John, 103
Shop & Ride, 29–30
Short, A.B., 12
Shoulder, The, 147–148
Simpson, Becky, 181
Sin Fronteras, 160–161, 162
Single Family Property Disposition–Homeless Initiative rule, 45
Single-room-occupancy hotels, 48–51, 59, 196
SIPS. *See* Special Initiative Programs
Sixth Street Shelter, 61–62
*60 Minutes*, 70, 151
Slaney, Dave, 227
Small Business Administration, 213, 217
Small Business Administration Technical Assistance Program, 217
Smith, Larkin, 203
Smith, Margie, 137, 198, 233–234
Sneed, Cathrine, 199–200
Social Security Administration, 56
Social service programs, 50, 52, 62, 66, 94, 137
  for children, 120–126, 133–140
Sojourner Housing, 56
Sojourner Truth House, 202
Solar power, 90–91, 95–96
Soup kitchens, 20–22, 229
South Dakota, 25–27, 210
Southeast Community Hospital, 148
Southeast Memorial Hospital, 148
Southern Christian Leadership Conference, 176
Southern Development BankCorporation, 207, 208
Southern Pacific, 200
Southern Ventures Inc., 208
South Plains Food Bank, 16–18
  and food dehydration plant, 18
South Shore Bank, 207
Spaulding, Gary, 206
Special Initiative Programs, 51–53
Specialty Equipment, 227
Spenard, Alaska, 83, 84
Springsteen, Bruce, xii–xiii
SRO. *See* Single-room-occupancy hotels
Standing Rock College, 25
Standing Rock Lakota Sioux Reservation, 22–25, 140
Steffanson, Williamur, 223
Steinbeck, John, 199
Step Up on Second, 146–147
Stone, Faith, 210, 211
Strange, Marty, 175
Street people. *See* Homelessness
Streett, Rosalie, 135–136
Strobel, Charlie, 67–69, 72
Sturgeon, George, 207
Suburban Job-Link, 194–195
Sullivan, Liz, 71
Sumerford, Steve, 115–116
Summerhill, Georgia, 124–125
Summerhill Neighborhood Inc., 124
Summerhill One-to-One, 124–125
Sunshine Gardens, 35
Superfund cleanup, 180
Supplemental Security Income, 56, 58, 71
Sustainable agriculture, 170, 171, 173, 193
Sweet Sorghum Project, 220
Sweet Tooth, the, 210
Sweetwater, Texas, 205–207

## T


Tacoma, Washington, 53–56
Tafelski, Joe, 164
Task Force on Housing, 51
Tassajara Bakery, 199
Taylor, Ina, 220
Teaching factories, 190–192
Teal, John J. Jr., 223, 224
Teen-Age Parent Program, 103–104
Teen pregnancy, 103–104, 138, 139, 222, 235
Tenants' rights, 91–94
Tennessee, 29–30, 67, 69–73, 141–142, 144, 181
Texas, 16, 31–34, 77, 85–89, 96–97, 136, 138, 148–149, 153 –155, 160–161, 177–178, 185, 205–207, 209
Texas Farmworkers Union, 160
Third & Eats, 1, 196
Thoreau, New Mexico, 115, 221–222
Thresholds, 72–73
Thurow, Lester, 190
*Time* magazine, 188
Tinsley, Sonya, 124, 125
Toledo, Ohio, 161, 163, 164
Toledo Legal Aid, 164
Tomlin, Patricia, 123
Tourism, 39, 130
Transitional housing, 43–45, 68–69, 94, 132
  *See also* Homelessness
Transportation, 108, 194–195
Trapp, Shel, 183
Treasure Valley Community College, 166
Tree Project, 200
Trinity Ministry to the Poor, 136–138, 197, 233
Truancy Center, 120
Tucson, Arizona, 40–41
Tufts University, 38
Tull, Tanya, 123
Turnagain Circle, 84
Turner, Kathy, 157–158
Tyra, Amelia, 105
Tyson Foods, 37


## U


Unemployment rates, 23, 25, 126, 220
United Farm Workers Union, 87
United Food and Commercial Workers, 172
United Nations, 97
United Steelworkers, 227
United Way, 71
University of Alaska, 4, 223
University of Tennessee, 144
University of Texas, 96
University of Toledo, 163
University of Vermont, 92
USAF Recruiting Service, 187


## V


Valley Care Cooperative, 228
Vance H. Chavis Lifelong Learning Library, 116
Van Stralen, Barney, 174
Van Stralen, Gladys, 174
V'BURG Inc., 51, 76
Velasquez, Baldemar, 162, 236
Venice, California, 15
Vermont, 91–94
Vermont Tenants Inc., 92–94
Vicksburg, Mississippi, 51
Vicksburg SIP, 51–55
Victim-Offender Reconciliation Program, 72
Viehmann, Suzanne, 43
Village Commons, 84
Virginia, 211
VISTA, 175
Vittori, Gail, 96
Vladimiroff, Christine, 16
Vlasic, 162
Voices of Summerhill, 125
Voight, Betty, 12, 13–14
Voight, Dave, 12, 14
Voting Rights Act, 176
Voucher system, 16–17


## W


Walker, Dorsey, 90–91
Walthill, Nebraska, 175, 212
Walthill Community Action, 175
War on Poverty, 163, 216
Warren County, Mississippi, 51
Washington, 53–56, 155–156
Washington, Booker T., 218

Washington, D.C., vii, 19, 109, 133, 134, 195
Washington, Harold, 49
*Washington Post*, 159
Waterloo, Iowa, 169
Watson's department store, 29
Webster, Carol, 59
Weiss, Jeff, 136
Welfare, 23, 58, 126, 130–131, 158–159, 229, 231, 233
  prevention programs, 235
  recipients, 82, 152, 159, 187
  reform, vii, ix–x, 108, 127
Western Organization of Resource Councils, 173–174, 236
West Garfield Park, Illinois, 81–82, 83
West Side Coalition, 183
Westside Isaiah Plan, 82
West Texas Innovation Center, 206–207, 209
West Virginia, 190, 192–194
Wheaton College, 111
White, David, 29
Whitehead, Stephen, 16
WIC, 22, 103, 115, 127, 159, 235
Willey, Elizabeth, 94–96
Willey, Steve, 94–96
Willging, Tom, 163
Williams, Cliff, 205–207
Williams, Doris, 206
Williams, Maxine, 210
Williams Food Manufacturing Company, 206
Wilson, William Julius, 194
Wind power, 95
Winthrop Rockefeller Foundation (WinRock), 207–209
Wisconsin, 8, 116, 117, 187
Women and Employment Organization, 194
Women Entrepreneurs of Baltimore, 214
Worker-owned businesses, 226–228
Working poor, 5–6, 36, 144, 165
  support programs, 133–139
World Hunger Year, xi, 133
Wright, Bonnie, 214–215
Wyoming, 121–122

## Y

Yellow Pages, 197
YMCA, 103
Young Leaders Council, 72
Young Life, 109
Youngstown Steel, 228
Young Writers' Conferences, 116
Youth Enterprise Agriculture, 218
YWCA, 213

## Z

Zainhofsky, Diane, 139
Zero-budget organizations, 3
Zipperer, Suzanne, 117
Z. Smith Reynolds Foundation, 113